MARGINS

MARGINS

A NATURALIST MEETS
LONG ISLAND SOUND

MARY PARKER BUCKLES

NORTH POINT PRESS • A DIVISION OF

FARRAR, STRAUS AND GIROUX • NEW YORK

North Point Press
A division of Farrar, Straus and Giroux
19 Union Square West, New York 10003

Copyright © 1997 by Mary Parker Buckles
All rights reserved
Published simultaneously in Canada by HarperCollins*CanadaLtd*
Printed in the United States of America
First edition, 1997

Library of Congress Cataloging-in-Publication Data
Buckles, Mary Parker.
 Margins : a naturalist meets Long Island Sound / Mary Parker
Buckles.—1st ed.
   p. cm.
 ISBN 0-86547-516-4 (hardcover : alk. paper)
 1. Natural history—Long Island Sound (N.Y. and Conn.) 2. Long
Island Sound (N.Y. and Conn.) I. Title.
QH105.N7B83 1997
508.3163'46—dc21   96-47946

All photographs by the author

Grateful acknowledgment is made for permission to reprint excerpts
from the following previously published material: *The Once and Future
King* by T. H. White reprinted by permission of Penguin Putnam
Inc. Copyright © 1939, 1940 by T. H. White; copyright © 1958 by
T. H. White Proprietor. "Baiting the Bluebloods" originally ap-
peared in *Audubon Magazine*, copyright © 1996 by Tom Horton,
reprinted by permission of the author. *Spartina* by John Casey copy-
right © 1989; *The Beak of the Finch: Evolution in Real Time* by Jonathan
Weiner copyright © 1994; and "Shorebird Watching" from *A Silence
Opens* by Amy Clampitt copyright © 1994, all reprinted by permis-
sion of Alfred A. Knopf, Inc. *Aristocrats of the Trees* by Ernest H.
Wilson copyright © 1974, reprinted by permission of the Dover
Press. *Galapagos: The Flow of Wilderness* by Loren Eiseley copyright
© 1968, reprinted by permission of Sierra Club Books. *Pilgrim at
Tinker Creek* by Annie Dillard copyright © 1974 by Annie Dillard,
reprinted by permission of HarperCollins Publishers Inc. *A Natural
History of the Birds of Eastern and Central North America* by E. H. Forbush and J. R. May copyright © 1927, renewed 1955, reprinted by
permission of Houghton Mifflin Company. All rights reserved. *The
Wind Birds* by Peter Matthiessen reprinted by permission of Donadio
& Ashworth, Inc. Copyright © 1967, 1973, 1994 by Peter Matthiessen. (Sittin' On) *The Dock of the Bay* by Otis Redding and Steve
Cropper © 1968 (renewed) and 1975 East/Memphis Music Corp.,
© assigned 1982 to Irving Music, Inc. All rights reserved. Used by
permission of Warner Bros. Publications U. S. Inc., Miami, FL
33014.

FOR STEVE

Author's Note

I am an inlander. The place against which I measure all others is a three-quarter-acre plot of ground in the middle of Mississippi. My parents bought it in 1950, when its low-lying half was planted in cotton. The upper half, where they built our suburban house, afforded a view of trees that had grown up between the furrows. A creek beyond the trees formed the property's rear boundary.

I was eight years old when we moved there. From my room I could look out across the back of the upper terrace straight into the trunks of the trees—oaks, and hickories, and hackberries with their pimpled bark. Trunks that emerged just below the drop-off had their lower portions hidden from my view. I thought of them as keeping secrets.

A log bridged the creek, which usually ran with muddy water. Once across the log, I was in a mythical realm. This was not just someone else's property. It was a delicious arboreal landscape garlanded with grapevines that swung me high into the air. Farther on, exposed tree roots formed hollows in the dark brow on which a hospital now stands sanitized and white. After school each day I climbed to one or another of the small caverns and curled up in it. I still recall how moisture from the root tips dribbled onto my bare limbs as I sat, rolled tight as a pill bug, at the crest of an earthen wave.

Nearly half a century later, when I smell the brine of a salt marsh, I am back among those musky roots that dangled in the air and excited my senses. I catch the marsh's fragrance on the wind as I round the path above a shell-washed beach. The marsh and sand are a short walk from the house my husband, Steve, and I occupy near the town line dividing Norwalk, Connecticut, from Darien, Connecticut. The location gives us access to water sheltered by a small archipelago and a segment of the more extensive Norwalk Islands. Beyond these land masses, which we see from our windows, the dots and dashes of tugs with their drawn-out loads punctuate the horizon of Long Island Sound.

When we moved here more than eight years ago, this world seemed as different from the Midwestern one I had recently inhabited as that land across the creek of my childhood has always seemed set apart. Like that land, the Sound beckoned. But I lacked the bridge of a boat. And so I began to know the water from on shore.

The part of the Sound nearest us was fifty yards away at the bottom of a cliff. I couldn't see it from the house. Soon I learned to judge its moods with my ear. Water lapping and rushing, the patter of certain ducks on takeoff, human voices present sometimes even in dense fogs—these and other sounds awakened my senses in new ways.

I had wanted to live on the water for as long as I could remember, perhaps as a way to balance my earth-enfolded upbringing. In late 1987 I made a pilgrimage to the home of Walter Anderson, the late Gulf Coast artist who recorded the rich life of Mississippi Sound in thousands of line drawings and watercolors that I admired. Anderson's widow showed me through the cottage in which her husband had lived between working trips to nearby Horn Island, now part of the Gulf Islands National Seashore. One wall of the house was lined with shelves on which bones, skulls, shells, and other natural objects lay. According to Mrs. Anderson, some particular quality in each of them had presented itself to her husband's eye. I departed that day deeply moved by Anderson's love of the water and eager for a situation in which my own eye, over time, could select what it would from among the waves and tides.

A little more than a year later I landed on the shores of Long Island Sound predisposed to like what I might find. I am neither a scientist nor a boater nor a diver, nor even a very strong swimmer. Though I consider myself a naturalist, for several years after I moved here I could hardly tell one kind of fish from another even in the markets; and I certainly couldn't catch anything. Steve and I had maintained a sailboat in lakewater. But neither of us knew how fast barnacles and other marine invertebrates attach themselves to boat hulls, or how hard they fight to stay put.

I spent most of 1989 touching my new environment as if it were a cake about to rise. When I tested its texture against that of my previous life, I found it pushed back at me in ways no other place had. In an effort to preserve some of these impressions, I jotted them down. The first note I made, on New Year's Day, reads as follows:

> Steve's old Boy Scout compass orients us. We face southeast, more east than south. Early-morning light on the water changed fast as low tide gradually revealed islands just offshore. I spotted a lighthouse through the telescope at the front window. I'm determined to experience things on the pulse.

By spring, after searching the local libraries and bookstores for information about the Sound, I realized how little had been written on the subject. The few books from prior decades dealt primarily with the waterway's social and commercial history, and with its geology. A few current volumes covered plant and animal identification, and one was designed with boaters in mind. Recent firsthand accounts about discovering the life of Long Island Sound had not been published.

Here is my attempt to fill that gap, by sharing my meetings and remeetings with the living things of this water and the land that surrounds it. The book is not a continuous narrative. It is a collection of writings amassed over several years.

In the spring of 1993 I acquired a used thirteen-foot Boston Whaler, a tough, stable little motorboat with a more or less flat bottom. The purchase has been empowering in the same way that a first driver's license is empowering. The Whaler transports me to channel markers where cormorants roost and shows me the delicate, fierce terns that catch their breaths on lobster buoys not far offshore. In coves it lets me bob through whole afternoons beneath branches from which ospreys come and go.

Many people gain access to the Sound by boat. Why more of them have not recorded their experiences on and around this water is still unclear to me. If there is a predominant reason, it may be the contradictory way in which the Sound is often perceived. Astronomical real estate values along these shores indicate that people want to live as close to the water as possible. (As a rule, in Connecticut and New York a private individual can own land down to the mean high water mark.) Yet public forums and area publications typically label the Sound "Problematic," with a capital P. Sewage problems and hypoxic problems and shellfish consumption problems and problems dealing with floatable debris and pathogens seem poised to overtake the waterway at any moment. Even geese and swans, classic symbols of a romance with the natural world, are viewed here as part of the mythology of disaster. If this body of water were a hospital patient, her personality would be lost somewhere in the written accounts of her condition. She would have *become* her condition, and thus a pariah instead of a living entity worthy of human concern and the best technology available.

There is no question that Long Island Sound has problems. I discuss some of them in the pages of this book. The chapter on salt marshes covers the most pressing ones identified by the government-sponsored Long Island Sound Study. What distinguishes my work from publications associated with that study and similar scientific writing is an intuitive, even idiosyncratic, approach to what I have found around me, and to the subsequent research that clarifies my observations. I hope that this personal point of view will complement those voices that speak out for the Sound in more technical or political tones, since many different voices are necessary to a total appreciation of this environment.

Conservation organizations, state and local governments, and the media will probably continue to focus on the important goal of saving the Sound. This is appropriate. Their work has already made a big difference toward this end. Yet it seems important, at this juncture, to temper the notion of salvation itself before the zeal of it becomes a substitute for understanding what is being saved. The perception that the Sound's sickness is her essence, and the consequential reluctance of people who live near this water to claim it as their own, can only lead to continued confusion.

An intimate perspective such as mine may offer one of the best hopes for saving the Sound, if in no other way than by inviting people who feel disenfranchised from this maritime world to discover it for themselves. The Sound is not just a resource available for recreational use but a place inherently sacred by virtue of being alive. It is capable of rewarding that childlike state of expectancy for which every adult yearns at some time. I have tried not only to personalize this water but also to internalize it. At different moments I have felt as much a part of this place as I did of my early years' sheltering roots. Meeting non-human organisms as equals, however briefly, may be essential to a true understanding of any natural locale. In an effort to maintain this focus I have attempted to parse some of the Sound's complexities and reassemble them on paper in the simplest terms that I could. To the extent that I have succeeded, I have acted as a translator of the Sound.

Discovering this water for myself has been my way of learning what there is to love here, and I now feel equipped to care whether or not the Sound is saved. My title word, "margins," rich in meaning, refers most obviously to those areas that join land, water, intertidal space, and air. These four life zones, which find certain parallels in the four elements, form the basis of this book's organization. I have found that in many instances the plants and animals discussed in each of the four major sections could have been treated almost as easily in other sections. This is because the Sound with its specialized habitats is also a single unified system. Its communities of living things are connected to one another and to me in ways I do not always fully comprehend, ways that have made my exploration of this water a spiritual quest as well as a physical chase. As long as I am privileged to live here, I hope to give this paradoxical place my attention. For it is through such surrender that I become centered, and that the Sound ultimately saves me.

In many respects this book is about belief in the capacity

of all of us who live near the Sound to override conventional thinking and see ourselves as part of a whole to which we may have been taught, unwittingly, that we do not belong. It is about belief in the related notion that the only factors impeding our embrace of this water are those limited perceptions we accept in ourselves. The book attempts to relate one person's discovery of snails and webbed feet and granite, of tentacles and feathers and mud and clouds and more than a hundred miles of salty liquid, and to do it in such a way that the reader is guided into what Walter Anderson once described as a "constant state of applause" for the natural world. In this way the work is about both science and magic. But it is about belief first.

CONTENTS

"So many things have been shown me on these banks, so much light has illumined me by reflection here . . . that I can hardly believe that this grace never flags, that the pouring from ever-renewable sources is endless, impartial, and free."

—Annie Dillard, *Pilgrim at Tinker Creek*

". . . and our hearts shall . . . correspond in breadth and depth and grandeur to our inland seas."

—Henry David Thoreau, "Walking"

MARGINS

INTRODUCTION
SETTING THE MARGINS

Between the hurdy-gurdy of Manhattan Island and the unspoiled nugget of land called Gardiners Island flows Long Island Sound. Neither island actually borders the Sound. The privately owned Gardiners Island, roughly 110 miles east of Manhattan, sits between the north and south forks of Long Island, while Manhattan is distanced from the Sound by the lateral arm of the East River. Yet the two islands, extreme in their differences, stand as physical and psychological gateposts to the Sound. What passes between the gates and overlooks the Sound from her shores is as varied as anything on earth.

Gardiners Island is contracted muscle. You can feel its strength and tension as you surge up and down the dusty grooves that pass for roads through a 1,250-acre stand of virgin oak, reputedly the world's oldest such tract. Bob Gardiner treats the whole of the woods as his personal roller coaster, urging his navy-blue van to go faster, faster.

"We'll find you some turkeys in here, Bird Lady," he yells at me over his shoulder: I had come here to see the island's famed osprey colony. The wheels throw half a bucket of dirt through the open windows.

"There are hundreds of them on the island," he continues. "Not the Thanksgiving turkey, which is a Mexican bird, fat and logy. We have the same wild turkey the Puritans found when they landed in this country, at the same time my ancestors did. Ben Franklin wanted it for the national bird, and Audubon painted it. He sketched here in 1820. The fowl tastes like duck—rich. But lean."

Bob Gardiner is rich but lean. At eighty-six, Robert David Lion Gardiner, sixteenth lord of the manor, is as energized as the land against which he tests his mettle. I don't know how he sleeps. Only once in an afternoon of touring did his arms and hands relax enough to loosen their grip on things round—steering wheels, boat wheels, gear wheels in the island's handmade windmill.

"There. Look there." He pointed. "That's one of three freshwater springs on this island surrounded by salt water. It's as pure as when the Indians stopped to drink from it. I always take a quaff."

Bob led his passengers to the perfect liquid and dipped in his cupped hands with great gentleness. Just before all the water escaped between his fingers, he drank and smiled. We did the same.

This is truly Eden, but it's a rambunctious one, not the peaceable kingdom in which lions lie down with lambs. Its Adam sees the non-human history of the island as being so entwined with the human one that it seems impossible for him to think of the two separately. A set of decorative plates Bob showed me illustrates his perspective. The two dozen circles were made in the mid-eighteenth century from melted-down pirates' gold, Captain Kidd and other pirates having figured prominently in the island's past. Yet the plates depict human forms not as pirates but as fishermen and other figures in natural scenes. Pheasants and quail share the gleaming surfaces with island plants.

On Gardiners Island, a land mass of 3,300 acres, the permanent year-round human population is in the single digits. The other extreme in population density is at the opposite end of Long Island Sound. Of the 24 million people living within 100 miles of this waterway, 1.5 million are residents of Manhattan. This means that, on average, about eighty-five Manhattanites share one acre of land. The repetitive click of heels on sidewalks, the spin and pop of electronic gadgetry, billboards that wink, dogs that bark—this is the city's well-known brand of variety. The water that eddies and swirls around Manhattan's east cheek appears to have caught the contagion of urban activity. Hell Gate, near Mill Rock at the tip of Wards Island, is the perilous north entrance into New York Harbor. The passage ushers in boats and ships of every description, from lumbersome tugs and cargo vessels to speedboats that skim along the surface like torpedoes. Every Fourth of July boaters gather here to watch the sky blossom into gunpowder roses and stars.

To the south there is an improvement in the temperament of the river, which rounds the tip of Manhattan and joins the Hudson in Upper New York Bay. Below the Verrazano-Narrows Bridge the water flows through Lower New York Bay before finding its way to the Atlantic. This convoluted passage is the western connection between the open ocean and Long Island Sound.

My dictionary tells me that when "sound" is used as a noun it can signify "a long passage of water connecting two larger bodies but too wide and extensive to be termed a strait," or "a passage connecting a sea or lake with the ocean or with another sea," or "a channel passing between a mainland and an island." This last definition describes Long Island Sound, which lies between our U.S. mainland on the north and our East Coast's largest island on the south.

Eight miles east of Hell Gate, across an expanse of river shaped like a piece of jigsaw puzzle, the Throgs Neck Bridge marks the Sound's western margin. Beyond the bridge the water opens up quickly in both directions. To the south, a few handsome inlets reach well into Long Island. The land that overlooks them is called the Gold Coast, after the mansions built here by Morgans, Guggenheims, and other wealthy citizens. Not surprisingly, these buildings, many of which are now open to the public, command some of the best views along the island's north shore. It was from such a vantage point that the narrator of *The Great Gatsby* declared Long Island Sound "the most domesticated body of salt water in the Western hemisphere."

The inlets themselves are the modified channels of north-flowing streams that once fed into an ancient river basin. The valley that made up the basin's trunk was oriented southwest-northeast approximately where the Sound flows today. The river predated glaciers that covered parts of North America beginning as long ago as 3 million years.

East of the Port Jefferson area, nearly halfway along the length of the Sound, Long Island's north shore changes character. A ridge of rocky, pebbly material extends from Mt. Sinai, on Port Jefferson's eastern flank, all the way to Mattituck Inlet. This is a distance of some forty miles, a long way for boaters to travel without a single harbor, inlet, or marina.

The bluff is part of a moraine, a pile of debris shoved by a glacier and then abandoned during the glacier's retreat. This moraine extends east above water all the way to Orient Point, at the tip of Long Island's northern fork. At Plum Gut it is submerged. It resurfaces as the small islands called Plum, Great Gull, and Little Gull, ducks beneath the water again at The Race, and re-emerges close to the Sound's north shore, where it is called Fishers Island. The glacially formed spine and one similar to it run nearly the entire length of Long Island, though not always near the water.

Long Island thus helps protect the Sound from many of the same waves and storms that batter her own exposed south shore.

The glacier that deposited the moraines approximately 22,000 years ago had scraped its way south from present-day Canada. Like a mile-high piece of earth-moving equipment—part bulldozer, part backhoe—the ice sheet had already gouged land from the north shore of today's Long Island Sound by the time it made its way across the original river basin. By then it was approaching the limit of its movement, the climate becoming too warm for ice. As the glacier stopped its advance, it dropped bites of bedrock. Thus, land plucked from today's coastal Connecticut, Westchester County, and the Bronx became part of Long Island's skeleton.

The Sound's north margin bears evidence of this glacial assault in its numerous named coves and bays. These indentations are relatively small. Their presence is a boon to gunkholers, who can travel easily from cove to cove almost the entire length of the Sound's northern shore.

To undertake this journey is to travel through wildly varying vistas, each cove, bay, and harbor having a different shape. Some are broad and shallow, with huge stands of salt-marsh grasses that bend double in response to waves. Others are narrow, commercial channels. Others still are a mix of hard-edged man-made features and softer natural ones. Some include sand beaches that relocate grain by grain over time according to the way the wind blows. Others are sandbars that can change address in a single storm.

Gulls in flight seem to stitch together water and sky almost everywhere along this shore. The long-legged herons of summer are more particular. They fish only in quiet waters, usually from the edges of coves. In winter, harbor seals sun themselves on reefs and eye the frigid boaters.

The salinity of the water that fills the Sound's coves and bays varies also. Long Island Sound is an estuary, a place where fresh and salt water meet. The fresh water enters via Connecticut's rivers, which run from north to south. Three of them—the Housatonic, the Connecticut, and the Thames—are responsible for the greatest share. Pouring into the Sound near her eastern end, the Connecticut River alone provides approximately 70 percent of the estuary's total freshwater load.

The mouth of the Connecticut (like that of many rivers) constitutes a small estuary of its own. This one, along with parts of the lower river and some tributaries, is commonly referred to as the Tidelands. Still pristine enough to be designated one of the Nature Conservancy's forty Last Great Places in the Western Hemisphere, the Tidelands host both the threatened bald eagle and the endangered Atlantic salmon.

The lower Tidelands have a population of ospreys, though it is neither as large nor as well known as the nearby Gardiners Island colony. Ospreys are powerful hawks that feed exclusively on live fish. The mix of fresh and salt water right at the Connecticut's mouth is obviously acceptable to menhaden and other fish that ospreys eat.

Coves and estuaries in the western Sound are less saline than those in the east. This is because 90 percent of the salt water coming into the Sound enters through a passage known as The Race, at the estuary's eastern end. Similar in disposition to Hell Gate, The Race is the Sound's main connection to the Atlantic. West from The Race the rivers dilute the ocean water more and more.

Understanding the significance of The Race is the key

to understanding the vital nature of Long Island Sound. This estuary is more than the sum of two radically different shorelines and the natural beauty and heavy development at her eastern and western extremes. The Sound breathes, and The Race is her link to the source of air. Only it isn't air she inhales and exhales twice a day. It's water, in the form of tides.

Atlantic tides have not always exerted such influence over the Sound. As the glacier that formed Long Island began to withdraw from this area, its meltwater created a lake. Contained behind the ridge of the moraines, the lake filled the pre-existing river basin for more than 2,000 years. During this time sediments suspended in the water settled out and accumulated on the lake bottom to a depth of several hundred feet. (This explains the shallow average depth—65 feet—of today's Long Island Sound.) Eventually the lake drained, the ocean entered the basin, and what had been an insular body of water was given rhythm as tides came and went through The Race.

Because of this remarkable geological history, the diverse landscape that borders the Sound is not separate from the Sound in the way that a child is separate from the cupped hands into which it is delivered. The Sound and the land that holds it evolved together, having been conceived together in the earth's womb, then delivered in stages—of land that was first scarred, smoothed, and shifted by the passing of glaciers and later set pulsing with salt tides.

As the Sound's tides rise today, the margins of the land respond. Tiny fish that seem to come from nowhere dart through the shallows. Fiddler crabs exit their burrows and start to battle over mates. The gelatinous egg cases of snails become moistened once again as they stand glued into the silence under an intertidal ledge.

Other organisms count low tide as their time of greatest activity, a time when, to us, every inch of shore seems imbued with an intelligence that says "Wait." Shorebirds feed on the eggs of horseshoe crabs at the ebb, and gulls fight over the sandbar with the most mollusks. Many small creatures have body rhythms so attuned to tidal ebb and flow that they do not change their habits even when they're removed from tidal settings for scientific observation. The tides are a part of who they are.

The tides that sweep in and out of the Sound are a part of who we are as well. Though we may not always know it, they help determine our moods. Tides bring news of the estuarine neighborhood, often delivering to one address the same package they picked up yesterday at another. They also create what we see. Our impressions of this water change moment by moment because the tides change moment by moment. Their margins are never final. This fluid artistry tells us that the Sound, as much as any one of us, is alive.

LAND

A paper birch stands at a bend and, without shrinking, peels itself year after year. Because the bark pulls away from the trunk over horizontal ridges, the loose strips and curls are perforated with random slits that suggest eye holes. I press a strip to my face like a mask. The view is small, monocular. It brings to mind my first meeting with Long Island Sound.

It was autumn, and the day was still. Grasses I didn't recognize stood tall around a cove of liquid pewter. Fallen leaves pied the coastline and drifted in rafts that blurred the margins of the land. The world looked old.

The sun blinked on. Blue sky appeared through the clouds. Twenty feet above me a gull screeched to a stop and scratched its head with its foot. Light winds batted at the water's surface. The glimpsed movements ignited the scene and called me.

THE SHORE

Many paths lead to water from where I live. Some are journeys of the eye through glass and screen. In winter my sight travels from the large coastal oak out to islands framed by its boughs and, far beyond, to splinters of sun that underline Long Island's north shore. This allows morning to begin while a sliver of moon still lodges in the oak's crossed limbs.

Some paths are recollections. After a season of record snowfall my back exulted as it pressed into the warmth of Sound-side bedrock. A few snows had been heavy enough to outfit this stone in white spots above the dark water of high tide. As the tide receded, a sharp line remained to define where earth began.

The best path is literal and direct. It runs from the bottom of my front steps to the top of the rocky slope overlooking the Sound. The first ten strides lead me through evergreens that serve as a windbreak for the house and garden. A dozen more and I'm across a lane and out onto turf browned by repeated freezings and the unending thoughtlessness of geese. The rest of the trip requires forty-six steps and is often breezy.

Simply to stand here and look out is to be entertained. Diving ducks court shamelessly on these sheltered waters from late autumn through early spring. There are buffleheads and oldsquaws and two species of scaups and red-breasted mergansers with their head crests like worn-out toothbrushes. These waterfowl are small, the sprightly buffleheads weighing only three-quarters of a pound.

The birds vanish under water to feed. This distinguishes

them from mallards and other surface-feeding ducks, called dabblers. It also makes guesswork of tracking a particular individual, since flock members often surface fifty feet from where they plummet. When thirty or forty ducks forage at once, the water gathers them and shoots them back to the top with alacrity, and whole stretches of liquid dance with the motion.

Before the cold lifts and the diving ducks head north, I'm likely to see the mergansers mate just a few feet offshore. A hen will swim low in the water with a wild look in her eye. A drake who's been flirting by dipping his angled, outstretched neck will try to seduce her, climbing on backward sometimes. I'll chuckle, knowing little of wet chivalry's trials. He will correct his mistake and find success. For an instant the locked pair may swim with the drake clutching the back of the hen's crest in his red beak, the hen not quite drowning. Then it will be over. The two ducks may never approach each other again, their species' habit being to put on flashy nuptial plumage and choose new partners every spring.

When the flocks are far from shore, I sometimes watch their dives and reappearances over the backs of browsing geese and pheasants. Then the ducks' fleetness forms a living fringe that extends the margins of the land. Occasionally the telescope picks up a raft of forty or fifty scaups out near the islands, which are several hundred yards away. When they're not feeding, these birds bob along the shelf of the Sound, their white abdomens bookended by dark breasts and rumps.

As the diving ducks become increasingly restless prior to their departure for nesting, great and snowy egrets and the black- and yellow-crowned night-herons arrive to stand motionless along the water's edge. They gather their bodies into S's and hunches and other uncomfortable-looking postures that they appear to hold for weeks at a time. By late in the month the sheltered waters of the Sound seem drained of quickness, as if skateboarders had somehow become supplanted by aloof royals.

The herons do not starve. Their energy is simply different from the ducks': it's spent in rhythms of boom and bust. After a long period of immobility, a neck lunges violently toward a fish in the shallows—the Sandman with a seizure.

Casts of characters replace one another here predictably over the course of seasons. Yet there are moments when the world seems unrehearsed. On April 17, the mewings of cedar waxwings caused me to look up into the crown of a cedar rooted a quarter of the way down the rocky shore. Thirty of the birds were beginning to feed there, fluttering while they tried to balance on the berry-rich branches. As they fell silent with feasting, the movement of their many wings gave the tree itself a sense of lightness, as if it, too, vibrated in the pale air.

I watched the acrobats for several minutes. In groups of three and four they began to fly from the needled greenery onto stones beneath it, where runoff from the previous evening's rain formed tiny rivulets and pools. Though waxwings are terrestrial birds, these individuals slaked their thirst just above the tide line before they flew back up to their tree. They dropped and returned, dropped and returned, with a regularity that bridged water and land like a tangible line.

Soon the entire flock moved to the deciduous tree next door. Its limbs were still winter-bare, and I could see the waxwings clearly. Their dramatic black masks hinted of bandits as the birds sat fluffed up against the cold. They peeled out, kissed the cedar in passing, and evaporated en masse.

A freshening wind off the water sometimes sends me inland a few yards, along a ragged lane that separates an old apple orchard from a grove of pines. I've seen as many as seven deer at a time explode quietly from these conifers, their tails erect and flashing white. Before I can breathe, they've leaped across the road and melted into the hardwoods and hemlocks that surround the gnarled fruit trees.

The end of this lane leads down to water protected from the wind. The route is an improvised affair—part road, part raccoon trail, part just the memory of picking my way along massive boulders and bedrock that give out onto sand. Slow going, it promises, to the extent that anything can, a close approach to creatures I don't otherwise see. In warm weather, if the tide is out beyond the derelict wall that forms a lagoon here, I have a chance of finding panicked flounders swimming among the clouds of seaweed. And sluggish, foot-long worms—blue ones, with apricot "legs" that move in waves. It is not possible—ever—to see the great blue heron at close range. As a pointed stone rises to bite me in the leg, the bird utters three nasal croaks and lifts off for more solitary shores.

Often when a big flyer leaves me to myself like this, I think about what a consummate spot I've come to. At odd moments in my previous, inland life I pondered what I would value most on land bordering water. Would broad stretches of sugary sand like the sand of the tropics be appealing? Would evergreens, marching along rock shores as in Maine? Or would I prize a wave-echoing sanctuary, a place to garden like the heaven Celia Thaxter chronicled in *An Island Garden*? Those flower colors, which artist Childe Hassam captured in the New Hampshire light!

Those spire-like shapes, and vines that shade a lookout to sea! Amazingly, miraculously it seems at times, I found it all—trees, stone, sand, a seaside garden—the variety being concentrated in this one glorious setting near a cove. At the cove's head, within close proximity of the water, mountain laurel rises ten feet tall. The plants grow close together; in places their twisted trunks limit how far I can penetrate. Behind the laurel hells, which is what the dense patches are called, open forest floor is covered in matted leaves and in remnants of the plant called, quite wonderfully, wild sarsaparilla. Young sassafrasses stretch toward the light of clearings.

A small sand beach lies across a road from the laurels. Cradling it are thirty-foot-high curved banks of rock and soil. Trees extend down the banks to about fifteen feet above the tide line. The lower stone is devoid of major vegetation except in the few spots that hold marsh grasses. The overall configuration is that of a giant U, with the beach tucked into the closed curve between two headlands.

Alternating coves and headlands are typical along the north shore of the Sound. Michael Bell, author of *The Face of Connecticut*, compares the arrangement to a meter of poetry. "Like Shakespearean couplets," he writes, "place names along the Coast are paired, a 'convex' name followed by a 'concave' name: Hammonasset Point, Clinton Harbor; Bluff Point, Mumford Cove; Indian Neck, Branford Harbor. And on and on down the line."

This beach and cove, like many others along the Sound, attract beer cans and other throwaways that remind me I don't live near wilderness. Juice bottles, and braided ropes, and pink ribbons that wished someone three yards of "Happy Birthday Happy Birthday Happy Birthday," and aquamarine sea glass, and one-quart plastic containers printed with the words "Ursa Super Plus SAE 40 Heavy Duty Engine Oil" above the red–and–white Texaco star are all here.

After storms huge windrows of oyster shells lie tossed together on the sand with jingle shells and clamshells and blue–mussel valves, slipper shells, the occasional perfect conch. The whole lot often ends up bound into bolsters by seaweed. Giant waves fling the heaviest shells, oysters mostly, well above the coastal stone and onto the dark soil and leaf litter. In the calm that follows they look like bits of tissue strewn across the landscape.

An enormous white oak rooted on the bank overhangs this beach. I collect a handful of its acorns when I find them. They remind me of the thoroughly adolescent notes I used to leave curled inside acorns from my parents' yard. I wrote my brief announcements ("Meet me on the bridge, James Dean!" "Read this and die!") on strips of paper the size of those found in Chinese fortune cookies. After I rolled the strips into circles around my fingertips, I sealed the ends with saliva, removed each acorn's cap, and scooped out the pulp. When the hollow became large enough to hold a single scroll, I stuffed one inside and put the cap back on.

I thought of the ark as a tidy package of anticipation, since its existence was a secret known only to myself. I placed it and several others like it inside a dresser drawer in the house. I hoped someone would lift the linens and find the treasures. No one did. Nevertheless, I still think of acorns as vehicles for communication between unseen parties and myself. They are my own digital chip. There's a message in that drawer, still.

Here along the Sound the oak itself is the message. A

predominantly oak forest hopscotched across much of southern New England during the 10,000 years that preceded the European immigration. (Historian William Cronon describes the precolonial woods as a "mosaic of tree stands with widely varying compositions.") The southern New England Indians burned and cleared many acres of woodlands. But their communities relocated seasonally, which gave altered tracts time to restore themselves.

British and other European settlers who began arriving here in the early seventeenth century hacked the forest down in the process of clearing land for fuel and housing and a more permanent style of agriculture. The largest, straightest trees—white pines, initially—were singled out for the masts of sailing ships. By some estimates three-fourths of the southern New England woodlands were gone by 1840.

In 1864 George Perkins Marsh's ground-breaking book *Man and Nature* called attention to the devastating environmental effects of deforestation. Within the next two decades, partly in response and partly out of fear about the economic consequences of deforestation, many Northeastern farmers abandoned stony land that they or their forebears had cleared, fenced, and impoverished; and they didn't stop moving until they reached Connecticut's Western Reserve in Ohio or other areas in the fertile Midwest. Ironically, the migration gave the Northeastern forest a chance, once again, to begin healing on its own.

Now, little more than a century later, the oak forest has made a remarkable comeback. Stone walls originally built along the edges of fields currently lace up returning woods. Oaks and their co-dominants hickory and tulip poplar extend today from southern New England all the way into Tennessee.

As the trees have returned, wild turkey, black bear, and other native pre-Revolutionary forest creatures have re-established themselves as well. (The connection between oaks and deer ticks transmitting Lyme disease has only recently become clear: the numbers of infected insects are now known to increase dramatically in response to extra-large crops of acorns produced every three to four years. The huge crops initiate a population explosion in acorn-loving white-footed mice, from whom the ticks are infected with the disease-causing organism.)

Though the success of these woodlands is sweet, the Northeast's second-growth forests are never free of threats to their future. Development, acid rain, and clear-cutting are just a few. Nonetheless, the very fact of the woodlands' presence in this populous region of the country is nothing short of astounding. As Bill McKibben points out in his book *Hope, Human and Wild*, this is one of the unheralded triumphs of the past one hundred years of conservation history.

———

Bedrock—the miles-thick crust of stone that wraps the earth, ancient matter twisted and pressed by an energy so unimaginably vast that a friend thinks of it as the erotic energy of God. I had never given bedrock any thought at all. I'd had no occasion to wonder how parts of neighbors' houses had been fitted into the soft spaces between huge, hard outcrops. I had certainly never imagined that the stony nakedness could make me feel connected to the planet through a more direct lineage than any I'd previously claimed. Living in a stone dwelling seems totally appropriate here.

Bedrock preselects the direction I move as I wander this coastal land. I travel the same basic north-south route the matter itself assumed millions of years ago, when this part of what is now the state of Connecticut was given its dominant grain by planetary forces squeezing it from the east and the west. Whole continents collided and rebounded like languorous bumper cars then. The gradual fender benders resulted in, among many other things, the predominantly north-south orientation of the Appalachian mountain range.

This major land feature extends from Georgia to Newfoundland and constantly sheds sediment eastward toward the sea, though the flat band of eroded sediments known as the Atlantic Coastal Plain no longer covers the bedrock north of Staten Island. Here along the Sound, low hills of the exposed stone plunge right into the water. Their north-south alignment is obvious along the Sound's upper margin, just as it is in the hills and valleys of Connecticut's interior.

A more recent story with a similar theme is told in features of the land right around me. Bedrock rises gently out of the north here. In some places it suggests a whale's rounded bulk. The repeated grinding and scouring of glacial ice moving south across this region resulted in a prominent asymmetry of the stone. When the ice rode uphill, it skimmed off the top layer of rock. As the glacier began to slide over a crest's far side, it loosened some of the bedrock and fractured it into boulders. This plucked leeward stone was carried along under the frozen mass. The rock that resisted and remained often has a jagged profile.

Moving across bedrock in the same direction that the

glacier traveled, therefore, is easy (though it's clear the ice didn't always head straight south). All that's required for the climb are leg muscles strong enough to make the gradual ascent to twenty or thirty feet. If I walk north as if opposing the ice's general forward movement, however, I can go only so far before I reach sheared-off vertical surfaces that stop me in my tracks. *Passage Interdit*, they say; and they are not to be argued with.

This bedrock is predominantly metamorphic stone such as gneiss. Most Connecticut granite, an igneous rock, has been metamorphosed to granite gneiss. It was formed some 400,000,000 years ago deep inside the earth. Erosion and shifts along fault lines have brought it to the surface. More than the actual force required to form the stone, this ungraspable age is what confounds me. My computer has to be coaxed to accept all those zeros. My brain simply closes down.

Yet there are living things that take the bedrock on. They are the small plants called lichens. Part algae and part fungi, lichens secrete acids that initiate the process of breaking down stone into soil that will support higher plants. Though the vast majority of the soil around the Sound is glacial in origin, the notion that even a fraction of it has arisen through the work of plants as inconspicuous as these seems almost beyond belief.

Some lichen species look like no more than sprayed-on crusts of paint. They're the size of coins, the shape of the moon. Other species are less regular, with rubbery lobes I can flick and peel. Lobes that measure only a fraction of an inch across are considered large. Still other species spend their entire lives trying to attain a height of two to three inches. British soldiers (*Cladonia cristatella*) is one of them. In a spot I know along my stretch of the Sound, this lichen grows where the original British soldiers invaded more than two hundred years ago. The scarlet structures that *Cladonia* bears are reminiscent of the soldiers' red coats. Lichens' typically more subtle coloring helps the plants blend into neutral host stones. The big question with muted lichens, in fact, is what's the lichen and what's the rock. Light-edged gray and gray-green varieties overlap everywhere; clusters of brown ones lack obvious margins.

It was a stroke of genius on somebody's part to leave the treasure sitting out where thieves could find it—if only they knew what to look for. To my mind, what to look for with lichens is beauty—piled-up beauty; beauty grainy as sand, delicate and vulnerable-looking as lace.

To celebrate unsuspected beauty and strength, I gave my husband a small rectangle of soil. I'd watched a bird dislodge it from a depression in bedrock near the house. Lichens paper the bedrock's vertical surfaces. Mosses, which are lichens' direct beneficiaries, scallop the horizontal ones. It was spring, and the moss was thick with spore capsules.

Steve placed the gift in a glass coaster with a shallow rim. He mists and waters it daily, calling it his farm.

"Will you take care of my farm when I go out of town?" he asks.

———

At a lower elevation than the lichen- and moss-dominated stone and immediately above the tide line runs a twenty- to forty-foot-high band of bedrock utterly different from anything else along the Sound's shore. The nature of the rock itself is not different. The distinction is in the community of vegetation that the margin of land supports. This is not a kind country. Winds sweep across it. Salt spray

Fifteen feet from the tide line a waist-high northern bayberry shares a depression with a pitch pine of similar size

bathes and bleaches it. In many places the sun beats down on it for most of the day, and fresh water can be scarce. The few species of plants that manage to survive scattered about this landscape are highly specialized.

I visited this zone in the early fall of 1995, after a drought had turned the already demanding habitat into a wasteland. A bee had flown into the emptied coffee mug I clasped as I wandered above the band early one morning. The day was fine, and the buzzing bee made no attempt to exit the pottery mouth. Since I enjoyed its amplified buzz, the two of us began traveling downhill together, the cupped bee my engine and I its train.

Atop south-facing bedrock above a cove we met a post oak that had shed all but a handful of its cross-shaped leaves. Post oaks, which tolerate impoverished soil, usually have sufficient grit to live on the most exposed headlands. This one was dying of thirst. Its trunk was embraced by an eastern red cedar, which looked healthy. But below it bittersweet, that supposedly indestructible kudzu of the North, appeared too anemic to choke even a stem of grass. A thorny bramble bearing wizened leaves grew with the bittersweet in a crevice that ran downhill from the duo of trees.

Raccoon scat was everywhere. There had been no rain to wash it away, and now the droppings decorated the tops of ridges all along the woods' edge. In the older piles I could see calcified crab claws a fraction of an inch long. Moss on a ledge that was recessed into the forest had turned a sickly yellow-green. Fallen twigs and branches lay in every direction. Except for the occasional squirrel scampering through dried ground litter and the rattle of blown leaves, the shore was eerily quiet and still.

The drought was even more evident in plants on flatter, maximally exposed bedrock. Fifteen feet above the tide line a waist-high northern bayberry shared a depression with a pitch pine of similar size. Like the prematurely fallen leaves, these woody plants looked sere. The needles of the conifer and the crinkled deciduous leaves of the bayberry had turned cinnamon, though more mature bayberries growing in another exposure were still green. The only prominent color anywhere around belonged to goldenrod, bronzy poison ivy foliage, and a two-foot-tall groundsel tree, a shrub often associated with salt marshes. The groundsel tree, with white fruits and iridescent underpinnings on its branches, grew in a protective V of stone.

There seemed to be very little hope for the pitch pine and its bayberry partner. To be sure, both plants are adapted to grow in pockets of sterile, acidic soil containing little or no humus. The pitch pine even has a long root that equips it to seek out moisture, where available. But two nearby pitch pines, gnarled and contorted after many years here, had turned the same rusty brown as the small tree. It was not a good sign.

If salvation turns out to be possible for the pine, it may arrive much later, via a cone. The scales of a single two-inch-long cone on the tree were sharply pointed and stiff (thus the plant's Latin name *Pinus rigida*). Sealed at their tips by resin, the scales will remain closed with the seeds of a new generation inside until heat from a fire causes the resin to melt.

Long Island pitch pines were among the trees that burned for a week on the western edge of the Hamptons during the summer of 1995. Only two days before the bee and I began our trek, I had seen the smoke from our cove, which is seventy-five miles from there. Not all the cones on those Long Island trees were adapted to remaining closed. But some were. After the fire they would open and release seeds capable of germinating. This helps explain why, except in spots where the burning of extensive underbrush caused temperatures to soar above expected levels, those charred acres will eventually become covered in new pitch-pine forests.

My bee had flown away when I wasn't looking. This left me on my own to cross a vein of quartz twelve feet wide. Once past the interspersion, I headed to a slightly higher elevation above a deeper cove, where I knew there was a prickly pear growing. A cactus of the genus *Opuntia*, prickly pear is usually considered a desert plant. Yet here it was in a maritime locale, the only cactus native to Connecticut. The recumbent growth of this patch is extensive. It begins near the top of a ridge and ends twenty feet downhill. The root system that supports such irrepressibleness appears confined to five inches of soil between scrubby trees and obdurate stone.

The prickly pear had bloomed the last week of June. Its yellow flowers, shallow and cupped, sat along the edges of fleshy oval structures. What looked like hundreds of separate stamens, also yellow, surrounded a green, six-parted female structure at each cup's center. The blossoms looked so vibrant yet fragile that it hardly seemed possible they had opened on this ridge of baking rock above salt water. Altogether they embellished their stark surroundings with a ruff of colored laughter.

Even in the dry autumn of 1995 the salt-tolerant cactus bore edible pear-shaped fruits on the fleshy pads. A cross between mahogany and pink, they blended with the burnished leaves of the few unparched deciduous coastal trees. This made the cactus seem as integral to its surroundings as the flowers had made it seem anomalous.

Prickly pears lack true leaves. Instead, like those of many cacti, their flat, succulent stems are capable of photosynthesis. The water stored in these stems equips the species to survive in a hard, dry environment. Prickly pears also collect dew. The drops coalesce on stem structures known as glochids. The British horticulturalist Anthony Huxley describes the structures as "masses of unspeakable miniature barbed hairs . . . which become readily detached and penetrate skin with alarming ease, where they produce intense and persistent irritation."

Deep-green poison-ivy vines that had been flushed with red only weeks earlier romped through the crevices around me. When poison ivy can't contain itself as a vine, it becomes a shrub or even a small tree. The plant is so prolific along the Sound's shores that there is hardly any way to escape it.

Early last spring, when the weather was warm but poison ivy still looked inconspicuous, I watched a macabre scene unfold. I was scanning the islands with the telescope. Two camera-laden photographers and a man who turned out to be a model were carrying clothing from a beached boat onto the sand. Several feet above the tide line that sand is rife with the poisonous plant. The party headed into it. One of the photographers stomped out a site for the model. The model stood (click). He sat (click). He reclined (click). The other photographer, a woman, adjusted the angle of the model's cheek each time a new pose called for a tighter embrace of a certain vine-clad tree, and thereby joined her fate to his.

These people faced hospital time. They had not reckoned with the Sound, whose margins contain all manner of surprise. The fungal and algal components of lichen, long believed to live in symbiotic bliss, are now known to wage war. Even in drought, mica in bedrock near the prickly pear hosts orange dots that turn out to be chiggers. From that same bedrock I've watched groups of lion's mane jellyfish turn themselves inside out pumping their bells against the whim of currents. With each thrust the gelatinous bodies became liquid caramel breaking the water's surface. Their labors helped save the jellies from being thrashed against stone. *That* day.

Another day, on sand near the pitch pines and bayberries, an upturned Atlantic slipper shell full of water hosted a mystifying skit. A dark, pinhead-sized creature that looked like an insect flung itself against the shell rim and bounced back to the center. It did this over and over. For what?

In spite of such apparent misery, the narrow band of hardship above the tides is capable of generosity. My first year on the Sound I found a contorted crabapple four feet tall growing here between stones. Every spring it leafs out and blooms in perfect pink and white, prolifically, as if it were growing erect and well loved on some suburban lawn. Though I know where it is, the crabapple always startles me. "What are you doing here?" I ask in May. It responds with a quick stillness.

JULY 19

4:49 AM read the numbers on the coffeemaker. Something has awakened me. From the kitchen I glance through a sleepy haze at the pink-and-blue light on the water's surface. The air is cool. The day has not quite arrived.

A sound catches my ear as I pass an east-facing window on the way back to bed. A hard object has struck the asphalt beneath the sill. I look across the road to a doe, who stares back at me. Our heads are twenty feet apart.

Damn. She's after my daylily buds. She's probably been here every morning, waiting for the gold to show in the long, plump bullets. These are my favorites—'Jerusalem.' Yesterday I counted fourteen buds on two tall scapes. Today I expected them to open.

In this summer of disastrous dryness I've kept 'Jerusalem' watered. Earlier I thrust some green metal fencing into the soil around it, the kind sold in short, arched spans. This has protected the daylily in previous years, since the plant is close to the house. But in the drought, when animals have taken food and water wherever they could, the barrier is obviously a joke. The deer have already snipped off one course of *Hemerocallis*. It's time for another. And so the white-tailed tribe and I are locked in a classic confrontation between gardener and pest.

I stare at the doe for a full minute, wondering how many deer ticks she's brought me in exchange for my bounty. Then I say in a breathy whisper, so as not to awaken Steve, "Go on." Her ears, which will be fully backlighted in another five minutes, look enormous as they stand out from her slender head. Her thin legs are bunched beneath her. "Go on."

She turns around slowly, her back trailing her head and tall neck, until she ends up in the same position from which she started. Undecided.

Suddenly it is no longer half-light. I am aware of the single notes of birds in the trees. Still, the doe stands looking at me and I at her. "Go on," I say once more. She slowly walks around the low berm that rises between the house and the drop-off to the water. Then she retraces her steps to claim the same position she was in when I surprised her. The creature testing me this way is as lovely as any I have seen.

I say "Go on" again. She circles her own body and then the berm before standing profiled against the Sound. She exhales a half hiss, half harrumph, three times, moving a few steps farther away as she does so. Soon she is lost from sight.

———

"If we leave now, we can get to Australia and back before dark," I say to Steve. Australia is what we call the bedrock at the very tip of a headland beyond beach and cove. It's so far out in the water that a lobster once swam between my feet there as I straddled two points at low tide. At high tide, Australia is gone.

Coming here is the ultimate journey. Since this land is

not-land for approximately two-thirds of the time, Australia has the mystique of every place where worlds meet. In late evening we often stand bathed in western light on the plateau's slippery seaweeds. The sky dims in stages. Since we are below a ridge, we enter shadow before the blush withdraws from the breasts of soaring gulls. Soon the near islands lose their luster. Then the far ones. What only moments earlier was a frame of darkness around those bright, distant mounds is now unanimous dusk. Sometimes a trio of American oystercatchers rises and circles in that instant before the glow is completely lost. The birds' persistent pipings somehow match the blowsy look of their flight, as if three perfect, suspended pale roses were belling while wind tore at their petals.

When darkness approaches in late summer, fishing boats gather in the distance. Some string themselves out across the horizon. Others form bobbing flotillas. Still others venture toward Long Island on a diagonal. The reds and greens of running lights turn on, and suddenly it's Christmas.

Once on Australia we had a private Fourth of July, in August. For fifteen minutes the faded sky above a fireworks barge anchored offshore took on the tints of morning. I never learned why. Even on ordinary midsummer days, celebrations billow in the bright colors of sailboats' spinnakers, and in the specks of kayaks and canoes. During the summer drought of 1995, when lawns along the Sound were parched and brown, the marsh grasses out on the islands remained fresh and green. Each day they painted a prominent stripe across my view, a reminder that intertidal plants abide by their own rules.

On a humid evening in July, Steve and I stood on Australia and watched two men rowing a shell in the distance. The peculiar flash of their oars had attracted us.

Though their movements were only milliseconds out of sync, we saw their blades pull the water in four separate strokes, we counted four distinct featherings after the lifts, and we watched four separate angles of the long, slender shafts turn into half a spider gone spastic. At just such wry moments as this the line between human life and all other life blurs, and Australia salutes one world.

LEEWARD—FIRST SPRING

"It has been my privilege to make intimate friendships with the forest's monarchs."

—Ernest H. Wilson, *Aristocrats of the Trees*

"Here's the other side," our realtor said. She gestured toward the back of the house she was showing us. I didn't see the small building—I saw the tree that embraced it. Thirty- and forty-foot limbs extended far beyond the house walls. One limb rose slightly as it left the massive trunk five feet above the ground. It swooped to within inches of the mossy soil beneath the canopy before it rose again to form an arboreal chaise. On the trunk's opposite side another limb repeated the pattern, giving the tree a balance that suggested the Hindu god Shiva posed as Lord of the Dance.

One bough stretched above our stopped car. As I hung out the window to see its tip, bronze leaves brushed across the blue autumn sky. The leaves were backlighted, and their veins and faintly haired edges showed. The foliage in the dimmer light under the branch was less bronze and more of a green-gold. Everywhere beneath the metallic dome the sun played through the moving branches and left momentary patches of pale gray on the smooth, deeper-gray bark. The leaves were tossed like coins.

I was transfixed. I had never seen a living thing of such generous, almost Byzantine, proportion. Aboveground roots swollen with vitality suggested the toes of an elephant's foot. They had a firm grip on the land. The years, probably nearly a hundred, had left pimples and gashes and swirls all over the six-foot-thick torso. The heavy look of these marks accentuated the teasing mood of the leaves and branches, while beneath the crown, a cavernous room with a floor space of several thousand square feet looked as cozy as a child's playhouse. The entire plant (also like Shiva) expressed seemingly contradictory ways to be alive. It settled the question of where we would live.

The tree, which has guided us through the last few years, is a copper beech, *Fagus sylvatica atropunicea*. As I've come to know it, I've come to respect it more and more. My reverential attitude is shared by many people who live along the shores of Long Island Sound. Like the tree and like myself, these people are, for the most part, European imports to the area. Some are from families that have been here for generations. Others are upstarts, newer to the place than myself. What we have in common, we naturalized New Englanders, is the strong conviction that something extraordinary is in our midst in the form of the copper beeches, which require the special propagation of a graft to stay true.

In the branches I read not just magnanimous play but the heyday of visible wealth along both shores of this water. Beeches, elms, and lindens denote a grandeur of scale characteristic of the great coastal Long Island and Connecticut estates that were developed as part of the nineteenth-century landscape movement in America. Proximity to water and a clear view of it were as important to these estates as the presence of specimen trees. Consequently, some of the more imposing old copper beeches can be seen from the Sound today, though their intolerance of salt spray dictated their being planted slightly inshore.

In the Norwalk Island chain the copper beech on Tavern

Island spreads above a house that once belonged to producer Billy Rose. Another grows on waterside property at the University of Connecticut's Avery Point campus (near Groton), the former estate of railroad magnate Morton Plant. The characteristic color of the trees is unmistakable on Long Neck Point in Darien, Connecticut, though not all these beeches are large. Boaters can see massive copper beeches, however, near the towns of Oyster Bay Cove and Cold Spring Harbor, Long Island.

Two mature copper beeches even traveled by barge from where they were originally planted near New Bedford, Massachusetts, some fifty miles northeast of the Sound, to what is now the publicly owned Planting Fields Arboretum in Oyster Bay, Long Island, on the estuary's south side. The trees bridged not only two regions of the country but also two great American dynasties. Copper and oil magnate Henry Huddleston Rogers, whose interest in horticulture benefited his home of Fairhaven, Massachusetts, had a daughter who married New York insurance executive William Robertson Coe. In 1913 the young Coes purchased the Long Island property. When they moved there two years later, the pair of copper beeches that Mary Rogers Coe had seen from the windows of her Massachusetts girlhood home moved also. The trees were sixty feet tall, weighed twenty-eight tons each, and (after their two and a half day winter barge passage and four days of negotiations over the removal of utility company wires) required nearly two more weeks of being moved through the streets of Oyster Bay before they could be replanted. One of the trees is still thriving.

Not all copper beeches planted near the Sound during that lavish era were installed right along the shore. Many now grace public parks, suburban lawns, and other spaces that can accommodate their immense growth. "My" beech, which stands sixty feet from a road, dominates a walled leeward yard that has undoubtedly appeared to grow smaller as the tree has come to fill the area.

In January, as Steve and I were settling into our house, we commented on how different the tree looked from the way we remembered it. Devoid of leaves and therefore of movement and high color, it focused our attention on the shadows that its bare branches cast on the ground. The lines were strong, almost black. The trunk formed the bold shaft of a sundial. From our windows we watched as the living timepiece marked our first moments on the Sound.

I checked in with the copper beech several times a day that winter. In the early hours I glanced at it idly between strokes of the mascara wand. Soft rains freckled and splotched the trunk, while downpours made the limbs look slick as a salamander. On clear days light struck the undersides of the branches in such a way that pale chevrons emerged there, and the silhouettes of owls' heads.

In mid-April the beech was different. I stepped across its lowest limb and sat down with my back against the bough's final, upward curve. The branches above me showed evidence of new growth. Leaf buds that had been pointed and severe since I'd moved here were twisting into new shapes as they began to unpleat their foliage.

The tree opened fast. As the leaves continued to unfold, rounded clusters of male flowers bearing stamens a fraction of an inch long emerged. Each cluster hung from the end of a silken-haired cord (a peduncle) that was an inch or two long. The dangling spheres at the ends of the mammoth branches made me think of ball fringe. Paired female flowers wrapped in scarf-like bracts of cerise silk stayed concealed in the burgeoning leaf tissue.

Each cluster of staminate copper-beech flowers hangs from the end of a cord

I returned a few days later and noticed a continual popping around me when I stood under the beech's crown. Small iridescent copper husks were falling as the tree sloughed off scales that had enclosed the germ of its leaves. The next week brought a second rain of tree parts, this one of spent male flowers in clusters still attached to champagne-colored strings. They drifted down slowly and silently beneath the canopy. I caught two. Others landed on the spreading base of the trunk. And between the toe-like beginnings of the roots. And on the few softly spined, open seed capsules left on the ground from the previous fall. And on sparse stands of grass, where they lay twisted into fantastic shapes. Still others stretched out flat with their knapsacks of spent flowers. Even a reservoir between two of the tree's roots—the personal water supply of our neighbor's poodle, Polly—was covered in old beech bloom.

For several days the corded flower clusters kept falling. Along with the earlier husks they formed windrows under the largest branches and matted on the soles of shoes and clogged drains and blew onto steps and filled odd spaces until the land all around the tree looked blanketed in pale plush. Polly raked her reservoir clean by dipping in her right front paw and dragging the debris out over the lowest part of the dam. This tree, with its crown so vast it seemed to make its own weather, was more generous than any other plant I'd ever seen. (In autumn I was paid for my appreciation in the currency of rustic stars—penny-hued seedpods that fell by the thousands and spilled their edible, triangular fruits over the ground.)

For all this bounty, the tree's essence is, to me, something more. Whatever spirits reside in the massive frame— and there's room for hundreds—sustain me in unexpected ways. Conservationist Aldo Leopold felt a "strange transfusion of courage" at the sight of his pine trees in snow. "It is in midwinter that I sometimes glean from my pines something more important than woodlot politics, and the news of the wind and weather," he writes in *A Sand County Almanac*. When I rub my hand along a sinewy limb of the copper beech, I feel a comparable strength pass into myself.

The copper beech also connects me to home, through the memory of an incident that occurred long ago. A late great-uncle of mine loved piney woods, by the acre and the foot. He owned a good bit of them. Against great odds a black walnut tree established itself in one of his evergreen neighborhoods and grew to such a size that it became legendary. One day it was missing. By way of explanation, the family surmised that an acquaintance who knew the value of board-foot walnut had used a helicopter to airlift the tree, roots and all, from among its needled cohorts. What's more, they said, the fellow had done it in the dead of night.

I would have none of it. Not that it made a bad story. It made a terrific story, particularly the night part. But I couldn't imagine how that most earthbound of living things we call a tree could rise into the sky.

I've traveled far since that literal time. Trees do rise. Noon's shore becomes dusk's tidal flood. Nothing that lives is without wide margins of adaptability that cause me to look up and find a rootedness I thought long buried.

————

A real comer that first spring was a horse-chestnut tree that grew fifty yards back from shore. Sets of sticky brown bracts enfolded its tight leaves. The upright leaf ends remained gathered even after the bracts opened. If I failed to notice for just one day in late April or early May, however, I returned to bursting choirs of small, many-parted leaves robed in apricot chiffon and to tiny, buxom flower buds, each one pale and green. The knobby buds were clustered on short stalks that came out of the central stem end, which seemed to be always rising, while on either side of the buds a long, thin arm stretched out Zorba-style and dangled a single leaf from the tips of its fingers. As the gauziness waned, the entire structure looked so cleanly proud that I expected it to vibrate when I touched it—maybe even to set off the ringing of bells.

The maples also seemed ready to get on with things. By

the time the tiny sugar-maple flowers appeared, the red maples' seeds were already ripening. The seeds were carried inside the double whirligig fruits technically known as samaras but commonly called keys. During a May gathering along a tidal inlet, soft Middle Eastern dips and other dishes served as landing pads for maple keys that arrived on every puff of wind.

Fruit trees and other showy trees of coastal towns went through color phases like birds changing plumage. Willows turned yellow-green as forsythia faded and the white blooms of pear trees disappeared behind new foliage. Crabapple pink followed in a week. Along my stretch of the Boston Post Road each lollipop crab flowered within five minutes of every other and, after a few days, littered the sidewalk with petals.

Though these green debuts varied in style, the Sound controlled the timing. In a typical spring the estuary warms more slowly than the land surrounding it, and the temperature differential creates cool breezes that blow onto shore. As a result, plants right along the Sound flower late in the season. Traveling north from the Sound my first year here, I saw more and more open blossoms until I reached a point about twelve miles inland, where the coastal slope gives way to the hills with their different climatological pattern. The diminishing impact of the Sound, in other words, was documented in buds.

By the time spring on the land was full-blown, it had already come and gone in the estuary itself. The season arrives in the Sound as early as January, one of two times of the year when plankton begin to multiply. Plankton are the organisms that form the base of the marine food chain. They can be microscopic or larger, larval or adult, plant or animal (phytoplankton or zooplankton). Their common denominator is an inability to propel themselves through the water. They are drifters, hoboes riding the liquid box-cars we call currents and waves.

A few years ago, a scientist friend tells me, the Sound took a miss on a plankton bloom. After I learned of this momentous absence, I began to think of spring's arrival on land as more of a gift than a given. If ancient planktonic patterns could fail, rhododendrons could refuse to blossom. Trees that overhang coves could dry up, as many did in the summer of 1995.

When everything runs as expected, however, the on-shore spring is one of three beginnings, the other two being the early plankton bloom and a second annual explosion of plankton, which occurs in summer. These two provide a context of arrival and closure around the terrestrial spring, and thus, for me, a change of perspective on growth itself.

Of course, trees aren't the only living things that usher in spring on leeward land. The whole galaxy of plants that grow in this area does. I was drawn particularly to the na-tive herbaceous wildflowers, many of which were familiar to me from other parts of the country. Others were as alien as their names—lousewort, pussytoes, saxifrage. Though widespread coastal development has resulted in a serious loss of wildflower habitat, I could still find pockets of trea-sure on my rambles.

Sometimes, however, I couldn't take a step. The stubby pencils of green that thrust through mossed soil near the copper beech began to unfurl as April made room for May. Each stem carried two or three light-green leaves. From subterranean runners the stem rose about three inches into the air and so near others of its kind that in many places an almost continuous verdure covered the ground in every direction. Occasionally I found myself surrounded by the tender growth, as if I'd been painted into a corner of spring's room.

These wild Canada mayflowers, which are lilies, require a very acidic soil. The oak forest provides this. Oak foliage decomposes into leaf mold slowly, as serious mulch-seeking gardeners well know. Along with the acidic composition of the region's bedrock, this reluctant breakdown contributes to the formation of a woodland soil that supports a very particular flora. It typically includes not only this cunning little ground cover but also rhododendrons, mountain laurels, azaleas, and other woody heaths and associated species. These plants grow prolifically here, so much so that when the pale laurels bloom in June, the land looks covered in snow.

Within this general environment, one habitat intrigued me more than all the others: damp earth only yards from the Sound hosted skunk cabbages. I know now that these curiosities are a regular feature of troughlike freshwater swamps along some of this region's most fashionable lanes. But that first spring their furtive-looking features—beaked, hoodlike spathes and knobby spadices pimpled with flowers—struck me as angst-ridden. It seemed odd that such moisture-loving plants should thrive under massive hardwoods that were within sight of salt-bleached rock shores.

In places only slightly drier than skunk cabbage swamps, Jack-in-the-pulpits were up and running by May 10. Or if not running, then Jack himself (also a spadix) was standing ramrod-straight in the nearly cone-shaped, overhung pulpit that gives this native oddity its common name. The delicate wild geranium (*Geranium maculatum*) shared Jack's shaded soil, while from under the arched stems of nearby Solomon's seal rows of bells pealed forth.

It was still April when I noticed mayapples in a clearing nearby. The youngest mayapples, quite yellow, could have been the rounded tips of small, closed parasols pushing through the ground. Toward the end of the month I returned to the same place and peeked under the fully opened double umbrellas of foliage. In the V's formed by the divergence of the upright leaf pedicels I found simple white suns. They nodded slightly on their supports. April apples, after all.

The ferns, or at least that tantalizing promise of them known as fiddleheads, also vied for attention in the dampness. I followed a trickle of water downhill and found clusters of the dark coils parting the earth every few inches. Some of the fiddleheads subsequently developed into leaves of cinnamon and interrupted ferns, both large, magnificent species with very showy reproductive structures. (Ferns do not bear flowers.)

These ferns are classified in the genus *Osmunda*, along with a third species, *O. regalis*, which I had not run across in the wild. A local nursery carried it, however. Its fiddleheads were still only half unfurled in the pots and were tattered with the same cinnamon-colored natal felt as the fertile fronds of its cousin. I packed the embryonic royalty home and installed it in the shade. Every year since then it has ruptured the soil and raised the perfect heads of its fiddles as winter bows to warmth.

———

Bright tulips and hyacinths climb from floor to ceiling in my study's drapery fabric, so that even before the lilacs outside the window opened that first spring I was surrounded by flowers. Single stems of newly discovered real flowers sat lined up in jelly jars across the back of my desk. I photographed old friends I couldn't bid goodbye right away—the intricate Dutchman's-beeches, for example—

and wedged the prints at odd angles beneath the bases of multicolored pushpins that stabbed bulletin boards hanging on the room's white walls. The large horizontal surfaces were littered with open field guides. The shelves held over-due books.

I used the study for writing and for collecting small cu-riosities. I also began pulling apart large ones. Blocks of marshy soil that I spread out on sheets of plastic wrap gave off a smell so simultaneously sweet and sour that I couldn't stop inhaling. When the morning sun warmed it, the soil grew musky. I carried various grades of the scent around in my nose for days.

The immediacy of such firsthand experiences both in-doors and out fueled my imagination and seemed to heighten my senses. The tufted green world of mosses was made even greener by the airborne droplets of moisture we call fog and by the pinpoints of water that coalesced on every surface. Early in spring some mosses produce spears so thin and pliant they're little more than upright threads. Crouching, I stroked across their tips: a hundred identical forms bent together in the space of a mere square foot. I'd made it rain.

When it really did rain, in an April warm enough for me to raise the storm windows, I found the sound jarring and realized that winter had dulled me. Gulls I'd seen flying silently and without forward motion into cold winds sud-denly were screaming. Once the rain began in earnest, it fell for days and soaked everything. The stone front stairs stayed so wet they made puddle noises whenever I went up and down them in my duck boots. The sounds seemed brand-new.

Land noises I'd never heard before reached my ear. Ring-necked pheasants in these suburbs have no concept of property rights but wander freely from lawn to lawn in that pausing-then-running-like-all-hell manner of theirs. The jewel-headed cocks are far from silent when they're just poking around my house. Their rather high-pitched voice is limited to a one- or two-note repertoire that frequently announces their whereabouts. In warm weather, to hear the note of a pheasant followed by the croak of a heron cursing intruders was to hear the land and water exclaim as one.

Gradually my senses united into one delicious super-sense, as if I were on soft fire and, happily, couldn't parse the physical impressions made on me by living things. In honor of that time of increased awareness and of similar times since, I keep before me a tray overflowing with cherished natural objects I began collecting then. I recognized some of the items as I gathered them. Others, unfamiliar, struck me as real finds and have, in fact, turned out to be exactly that: I've run across only a handful of sea urchin shells near the Sound.

Walk bouquets have a place in the tray. My late friend the poet Amy Clampitt and I each made one during a stroll we took along these shores. Walk bouquets are casually assembled tussy-mussies of dried grasses and other uncultivated objects that beg to be picked up. Mine contains an old pussy-willow catkin and several unusual twigs.

Seeing the bouquet brings back the memory not only of excursions with Amy but also of the living things that attracted her. The shape of a tall evergreen growing at an intersection of stone and soil was one of these. Amy had once thought she might be a visual artist. This conifer with its rough trunk and Oriental-looking tiers caught her painterly eye. As she stood absorbing details of the twenty-foot-tall tree, her own slight frame looked even smaller than usual, and her wonderfully birdlike voice was only temporarily silenced.

Besides the bouquets, other tray items—sometimes separate, sometimes grouped—include an inch-wide horseshoe-crab shed with all ten leggings intact; four whelk fragments and four twisted lengths of whelk-egg cases (probably not relatives); and a complete blue-mussel shell, the valves of which open enough to admit my index finger. The bivalve may really be a cobalt butterfly.

Two glossy horse-chestnuts rest in their bristly shells. One rattles, one doesn't. There are Siamese-twin oyster valves (big ones), the small carapaces of several types of crabs, an unidentified bird bone, and too many jingle shells to count, most in sublime shades of yellow and apricot. One looks like a potato chip.

My oblong owl pellet and four fragile cicada sheds are balanced for the moment atop a water-worn stone. Next to them is a post-oak leaf with salt crystals stuck to its edges. I pried it loose from what had been a tide pool before all the water evaporated.

This collection forms a tactile portrait of the land around me. I try to keep it from looking arranged, since it suggests the rich randomness of the Sound's margins. From time to time I remove all the items, dust them off, and put them back together in a way that seems to refresh them and me. In summer I add recently dried roses, their colors still intact. In autumn I scatter the lightweight seedpods from the copper beech over the surface of the collection. Some fall into the spaces between heavier objects and stare up at me from the darkness. At the center of the coffee table in our busiest room, even in winter, the outside-in mélange bespeaks wholeness—cycles of night and day, rainfall and evaporation, spring and fall. The miracles of photosynthesis and transpiration. These mercies call into being every living thing. I touch their incarnations.

CANADA GEESE

"When the wild geese saw the tame geese, who walked about the farm, they sank nearer the earth, and called: 'Come along! Come along! We're off to the hills!'

"The tame geese could not resist the temptation to raise their heads and listen, but they answered very sensibly: 'We're pretty well off where we are. We're pretty well off where we are.'"

—Selma Lagerlöf, *The Wonderful Adventures of Nils*

"Whenever we introduce an alien to a new country we also change life for the natives."

—Jonathan Weiner, *The Beak of the Finch*

Two Canada geese ate their way across my lawn this morning. At some veiled signal they alternated watch: the long black neck of the one that had seemed the more ravenous rose and, with horizontal head and beak, formed a question mark against the water's shine. This pair, probably lifelong mates, will feed near my stretch of coastline for the rest of the winter. Others will no doubt join them. Early in spring each twosome will adjourn to a nesting site on a nearby island or pondside, and I will not see breeding Canadas at close range for a while. But the conundrum symbolized by those rising questions of feather and bone will not disappear—how have these magnificent waterfowl, birds once thought to fly to the moon each winter, come to live among us year-round?

When it snows, I clip on my old cross-country skis and explore the Canadas' feeding grounds for clues. There are no right-of-way rules for skiers in these parts, though perhaps there should be. Everywhere are signs that whole armies of the waterfowl have encamped. Where my skis leave two parallel grooves in the snow, the geese leave toeprints in intersecting lines. A little larger than my palm and the shape of a fat kite, the prints consist of five marks each. The three most prominent ones record the toes themselves. (A fourth, raised toe leaves little impression.) The other two marks, which are sometimes fainter, connect the first three and show the extent of webbing. The tracks do not appear side by side. Instead, each one presses into the white landscape at a slightly drunken angle to the one before and behind it. Where many impressions overlap, mayhem reigns.

I can count on recognizing these prints and the cigar-shaped droppings among them, but one day I realized I'd had the birds marching backward through my head. The narrowest part of each print indicates where a goose's toes join the rest of the foot. Yet the arrow that this small angle creates points to where a Canada has already been. The imprint looks like a mistake in design, and each time I see it I have to stop and puzzle it out all over again.

Every winter evening, flocks of as many as two dozen geese leave our shore to roost overnight among the chain of islands beyond. Steve and I often watch them clear a dam or bridge as they honk and burble monosyllabically amid the rustling of their great wings. The short trip seaward makes sense, since islands typically harbor few of their predators.

Many mornings, instead of being greeted by the flocks wheeling back to the mainland in slanted flight formations, we observe a most decorous procedure. The geese line up one behind the other, still in gaggles, and swim slowly in. When a coral light coats the water, the silhouetted birds glide across the colored pool with a breath-holding stillness. No webbed foot shows. No neck turns or twists. There is only the even slide through a sun brought low. We have never found a satisfying explanation for this avian ritual other than this is what sleepy geese like to do.

Steve called my attention to the faster rhythm of the birds' drinking. In late January the ice covering most of the local brackish ponds was beginning to break up. One afternoon we trained our binoculars on two dozen Canadas sipping the newly liberated water from a pond edge. Several of them stood with their long necks bowed and their beaks thrust under the surface. As they alternated raising and tilting their heads to let the water trickle down their throats, they suggested a noble clockwork.

The next day I saw a young man idly tossing rocks onto the same pond, which was still frozen in patches. The nearest geese—perhaps the drinkers—waddled en masse away from the annoyance and then turned to watch. Their necks and heads moved in unison this time as they mirrored the up-and-down trajectory of the stones.

The choreographed flock life that's so entertaining to me is necessary to a goose's survival. Polly, our neighbor's dog, often rounds a curve of road leading onto a mowed field where as many as sixty of these waterfowl gather to feed. She trots along nonchalantly until she reaches the very edge of the open space, which is about a hundred feet from the geese. She pauses. The white chin strap of one bird flashes in the light. Polly's off, streaking over the ground with her tongue flapping. I can almost hear her thinking she's going to startle the birds this time. But she never does.

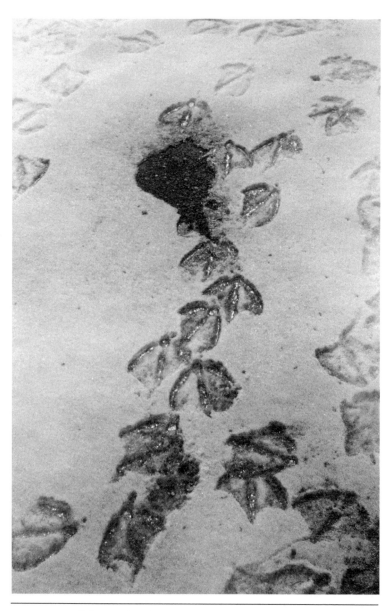

*Whenever I see goose toe prints, I have to stop and
puzzle them out all over again*

Canada geese (*Branta canadensis*) have a wide view of the world. They can see almost as much with a single eye as I can with my binocular vision. That's why they don't need to face Polly to know she's nearby. By the time she approaches the browsing flock, the sentries (which browse little) are already initiating a warning. Ornithologist Albert Hochbaum describes it as "a nervous uptilting and shaking of the head . . . As one individual begins this action, its companions become alert, and the movement is repeated by all members of the flock. When shaking reaches a certain degree of intensity, the birds invariably take to the air."

Lift-off is not possible for Canadas in every season. After the four to nine goslings are hatched in spring, the youngsters are herded along on the water between the parent birds. Like the goslings they shepherd, the adult geese cannot fly. During the latter half of the brood period, which extends from spring through most of July, the adults molt their feathers, including their flight feathers. This shedding makes the adult birds vulnerable to dangers that they can escape at other times of the year. It explains why geese leave the land in summer and congregate in the middle of ponds, where they often float along with a duvet's worth of their own feathers. It also helps me understand why geese who can clip spring grass faster than a machine can mow it will seek summer handouts from boaters in coves.

This short-lived flightlessness is of minor consequence compared with what Canadas suffered here at the turn of the last century. Some of the large estates then being developed along the Sound went to great lengths to attract wild Canada geese, which did not breed in this area. Migrant geese injured in hunting were pinioned and used as live decoys by the private collectors, and by game breeders as well. (Pinioning means amputating the wing at the wrist on one side.)

Some of the flightless geese escaped. *The Atlas of Breeding Birds of Connecticut* states that descendants of those that did not were released "after legislation abolished use of live decoy flocks in 1935." At least a portion of the resident Canadas along the Sound today are believed by some people to be the great-great-greats of those once-grounded birds. Others of the geese are assumed to be former winter migrants who settled into the comfortable life here. And there are still other origins suggested for the birds, this whole question being nothing if not scientifically controversial.

If today's Long Island Sound geese are, in fact, the descendants of migrants, they do not know their species' historic travel routes along the Atlantic flyway. Among geese, swans, and cranes, migration involves both instinct and learned response, and some concept of it must be passed from one generation to the next. This type of education may have been interrupted here. Scientists tell us that today's resident birds no longer have even a trace of the racial memory that once guided their forebears to historic breeding grounds such as the tundras and lakes of northern Quebec and the upper Canadian Maritimes.

Many waterfowl biologists downplay the role of escaped decoy birds in the history of today's resident Canadas. Milan Bull, director of the Connecticut Audubon Center in Fairfield, says there is no evidence that significant numbers of those birds existed. "Our resident Canadas are *Branta canadensis maxima*, an introduced, non-migratory bird native to the Midwest, and only remotely connected to live decoys or pinioned birds," he claims. Professional game managers were delighted to stock the twelve-pound *maximas*, since they wouldn't fly away. And state agencies had every confidence that should the geese overpopulate, they could be controlled very simply with a gun. Concentrating their numbers in areas where hunting is prohibited, however, the geese have proven smarter than their would-be managers.

Wherever the Sound's resident geese came from, one thing is certain—the birds consider *these* shores and *these* waters their natal territory, and are thus significantly different creatures from their past and present migrating kin. Even the residents' reproductive life has changed. Well nourished, the local birds start breeding at two years of age, whereas migrants begin at three or four. The stay-at-homes also have hatch times early in the season, which may help explain their relatively high survival rates. These factors have contributed to huge recent increases in the numbers of non-migratory geese. Connecticut had an average 9,000 nesting pairs of the birds during each of the last three springs, while in the same time period there were an average 7,000 breeding pairs in New York's Westchester and Rockland Counties and on Long Island.

While the residents' numbers have burgeoned, there have been decreases in the numbers of geese that still travel to and from these shores. At least two factors are responsible for this. Migrants have suffered severe weather conditions on their breeding grounds for the past few springs, and in Canada the birds come under heavy pressure from hunters.

Ironically, the Canadas that now remain near the Sound throughout the year (which represent about 85 percent of the geese seen in the area) may function as live decoys for the flocks that still do migrate high in the sky. Some observers hold the residents responsible for short-stopping by one hundred miles or more the migrants' autumn journeys south. In Southern states where the geese once wintered—primarily North and South Carolina—populations of the waterfowl have been reduced by as much as three-quarters since the middle of the century. But influences such as new food sources linked to changing agricultural practices are involved here and make short-stopping a controversy all its own.

———

Many people who live near the Sound consider Canada geese their adversaries in battles over property rights. There's no question that geese and people have similar tastes in landscape. Relatively open countryside dotted with ponds and lakes, the whole of it accessible to the sea or some other body of salt water, is what the traditional breeding ground of our Canadas' ancestors looks like. It's also what we along the Sound have been busy sculpting for ourselves since the end of World War II. In the 1960s and '70s alone, there may have been as much as a 50 percent increase in back-yard ponds in Connecticut's Fairfield County. Not unexpectedly, the geese feel at home in this environment.

Even the arrangement of elements within our suburban and exurban spaces welcomes today's geese. Some of the outdoor public areas we've designed for our own enjoyment are grassy tabs of communal property that extend into sheltered waters. Mamaroneck, New York's forty-four-acre Harbor Island Park is a good example. Surrounded by quiet salt water on three sides, it gives the birds every opportunity to elude threats. The park is so attractive to the geese that the village of Mamaroneck has engaged a specially trained border collie to chase them away.

A few miles inland, where agricultural fields may offer migrants substantial food, resident geese are drawn to ponds that have had islands built in them. This provides seclusion, which Canadas need for nesting. The land around such ponds is often planted in grass that gets mowed regularly. The geese like this, too, and not just because grass is maximally nutritious when young and tender. The openness of such habitat lets the birds see what's around them and helps guarantee their safety.

Manicured corporate headquarters and golf courses may be the most irresistible carrots we dangle in front of the geese's bills. The water hazards that the links contain offer refuges where small flocks can gather in relative safety. Golf-course grass is kept meticulously groomed. And toys such as the balloons and plastic whirligigs often positioned to keep Canadas off smaller, private greenswards throughout the region are deemed inappropriate where unobstructed views down fairways are required. For these and related reasons the third hole of the Yale University course in New Haven, Connecticut, has far more geese than golfers on many days. It's typical of entire courses throughout the area.

Even where the Sound's shores and adjacent lands have not been extensively developed, the Sound itself acts as a magnet to Canada geese. Because salt water is slow to freeze, the estuary provides the basically herbivorous birds with a variety of marine vegetation twelve months of the year. Small crabs, mollusks, and similar creatures probably supplement this diet. The Sound's reliable foodstuffs help sustain the waterfowl in harsh winters particularly, when dining only on frozen or snow-covered terrestrial vegetation may prove difficult.

In exchange for the use of "our" open space, the large numbers of geese near Long Island Sound leave messy droppings that carry the threat of salmonella bacteria, coliform bacteria, and other harmful pathogens (though coliform counts in goose droppings are very low compared to those in the droppings of dogs, cats, and gulls). The goose-droppings issue comes to public attention primarily in warm weather, when parks and beaches swarm with the birds, along with people and their pets.

Health plagues that threaten public reservoirs such as the 30-billion-gallon one in Kensico, New York, just north of White Plains, are often thought to be goose-related. Typically, 90 percent of New York City's drinking water has moved through the Kensico facility. For several years prior to a 1993 cleanup the reservoir was bypassed. The droppings of some three thousand Canada geese and ring-billed gulls, along with non-avian pollutants, had made the water unsafe for human consumption.

In spite of such problems, our dance with the geese is not without its cartoon aspect. The list of techniques that communities have used in an effort to become goose-free is both long and futile, particularly since hamlets that receive the exiled birds may volley them (or their cousins) right back. The town of Greenwich, Connecticut, alone—allegedly the Canada-goose capital of the Sound—has installed electric fences, deployed venal-sounding explosives over the birds' heads, floated helium balloons, paid raucous students to sprint across beaches, and considered any number of the several thousand other goose-busting suggestions received at Town Hall, all to no avail. Where there has been a modicum of success, as on a Greenwich golf course that uses families of counterfeit swans to help keep geese off the greens, constant vigilance is required to make the lesson stick. The geese are street-smart by now, a trait that may play out in their continuing evolution in ways we may not yet have dreamed.

In the meantime, no single long-range, socially acceptable solution for controlling the Sound's Canada goose flocks is at hand. Piecemeal efforts that have been successful in other areas seem to work here on a limited scale. Communities in Minnesota and New Jersey, for instance, are experimenting with harvesting Canada geese for soup kitchen use. Canadian sculptor William Lishman has imprinted newly hatched goslings on an ultralight aircraft. For several years now the youngsters have followed the craft to their ancestral wintering grounds and returned to Canada on their own the following spring. The 1996 movie *Fly Away Home* is based on Lishman's experience. Yet playing lead goose for tens of thousands of birds is infeasible.

It's a dilemma. Nevertheless, these fabulous creatures who have stirred feelings and inspired poetic thought for centuries still delight me, as they do many others. I agree with conservation writer Ted Williams when he says it cheers him to know there's "a symbol of wildness that humanity has not been able to crush which, instead of going gentle into that good night when we convert the world to asphalt and green monoculture, takes over and doesn't get out of our way." Since neither the resident Canada geese nor the vast majority of Northeastern human beings are native to these shores, perhaps the final test of who owns the land around the Sound will come many decades from now, when the species with the most offspring left standing and feeding and stretching in the morning light wins.

Owls

" 'Oh, owl!' cried the Wart . . . 'Look, he has decided to talk to me!' "

—T. H. White, *The Once and Future King*

It's early morning, frigid, January, and Saturday, circumstances guaranteed to keep me in my fuzzy bathrobe for a while. Tucked into a fireside rocker by a window overlooking the Sound, I'm reading E. B. White's delicious Yankee prose:

> There is a fraternity of the cold, to which I am glad I belong. Nobody is kept from joining. Even old people sitting by the fire belong, as the floor draft closes in around their ankles. The members get along well together: extreme cold when it first arrives seems to generate cheerfulness and sociability. For a few hours all life's dubious problems are dropped in favor of the clear and congenial task of keeping alive. It is rather soothing when existence is reduced to the level of a woodbox that needs filling, a chink that needs plugging, a rug that needs pushing against a door.

As I savor this, a small boat outfitted with a davit and lobster block heads west beyond the lighthouse. Its silhouette is stark against the water's blinding whiteness. On land nothing moves but one perched crow, also silhouetted. Storm windows mute its caws. Yet they are evident in the bird's hunched rocking. The sight is reminiscent of another colorless morning on this water. Devoid of today's coziness, that time suggested a siege.

Not far from here a woodland path loops around strong-boned faces of bedrock and a freshwater sink edged with ferns. Its outer rim skirts salt marsh. A section of the trail farther upland feeds into an allée of ancient mountain laurels. In winter long strands of crusted snow rest on the plants. Strand segments slip below the limbs to hang like ropes of pearls.

I love this combination of landscape features, and I often walk here early in the day. As I approached the trailhead one wintry morning, I glanced out toward the Sound. Red-breasted mergansers were feeding in a cove, and I paused to watch one execute the grace-note leap that becomes its dive. Before the duck surfaced, I heard an unfamiliar noise. It wasn't quite human, or even mammalian. Yet it didn't suggest a bird. It scooped upward through about a major fifth and sounded like a door squeaking on its hinges.

A moment later an astonishingly lovely and loud trill rose into the air. It seemed to originate very near the squeak, from a spot about fifty feet away. I saw nothing. Soon I heard the squeak again, followed by the musical tones. Just off the trail, oak leaves suddenly danced above the frozen soil. An enormous pair of flapping wings and a distinctive muffled hooting, as if from far away, told me I'd found a great horned owl (*Bubo virginianus*). Because I couldn't really see it among the foliage on the ground, I left, excited, to fetch the telescope. As I was returning, I noticed crows flying as if possessed.

I quickly set up the scope and tripod. Through the eyepiece I saw the owl facing away from me at an angle of about one hundred degrees. As it came into focus, it spread its wings and lifted its tail. Leaning forward in this posture, it sounded a trio of soft-pedaled hoots.

Then I noticed a second pair of spread wings. They were beneath the first pair, almost entirely camouflaged by the ground colors. The owl that was hooting had another great horned pinned on its back. The subdued animal lifted its head, and I could see that its left eye was pecked out. The dominant owl, whose face was bloody, threw its tail up again and gouged the victim with its beak. Whenever the weaker owl rallied, the conqueror inclined itself like this and delivered its triple *Whoo*.

Two extraordinary things happened then. After a silence the wounded bird gave a call entirely new and soothing. It was soft as a lullaby, almost like a musing. Simultaneously, the dominant owl brought me into the drama, intermittently swiveling its head and fixing me with huge yellow eyes. I kept my own eyes hidden, one behind the telescope and the other behind a mittened hand. It seemed ludicrous to think the bird known to French Canadians as *le duc d'Amérique* might abandon its captive to pursue a lanky, shivering species cowering behind three metal legs; nonetheless, I felt vulnerable. But I wouldn't leave.

After what felt to me like hours of trying to remain invisible, my feet ached with cold. While the stronger owl was preoccupied, I turned my back to the combat, shook out my legs, and walked away to thaw. As I returned to the scope a few minutes later, the forest began to resonate with crow call once again. The subjugated bird had freed itself and was sitting on a low limb of a tree in the bend of the trail, silent. Crows taunted it even more as it flew to an evergreen and disappeared into the needles. From farther away came a three-note hoot.

The continuing cacophony lured me around the entire path, but I didn't find the other owl.

———

What had I witnessed? A duel? Child abuse? I had no clue. The encounter was stamped with the most familiar elements of owldom—mystery, ferocity, and dramatic vocal sound, to say nothing of sheer strength and will. The experience was typical of how human beings see these birds in the wild, if we are fortunate enough to see them at all—in tantalizing bits and pieces, more holistic impressions being hard to obtain because of owls' nocturnal lifestyle and penchant for privacy. I wanted to know what really had happened. I thought I knew where to find out.

R-A-P-T-U-R-E, the library assistant typed into the computer. In freezing weather, between two birds with temperaments of steel, could it possibly be rapture? I'd suggested this, though not this, as a means of locating a volume of Arthur Bent's life histories of North American birds. I needed information on the owl as a bird of prey, or raptor. That my key word was heard as "rapture" seemed providential, as though the ecstasy of courtship and mating instead of some rawer instinct held the key to the episode on the trail.

It is true that great horned owls, found in many habitats throughout the United States, mate and nest earlier in the year than any other bird. It is also true that along the shores of Long Island Sound, where winter temperatures are relatively moderate, the birds begin pairing as much as a full month ahead of their inland counterparts. It may or may not be true that these owls therefore get a thirty-day jump on rapture. All that's known is that in the coastal birds hormones are boiling by New Year's. The conflict I saw occurred January 8.

My guess is that my movement broke up what would have been a fatal fight for at least one of two males in hot competition over the same mating territory. Since most owls rely on excellent binocular vision for hunting, the loss of the weaker bird's eye may have been a death warrant anyway.

The veteran New England owlers I consulted all supported my interpretation. Yet it's odd that strixine (owlish) literature doesn't contain similar accounts. It's odd also that my account reminded none of the seasoned birders of incidents they had seen. It made me think my sighting was very rare, if not unique.

Owls' lives are not well understood, even by other owls. During courtship the dignified great horneds and other members of the Strigidae family face serious sexual challenges. Not the least of these is the fact that in spite of possible cues from the ear tufts, great horned hens can't always recognize great horned cocks, and vice versa, without a fair amount of ritualized dallying. This confusing state of affairs is tied to what biologists call reverse sexual dimorphism. It's a fancy way of saying that in most owls the females are bigger than the males. In great horneds the difference is slight.

In the book *Owls: Their Natural and Unnatural History*, John Sparks and Tony Soper comment on their subjects' gender plight: "The approach of a mate which, to all intents and purposes, shows the same characteristics as a rival, is a delicate and danger-fraught situation." Jonathan Maslow, author of *The Owl Papers*, employs understatement to illustrate the same problem. "Owls are built for destruction, not tender romance," he writes. "Imagine a caress in the dark from those ganghook talons, or an amorous peck from that stiletto-sharp beak. A muffed show of affection could do a lot of damage." Even a great horned with a light touch, then, needs some non-tactile means of sorting out a mate. Ah yes, the famous voice! This, as it turns out, is the great horned's one completely reliable courtship clue. The land-owning cock begins to advertise his worthy status with a loud, insistent hooting campaign. If he's lucky, his various calls are picked up and decoded by the ears of an available hen, owl hearing being superb due to funnel-like ear flaps and deep auditory slits behind facial disks shaped to catch sound. Even when the male's come-hither solos don't reach the ears of a female great horned, they are not necessarily lost to the world. Female human ears may come to count on twilight hooting as an evensong of sorts. Mine had yet to hear the far less mellow noise to which the hoots can lead . . .

———

A great advantage of occupying a house open on one side and backed by trees on the other is that I can study the way it gathers sound, to improve my birding. For instance, I've learned that the early-morning chirruping out the waterfront windows comes from house finches. They nest each spring in ivy that climbs the chimney between two casements. For months the birds flit throughout their neighborhood as if swapping homey tips and commenting on the weather. Occasionally I catch a glimpse of scalloped raspberry flight, or I see winged shadows suspended on the deep window frames. On the whole, though, my finch education has been aural.

If I enter a room under the trees, I no longer try to

distinguish the finches' bubbling communiqués from other birds' calls. In spring dawns, north-flying warblers move from branch to branch outside the rear windows, during stopovers along routes that roughly follow the Sound, and I concentrate on *their* songs.

The great horned owl completely foils my attempts to bird through particular openings in my walls. Its voice will not be contained but reverberates through all the rooms at once, at almost every season, day or night, whether the windows and doors are open or closed. Sometimes the very stones of the house seem overlaid with owlish sound.

Angus Cameron and Peter Parnall experienced something like this, I surmise. In *The Nightwatchers* they say of great horneds: "The profoundly deep resonance of these feathered bassos seems to originate inside the sounding bones of one's very skull." What must the *owl's* broad skull feel like during a hoot!

At 5 a.m. on September 15, two great horneds near the house awakened me with repeated antiphonal calls. *Whoo, whoo-oo, whoo, whoo . . . Whoo, whoo-oo-oo, whoo-oo, whoo-oo.*

I listened, sleepily, before stumbling to the piano to double-check the interval between pitches: a step and a half. When the lower call sounded, the higher followed right away. Then silence. I was hearing the birds' haunting signature vocalization, which carries up to a mile. The deeper tone is produced by the male's large syrinx, the uniquely avian voice box. To me, the calls of that groggy Indian-summer dawn seemed identical to the previous winter's courtship duets. But the season seemed wrong for the degree of ardor indicated by the close spacing of the two serenades.

My friend Julio de la Torre explained. The September

vocalizations were the owls' way of connecting with their lifelong mates again after a summer apart. Julio, the madcap originator of the Stamford Museum's owl prowl and author of *Owls, Their Life and Behavior*, admires the powerful great horneds' independence. "These creatures are like Roman senators," he said. "Though the actual sequence of some of their behavior is encoded, the birds basically do what they want to when they get good and ready." As late as March Julio once observed an unmated pair compressing all their bonding activities—vocalizations, preening, dancing, and copulation—into an unforgettable all-night festival!

For most great horned owls, mating and nesting occur in January and February. What follows leaves little room for improvisation. It takes the birds roughly a month to incubate and hatch the two or three eggs that the female lays in a well-concealed old nest (typically a red-tailed hawk's). The owlets need another six to seven weeks of being intensively fed before they can leave the nest. This schedule affords the parents ample hunting time in spring before tree leaves open and hinder vision. Even after the owlets fledge, it takes another four to five weeks before they can fly.

Altogether this programmed regimen spans nearly four months. For most birds this would be an eternity. At the end of this period, typically around the first or second week of June near the Sound, the young great horneds are still far from self-sufficient. They often continue demanding food from the adults well into autumn. The success of these feedings, of course, depends on how well the mature great horneds perform their most obvious non-programmed activity—hunting.

One April I found an adult great horned's primary

feather. It lay unmussed at the far end of a hundred-yard swath of mown turf that parallels the shore. I fingered the feather's serrated leading edge, through which air easily passes. This adaptation provides a noiseless wingbeat that allows owls to sneak up on potential prey. The feather was my first clue that the birds might be roosting in trees along the water while they devoured the catches their talons had impaled.

Weedy undergrowth borders one long side of the noted greensward, while the opposite side drops off through trees and shrubs to boulders lapped by the shallows. About sixty feet of open land separates the two. Both unmanicured margins are textbook examples of the vegetative edge, a favorite haunt of many birds. Any great horned that can't snatch rodents from a sideline or small fish from the quiet water below isn't worth its predatory stuff. From a place as advantageous as the one I know, the raptors can even swoop down on unwary gulls and herons, which they also relish.

The benefits of an edge effect are apparent all along the Sound's northern and western shores, where biologist Dwight Smith estimates that great horneds nest every two to five miles. In the Bronx the birds take advantage of the large tract of public land known as Pelham Bay Park. Jonathan Maslow immortalized both the birds and this site in The Owl Papers, calling Pelham Bay "little more than a smear of Long Island Sound." Alison Beall, naturalist at Marshlands Conservancy in Rye, New York, tells me that great horneds have nested near her for the past fifteen years. And toward the eastern end of the estuary Hammonasset Beach State Park regularly hosts the bird.

Great horned owls are at home in the Sound's waterfront

and near-waterfront suburbs as well. A number of species including Norway rats, gray squirrels, semiferal cats, raccoons, opossums, and other medium-sized mammals have kept pace with the local increase in human population. The developed back yard seems to sprout the small meadow voles on which great horneds snack, and the compost pile produces fine crops of insects and grubs, on which the skunks that owls love love to feed. Even the woodsy bird feeder attracts creatures that great horneds eat. The result of all this is that the diverse food base has become a strixine smorgasbord worthy of the great horned's hunting talents.

The lawn I was monitoring came to life in a new way the first week of May: a bleach-topped great horned juvenile sat perched on the tip of a tall pine bordering the turf. Its eyes were piercing, but they also had a startled look. Perhaps I was the bird's first human being, as it was my first young great horned and the only one of its species I was ever able to study face-to-face along the Sound.

I found the owl again a week later when I first noticed the brunch that awaited it under its favorite evergreen. The treat was a rat, perhaps one from the nearby seawall, where I'd seen the rodents at low tide. I assumed that the parent bird in an adjacent tree had left the rat after a dawn hunt. I couldn't explain why it was still intact. Perhaps it had already crossed the line that separates fresh meat from carrion, which these strictly carnivorous owls rarely if ever consume.

I didn't see the youngster for a few days after that, so I did some reading. I learned that when young great horneds are hungry, they shriek. Long Island author Lewis Walker describes the noise as resembling "short blasts of escaping steam." Walker continues: "The sound is emitted with considerable volume."

From the combination of this restrained description and my own experience I can only conclude that Long Island's starving great horned youths must be vocally anemic compared to those that inhabit the Sound's north shore. In the dead of night I was awakened by a hissing scream so loud it catapulted me from the sack. After I composed myself, I taped the intermittent cries. That recording sounds completely otherworldly, harsh, and besotted with misery. It taught me that I can have a nightmare whenever I want one simply by pushing a button that says PLAY.

———

One day, as I was poking along the edge of an orchard near my house, I stumbled across three plump, gray, torpedo-shaped objects about two and a half inches long. They lay near the base of a hemlock's trunk, beneath what resembled white paint splashed like oversized raindrops across the tree's lower boughs. They were clearly agglomerations of fuzz and bone, but didn't fall apart when I handled them. Perplexed, I dropped them into my coat pocket and returned home.

The objects turned out to be great horned owl pellets, among the more arcane of the not-so-worldly goods I collect. Similar to cat fur balls, they are composed of all the material the bird's digestive system can't handle. That's quite a lot, since these voracious owls bolt small rodents whole—skulls and all—and eat crudely torn parts of much larger animals. The whitewash on the tree limbs was what had made it through the usual channels.

An owl pellet rests in an oyster valve

Pellets are regurgitated by several types of birds and other creatures. The ones that owls form are a boon to scientists interested in the checks and balances of predator-prey relations and provide a good deal of information about strigine eating habits. Alexander Wetmore, one of the North American deans of ornithology, reportedly scrutinized more than 1,200 barn owl pellets to arrive at the following bone tallies: 1,987 field mice, 656 house mice, 210 rats, 92 sparrows and blackbirds, 4 frogs. This makes an impressive statement about the ecological value of owls as predators. If scientists of the twenty-first century can see a reason for it, perhaps they will analyze with equal zest the grungy accumulations of orange peels, tea bags, cigarette butts, fried-chicken bones, and other human indigestibles found along commuter rail tracks and at the base of urban chain-link fences.

As for my own activities with pellets, I can tell approx-

imately how many squeakers a great horned ate for breakfast by leaving the pellets immersed in warm water for
several hours, then wielding a pair of tweezers. That's
about as far as I care to go. I do like the surprises I read
about, though. In *One Man's Owl* biologist Bernd Heinrich describes how he rehabilitated a young orphaned great
horned in a Maine cabin. More than once the bird cast a
pellet that not coincidentally matched its benefactor's green
dishrags.

Editor John A. Burton included three colored portraits
of pellet parts in the volume *Owls of the World*. All of them
are fascinating, but the one labeled "Contents of long-
eared owl pellet" is stunning as well. It's created from a
block of rodent fur, ranks of tiny, fine bones all nestled into
concentric packets, and additional lines of bones both
chunky and delicate. The chunks are vertebrae; the other
bones, mouse femurs. Mice femurs?! I'd like to hang the
picture on my wall.

———

Unless you count Papageno from Mozart's frequently performed fluty opera, you don't hear of many bird catchers
these days. Or do you? The traditional German *Vogelfänger*
or French *oiseleur* may simply have become transformed.
The bird catcher was a man who dressed as a big bird in
order to snare little ones, primarily for the dinner table.
The question of what made him obsolete seems secondary
to an understanding of why he wore feathers in the first
place, and of how effective they were.

The answer is clear but not simple: mobbing. This is the
incompletely understood panic reaction that crows and
other birds have to hawks (diurnal birds of prey), to owls

(nocturnal birds of prey), and especially to great horneds, the undisputed and generally unadored king of the avian food chain. Though crows occasionally toss great horned owlets from the nest, great horned adults consider crow one of their tastier regular meals.

Strangely enough, while crows may panic at the sight of a great horned, they don't run away and hide. Instead, they marshal their cohorts and take turns trying to impress the raptor with their great numbers, incessantly heckling it, like the ones I heard on the looping trail. Inland common crows frequently winter along the Sound, and they mob right along with their year-round, nearly identical water-side cousins, the fish crows. This aggressive behavior does seem to protect the mobbers, perhaps because great horneds hunt more by surprising their prey from behind than by nabbing obvious tormenters outright.

Mobbing, then, may be the original approach–avoidance conflict, which the bird catcher could have exploited to get small birds to come near him. A sixteenth-century edition of Aesop shows such a figure wearing what amounts to a blind designed for one person. It looks like a portable, natural cape not unlike the "trees" that grade-school children are wont to waltz around in onstage. A stick emerges from Aesop's blind, and on it sits a large, live decoy owl. It is a small step from that owl to the man-sized bird that Papageno represents.

Some recent midnight when no one was looking, the bird catcher exchanged his feathers for ridges of molded plastic as he metamorphosed a step further into an artificial great horned owl. The thumpable gray-brown model, which costs about $13, is supposed to reduce the number of owl-hating birds not by snaring them but by frightening them away from property they would otherwise foul. To this end it is prominently positioned on boats, on docks, in gardens, and along seawalls up and down Long Island Sound.

If mobbing leaves serious owlers confused, which it does, think how the owners of these strixine copycats feel. According to most of the ones I know, animals that are potential great horned prey are quick to catch on to the ruse. Very soon they neither mob the fake nor flee it, but simply proceed as if it were not there.

The mobbing of a real great horned, on the other hand, is one of this land's dominant sights and sounds. From inside the house in early morning I often hear mobbing start in the rasping cough of a single crow. Quickly it grows into a roar. The mobbers accompany the owl as if they were its jesters, but they may lose interest if the great horned lingers too long in one tree. Then they drift away still sputtering. Usually, however, their patience is greater than the raptor's, and they stream after it each time it flies. Bernd Heinrich likens the sight to a "ragged plume of black smoke."

More than once, when standing under a copper beech near shore, I've spotted a mobbed great horned as it ducked into the tree's dark foliage. It instantly disappeared, causing its enemies to reach a new pitch of fury expressed in black cartwheels and venomous tones. I've tracked mobbing parties behind horse barns and over the roofs of houses, above mixed stands of hardwood and evergreen trees. I've even raced the streaming flocks the way cars race hot-air balloons—waiting, but not for a crash.

AIR

O n the ground around me, fruits from the plentiful hickory trees are darkening to mahogany amid the riot of summer growth. Occasionally, if I'm lucky, I find a green fruit, one that hasn't broken apart. Its acrid smell is so strong it makes my nose twitch. Yet I inhale and inhale. My childhood rests in this scent, as in the songs that hickories sang to me each spring.

My father began our ritual whistle-making by selecting a pliant young hickory branch. With the sharp pocketknife he always carried he cut it from the tree, then stripped it of greenery. Ideally this resulted in a switch about three-quarters of an inch in diameter and at least a foot long.

Next he sliced the wood on the diagonal at one end and on the opposite diagonal at the other end, giving it the look of an end-blown whistle similar to a recorder. I can still picture the evolving instrument lying across my father's blunt fingers as he extended his hand to my eye level for inspection.

Very carefully he cut off the tip of one diagonal, notched the branch about an inch below the cut tip, and removed the wedge of wood that the notch yielded. Halfway down the cylinder's length he scored the bark all the way around. The scoring was the first step toward the creation of a casing on the half of the branch that included the notch and cut tip.

In order to loosen the bark on this half and encourage the

developing casing to allow the inner wood to slide up and down inside it, my father tapped along the outside of the branch with his knife. Holding the branch down in front of him then, he put a portion of the loosening segment into his mouth, and looked as if he might swallow it—he closed his lips on it. With a flattened palm on either side of the branch he gently rubbed his hands back and forth. This usually caused the bark to let go completely. He continued to moisten the now separate casing, to check it, remove it and moisten the wood inside, check again to make sure the bark wasn't splitting (perhaps he even made some sort of reed), until finally the casing housed an easily movable piece of wood—a smooth, creamy core.

When all this was done, he removed the whistle from his mouth and placed just the cut tip between his lips. Then he blew. A piercing note came from the blast. When he wanted to make the sound melodic, or at least not static, he pulled the heartwood out from under its casing and pushed it up again, producing a musical glide.

The Boston Pops in our front yard could not have delighted me more. The sound was unique, sharp like birdsong yet mellow. If my father took the time to craft a second whistle, he made it larger or smaller than the first. This meant we had two different ranges in which to work when we performed together. Between his rising line and my descending one, we could play absolutely anything that didn't require a tune.

To my knowledge I was the only person in the United States ever instructed in this fine art. Yet it has always struck me as odd that learning to make and play hickory whistles is not a part of everyone's normal maturation, like learning to brush teeth and catch tadpoles. In my mind it is a rite of similar stature and the surest sign of caring between members of two generations.

I realize now that my father, who was a biologist, enlisted the trees not as servants but as partners in music. This must be what he wanted me to grasp about the entire experience—that, though he himself had great whistling gifts (which I failed to inherit), the best sounds were made by breath moving through wood. Trees were equal in importance to our personal streams of air, one being no more sacred than the other.

This is a powerful concept to carry into adulthood: I think whistle music provided my earliest hint of earth's agreement among air, plants, and animals.

OSPREYS

"What do you know about ospreys?" I asked a friend at the dock.

"Nothing," he replied. "I just love them."

Does anyone who can recognize the birds not love them? As ornithologist Alan Poole says, even "New England clammers, normally reticent men, wax garrulous when Ospreys are mentioned."

I've seen my stylish neighbors, parents of a four-year-old daughter, raise their binoculars and stand slack-jawed in the summer heat for an hour. If the right distant speck finally appears above the trees, they grab the child and bolt for the dinghy. "It's an osprey! Don't lose it!" they order each other. They scramble for oars. They jab the sky with their fingers. They wind their heads on their necks like owls. They paddle in drunken circles. The four-year-old sits quietly in the stern, awestruck by the approaching grace.

The bird is wonderful to follow. Gradually, even excitable adults calm down and adopt the deliberate pace of the nearly eagle-sized creature before them. Its six-foot wingspan, distinctive whistle, gleaming white breast, and M-shaped silhouette make it hard to confuse with any other species. And when an osprey soars high overhead on the thermals of early fall, the sun above it washes out the pale shading of its wings. What's left is a dark cipher in the sky. I read it as a serifed boomerang, a broad omega carving up the light.

While a flying osprey resonates with poetry, a fishing osprey appears mythic, like Icarus drawn to water as well as to the sun. One late-summer day I saw an osprey circling high above a Soundscape of brackish coves and fresher pond water. A tree-lined river flowed nearby. For several minutes I stood on shore and let my thrown-back head trace the lazy gyres. Thin triangles of light showed between the flexed wing tips. The bird changed direction four times. Just cruising, I thought. Some flash in the water must have caught its eye from that amazing height. It lowered itself, hovered briefly, then flung its wings out behind and dropped like a landslide, crashing feetfirst into the shallows. Curtains of spray closed around it. I thought the water had swallowed it whole.

If the bird was stunned, it recovered immediately, lifting off and shaking itself like a retriever suspended in space. That was when I saw the fish in its talons. It looked like a silver bullet and must have weighed at least half of what an osprey weighs, which is about three pounds. The airborne raptor shifted the catch to a head-first position. With its glittering prize in both feet—one behind the other—it flapped toward an oak branch far above me.

After a brief respite the bird thrust the sharp hook of its beak through scales and into tender flesh. As it ripped a bite free, I saw the fish (a herring) convulse beneath feet adapted to hold down prey against a limb. The osprey twisted off three more chunks before lifting its wings and sailing out over the water, half a meal in tow.

This elegant wild animal, also known as a fish hawk, is the one diurnal raptor that eats fresh fish and not much else all year long. No other large bird in North America has a foraging style anything like it, the bald eagle being basically a land-based angler. In fact, with the possible exception of an oceanic bird called a gannet, no other

A young osprey occupies a nest on a man-made platform

large creature of any kind—including a human being—
performs such brilliant split-second-timed feats at the
meeting of water and air.

This unique hunter possesses nesting instincts that can
appear odd. The bird builds on utility poles, atop channel
markers in rushing rivers, on man-made platforms, and so

close to rocketing trains that it must know their schedules by heart. This may exemplify the kind of compatibility with people and their structures that led the late birding wizard Roger Tory Peterson to state, "Of all the raptors, the Osprey is the one that can live most happily with modern man, if given a chance."

The bird's utter wildness paired with its particular brand of tolerance for what we call civilization is without parallel. Yet tolerance has been forced on ospreys. Along the shores of Long Island Sound most of their traditional nesting sites—old and dead trees—were destroyed for human development decades ago. The osprey adapted by accepting the alternative it found, nesting platforms. Now commonplace along marshy waterways, the yard-square structures mimic treetops open to the sky. New England ospreys are often choosy about the longitude in which they build, however. Before 1994, when the birds adopted platforms erected in Greenwich, Connecticut's Cos Cob Harbor, that vicinity had had no nesting ospreys for at least two hundred years. In 1993, in fact, the birds nested nowhere in Connecticut west of the Housatonic River.

On Long Island the east-west distinction is blurred. Mill Neck in Oyster Bay hosted what was the westernmost nest until 1993. That site still holds its distinction among Long Island nests near the Sound. But a new nest was recently discovered on Staten Island. Ospreys are also found in Jamaica Bay, on Long Island's southern shore, as well as in the Hempstead area.

Connecticut's birds and the local New York coastal ones are together generally referred to as the Long Island Sound ospreys. Rhode Island and Massachusetts birds are often grouped with them to form what is traditionally known as the New York to Boston population. This large discrete breeding group currently occupies between 350 and 400 active nests.

Looking east of the Sound within this group, one finds ospreys on Nantucket Island, off Cape Cod, Massachusetts. This is a recent development. But Martha's Vineyard right next door has had the birds for years. Vineyard home owners routinely have nesting platforms installed right on their property by a naturalist with a long waiting list. No doubt residents with established nesters can be as smug as Europeans who jealously watch after their rare chimneytop storks.

The idea of an artificial osprey nesting site is not news in the Northeast. In the early years of the century cart wheels were used for this purpose. What is news is the recent breeding success the platforms have promoted. It makes the osprey seem like a miraculous survivor, a child snatched from the fire. For the conditions that immediately preceded it were so disastrous that in the 1960s at least one ornithologist predicted the bird would entirely disappear from the Northeast within a decade.

———

Jerry Mersereau cracked the door of his Subaru wagon, cocked his eyes skyward, and tucked his head below the ladder lashed to his roof. Then he leaped from his vehicle to pump my hand in greeting. The obscenely early hour of this Exit 70 rendezvous obviously didn't faze the wiry man, his jeans-clad frame dancing in the June breeze. But the wisps of gray beneath Jerry's blood-red baseball cap belied his youthful appearance. From a lecture I'd heard him give I knew that he had been involved in osprey care along eastern Connecticut's Interstate 95 for more than three decades.

No one understands the osprey's former desperation better than the handful of licensed bird banders and researchers who finally made sense of it. They have a special claim on the Northeast's favorite bird and provide a unique perspective for the dozens of new volunteers and professionals who join them in celebrating the creature's continuing recovery. Jerry was one of those original banders.

Before the 1940s ospreys were so common between New York and Boston that no one bothered to make a comprehensive count of their nests, though some estimates set the number as high as 2,000. In the 1950s the number of birds all around the eastern end of Long Island Sound began to plummet. By 1957 the reproduction rate of those ospreys near the Connecticut River mouth had dropped to about 15 percent of normal. No one knew why.

In an effort to comprehend what was happening then, Jerry Mersereau and Yale student Peter Ames focused on one colony of ospreys within the larger Connecticut River group. They chose the birds of the 500-acre, state-owned Great Island Wildlife Area, right at the river's mouth. I was going there today to watch Jerry band the descendants of those much studied birds.

In 1960 Jerry, Peter Ames, and others began their most concentrated work by providing Great Island's ospreys with elevated nesting platforms procured under the guidance of Roger Tory Peterson. He had moved to Old Lyme several years earlier in order to be near ospreys, which were now disappearing before his eyes. Soon the raised nesting structures confirmed what their population problem was *not*, namely tidal flooding and predation by raccoons. Even nesting twelve feet aboveground, on sturdy platforms that had poles sheathed with metal predator guards, the Great Island ospreys continued to suffer heavy losses.

The crisis worsened. By 1964 the two hundred osprey nests that had historically surrounded the Connecticut River mouth were reduced to a mere two dozen, and the Great Island population had fallen accordingly. That same year Jerry and Peter Ames published a co-authored paper explaining the somewhat inconclusive results of their field research involving the Great Island platforms. Their work, along with Ames's later independent analyses of osprey eggs, a study of British birds, a tip from a friend of Peterson's about diminishing eagle populations, and many other efforts slowly pointed to exactly what *was* wrong with the raptors—poisoning by the pesticide DDT and its metabolites. DDT, which promised to make the mosquito bite obsolete, had been abundantly sprayed in Connecticut and on Long Island in the middle and late 1940s. It had been sprayed particularly heavily on salt marshes, where fish swim while mosquitoes breed. The osprey's pesticide-laden prey, once ingested, was nothing short of a killer.

By now the way DDT poisoning works is well known. It inhibits calcium deposition in eggshells. This results in thin shells and therefore ultimately in depressed breeding, since the shells crack easily under the weight of the incubating birds. As recently as thirty-five years ago, however, this mechanism was not at all clear.

A Wesleyan University student named Paul Spitzer finally proved that it was indeed weakened eggs, and not some aberrant behavior on the part of the parent birds, that was keeping the osprey hatch rate far below normal. Spitzer demonstrated this by means of an imaginative experiment that involved swapping unsound Connecticut River osprey eggs for intact Chesapeake Bay ones. The Bay eggs continued to develop normally under the Connecticut parent birds, who readily accepted them. But the Connecticut eggs failed to hatch even when placed in the Chesapeake Bay nests. Virginia researcher Robert Kennedy kept Spitzer supplied with enough eggs for his shuttle by taking advantage of the osprey's habit of double-clutching, or laying a second clutch of eggs if the first is removed.

Spitzer's experiment was completed in 1972, ten years after the publication of Rachel Carson's ground-breaking book, *Silent Spring*. The real issue raised by that book and underscored by many other sources was the viability of an age-old dream as popular as it was deluding—that the natural world could be controlled through technology.

The start of the comeback for ospreys—as well as for salmon, blue-claw crabs, hawks, eagles, and other non-target victims of DDT—can be traced to a single event in 1966. In the eastern Long Island town of Brookhaven a citizens' organization had filed a class-action suit against the Suffolk County Mosquito Control Commission, charging it with the irresponsible use of DDT. In November, after a week of heavy testimony and cross-examination, the citizens' group won the case. This led to a court-imposed ban on DDT, and later to a statewide ban, and then to a nationwide one. What had begun as a skirmish over life in the waters surrounding Long Island had developed into a battle of monumental import.

The scientists and attorneys who were the architects of the original winning strategy eventually formed the core of the Environmental Defense Fund. This public-interest group, which set a precedent in fighting the abuse of natural systems through litigation, helped point out an important ecological link between ospreys and people. It demonstrated how toxins that become concentrated in the fatty tissues of birds at the top of the food chain can also become concentrated in fish-eating human beings. The osprey, long the fisherman's friend, had earned its distinction anew.

———

Great Island's public boat-launching area is a slope of blacktop wide enough to accommodate two small vessels at once. On the morning I met Jerry Mersereau, beach roses, sumac, and sweet-scented honeysuckle jockeyed for light in a thin unmowed strip above the ramp. The plants looked as constricted by their narrow blooming space as the sweep of green cordgrass below them looked boundless and without form. Nothing about this salt marsh suggested the definiteness of an island.

This is perfect osprey nesting habitat. The shallow tidal water that flows along the banks and shoals of the marshes supports flounder, which spawn in winter. These fish are still small when ospreys return to the Northeast from Central and South America in early spring. Nevertheless, they make an important contribution to the birds' diet. The flounder surge in on the tides until May or June, then head for the colder deeps.

By that time in the season osprey nests often hold ravenous young birds. In providing for them the adults may concentrate their hunting over more exposed bodies of water like the small estuary at the mouth of the Connecticut. It is deeper than the marsh, and (though its spring fish runs were low in 1995 and 1996) by summer its waters typically host plenty of bunker and other schooling fish from offshore. They swim near the surface, an important factor to ospreys, whose outstretched, fish-grasping legs measure no more than about twelve inches.

Standing at the foot of the Great Island launch ramp, Jerry hailed the man sashaying his blue-carpet-lined craft in the falling tide of the main waterway. The boater headed in our direction. Wading out a few steps, Jerry held the extension ladder he'd brought from the Subaru, and the boater grasped its end firmly. After the two of them carefully set it in place along the gunwale, Jerry and I climbed aboard.

"I'm Dave" was my taciturn introduction to Dave Girardin, an avid bird photographer who has filmed nearly as many ospreys as Jerry has banded. Dave slid his engine into forward, then propelled us away from the gasoline-heavy water of the launch area up a tidal creek to the north.

The world changed. The brown ribbon of peaty substrate that supported the cordgrass was becoming more and more exposed as the water ebbed. Like an organic compress, it wrapped itself around the rich marshy smells and squeezed them into a contradictory sweetness that threatened to overwhelm me when I inhaled. Footed in the peat, a well-supported, man-made osprey platform about a yard square rose twelve feet above the glistening salt meadow ahead of us. The wooden structure was crowned with an elaborate two-foot-high nest made of tree branches that stuck out stiffly in all directions. A tall, irregularly shaped tree trunk had been driven into the marsh about thirty feet away from the platform. It was slightly taller than the nest's topmost sticks. Jerry said it served as a perch for the adult osprey away from its nest.

There was no bird sitting on this perch pole when Dave nosed his boat into a convenient peat ledge. He cut the engine, bathing us in quiet. *Yewk, yewk, yewk* came a repeated series of calls far above us. I shaded my eyes to see two adult ospreys, obviously the parent birds, flying round and round.

We all climbed out onto the semisolid land. Dave and Jerry drove the blade of a wooden oar into the peat to serve as anchor, then wrapped the shaft with the painter. They removed the ladder from the boat, and Dave planted its pair of metal feet on a hummock of salt hay below the platform. He leaned the ladder's other end against the edge of the nest, climbed up, reached in, and scooped up an osprey chick. It was as simple as that. The parents continued to circle and call but never attempted to harm him. I will not forget the sight of that nestling against the cerulean heavens. The creature was basically a pair of interminable, drooping wings, its body an afterthought. Had Dave not looked so purposeful, he could have passed for a child holding a floppy-eared stuffed rabbit. "This little bird's heart is going," he said. Grasping the ladder in one hand and the bird in the other, he descended. He set the chick on a cowlick of grass in the cool of my shadow.

It collapsed, a rag doll. The altricial bird (one helpless at birth) was only four weeks old. Unable to hold its head up, it lay in silence with its wings folded under and its downward-curved beak half buried in cordgrass. Most of its body weight was on its breast, and its rump was in the air. Yet even in this undignified position the Cornish-hen-sized youngster had presence.

Twice more Dave climbed the ladder and gathered the prizes, working as fast as he dared in order to shorten the time the parent birds were kept from the nest. When all three chicks were lying on the ground and he was preparing to trip the shutter, he commented, "Three is the normal clutch."

Seeing the docile triplets all lined up, I recognized the pronounced differences in their size and development. Because the female lays eggs a day or two apart, her chicks are in various stages of growth. This is typical of raptors.

These month-old birds were on the cusp of developing the black-and-white-feather pattern ospreys wear for their first year. Now, however, they were an endearing hodge-podge of unfinished business. Pale-blue feather shafts showed here; a stubby tail-in-progress peeked out there. Buff and black tones seemed to emerge randomly within a plumage struggling to define itself. The only features the chicks seemed to have in common were their orange eyes (the adults' are lemon-yellow) and an inch-wide stripe of white natal down that ran along their backbones. The line may be a form of camouflage, since from the air it makes the facedown juveniles virtually indistinguishable from the sun-bleached sticks of the nest.

As I knelt and stroked the birds' soft heads, I heard Jerry say, "Their only job is to grow." Of course, I thought. They'll catch up with those long wings, which are as un-manageable now as those of Baudelaire's Albatross/Poet. In just two to three weeks, Jerry added, the chicks will be testing their wings as they helicopter above the aerie.

The thought of such rapid development made the youngsters seem like shells of birds just waiting to be fur-nished with the strength to fly south across the greater part of two continents, along the same route their parents would have taken a few days before. They would not re-turn home for at least two years. Sometime from now I will see an osprey west of here on a day leaning toward autumn. The orange eyes that mark even the older non-breeding immature will flame out from the dark eye stripe, and light-edged feathers will drip from the shoul-der like a dramatically lapped fur robe. I will wonder if the magnificent creature before me is part of a popula-tion from as far north as the Maritime Provinces. I will hope it might be an osprey that started life as one of the

disproportionate Connecticut nestlings I'd seen on a morning in June.

I will have a clue.

"Ospreys are all big in the feet when they hatch,"
Jerry stated. "The feet won't grow much larger than they
are now." As he talked, he knelt and reached into a
compact blue tote bag he had brought with him. It
rested on the matted salt hay. Jerry lifted out two stiff
metal loops strung with aluminum bird bands. They
looked like a matched pair of necklaces. He checked the
sequence of band numbers against a master list from the
U.S. Fish and Wildlife Service, the bander's licensing
agency. The orders tallied.

Wasting no time, Jerry unfastened the clasp on one of
the big metal loops, removed a band, and placed it in my
upturned palm. It was so light I could hardly tell it was
there. "That's a size eight," he said. "It fits an adult osprey
as well as a month-old juvenile. A nine, which is the largest
band the Feds make, fits golden and bald eagles."

Bird banding is the most reliable means of learning
where various species winter, what their family life is like,
how long they live (ospreys can exceed twenty years), and
other valuable information. I had seen birds waiting to be
so marked only once before. They were tiny creatures that
had been trapped by a fine net called a "mist" net.
Stretched across an ornithologist friend's back yard, the net
held its feathered captives in not particularly merciful-
looking positions.

I have a vivid recollection of the doll-sized bands my
friend used. They were simpler than the one I held, really
just interrupted circles. I asked Jerry about the difference.
"We used to band ospreys and other raptors with those,"
he said. "They're called ring bands. But the big birds can

open them with their beaks. That's why we went to the kind of band you're holding, which is called a lock-on band." He showed me the overlapping tab, which provided additional security.

Jerry lifted the dream-weight aluminum from my palm and opened it deftly with a pair of pliers from his satchel. Then he turned to Dave, who was holding the first juvenile removed from the nest. Jerry reached between Dave's first two fingers and gently extended the bird's left leg until it was almost straight. He closed the band around it above the foot and below the first joint. "You just line up the metal edges, press the tabs together with these flat pli . . . Yahhh! Fish juice!"

I hadn't noticed the chick's full, rounded crop under the neck. The enlarged gullet is basically a holding tank for food waiting to be fully digested. This one bulged like an Adam's apple. Jerry paid no attention to his sopping hand, but continued banding. "This band won't come down over the foot," he said. "So there's no chance of the bird starving because it can't fish. It won't ride up either. The chick probably doesn't realize it's there."

After Jerry had banded the other nestlings and Dave had returned them all to the nest, I climbed the ladder for a final look. Of the seemingly boneless threesome only the oldest sat propped up. It looked unnatural, like a freshly plumped pillow. It wasn't going anywhere unless it fell from its high-rise home. The female parent would probably feed it if she found it on the ground. But the young bird would be at the mercy of whatever might beat her to it . . . if it survived the twelve-foot drop.

The parents were circling and calling low over the nest as we boarded ladder-first and cast off into the waterway. We had kept them away from their charges for exactly nine minutes. "The adults always get nervous when we leave," Dave said. I could have sworn I saw one of them look down and count the chicks, ticking them off with three tilts of the head.

———

Our second banding destination was not on Great Island proper but on an adjacent patch of marsh known as John's Point. The platform there stood only twenty feet from the waterway we were traveling. But the peat within that short distance was more heavily pitted than at our first stop. Jerry and Dave had mastered the fine art of distinguishing solid ground from the depressions' grassy coverlets. I hadn't, and I kept twisting and falling into holes as deep as my knee boots.

When I finally slogged my way to the pole, I looked up. An osprey nest rose four feet above the platform on which it was built. It dwarfed the nest we had just left. Obviously it had been added to year after year by the returning residents, who mate for life and keep augmenting their homes.

Dave began to retrieve the chicks one at a time, as he had done previously. This time he didn't stop at three. Here were quadruplets, almost as rare among ospreys as they are among people. "You're an old sport," he said to the last bird, which he brought down and handed to me. It felt like a bucket of water with no bucket.

The quartet ranged in development from the small, floppy runt (which Jerry addressed as Number One) to the obvious Schwarzenegger of the clutch (Number Four). This last chick could sit up on its haunches without continually falling forward. And when Jerry slipped an index finger inside Four's rounded ebony talons to untangle some fishing line, he said he could actually feel pressure, though no pain. Fouled monofilament line, routinely tossed overboard by fishermen, is a favored osprey nest material and presents an ongoing threat to the birds' mobility.

While Jerry's skilled hands continued their work, I got a good look at a chick's feet and toes, the parts of its body that will keep it in business. Scales, not feathers, covered the entire shank. The four toes, which can be used in an arrangement of 2 + 2 or of 3 + 1, give an adult osprey increased maneuverability and gripping power. This is particularly important as the bird comes to land on a perch with a fish in its talons. The adaptation sets ospreys apart from all other hawks and helps explain their somewhat controversial solo position on the phylogenetic tree.

The most interesting foot feature, and the hardest to see, is the set of tiny spines on the underside of each toe. Technically known as spicules, they are designed to aid the bird in holding on to its wet, wriggling catch. Spicules have also been blamed for osprey drownings. Alan Poole, the widely acknowledged authority on these birds, discounts this in his 1989 book, *Ospreys: A Natural and Unnatural History*. Ornithologist Arthur Cleveland Bent had discounted it earlier. Yet no airtight explanation is offered those who have seen the raptors pulled under water forever, possibly by having eyes bigger than their stomachs.

Jerry finished checking and banding the foursome. Then we replaced them and motored slowly back toward Great Island. As we approached another platform, he said that he'd recently found only a single egg and no chicks at all there. He'd been authorized to take the egg for chemical analysis by the state Department of Environmental Protection.

While the engine idled, Jerry climbed and fetched the

osprey egg and handed it down the ladder to me. Nestled in my cupped palm, it felt much like a jumbo hen's egg. The rich tan speckling typical of these eggs is concentrated on its larger end and is quite lovely. The blue ground cover, however, concerned me. White and cream are the usual backgrounds. The sky-colored tint, perhaps along with the exaggerated pungency of the shell, may have indicated serious trouble.

"Great Island had six active osprey nests this year," Jerry said. "But they yielded only the triplets we banded at our first stop. We don't know what caused the other five to fail. Whatever it was did not affect nests near Great Island.

"Incredible as it may sound," he continued, "DDT is still used in much of the osprey's winter range. This egg may tell us if, somehow, the Great Island birds alone could have ingested DDT-contaminated fish before returning here this past March."

———

The top of the latticed street barrier that marks the entrance to Hawk's Nest Beach near Old Lyme had sprouted flowers. You couldn't miss them. Primary-colored zinnias on short, stiff stalks and pastel cosmos blossoms on tall willowy ones intertwined with other New England summer blossoms to form a welcoming trough bouquet. It guided us into this coastal community, where we would meet two osprey enthusiasts, and it would see us off to meet more osprey watchers farther along our banding route.

Side-by-side cottages with porches positioned to catch the sea breeze said RENTAL in boldly lettered signs on their identical façades. A local resident owned most of them, Jerry said. As he drove past tennis courts and baby strollers, other permanent residents began to announce themselves in mailboxes and street signs bearing reference to ospreys.

Eventually the land narrowed to a sandy point on which two rows of weathered houses faced each other across a lane. Behind the inland row was a small, picturesque salt marsh surrounded by woods on three sides. It held two osprey platforms visible from the front of the home of Nancy and George Terpenning. Now in his seventies, George (known to all as Terp) has been coming to Hawk's Nest Beach since he was two. He is one of the few people living here who remember when the ospreys nested in trees.

"The hurricane of 1938 took out most of the birds' natural nesting sites along this beach," Terp said. "We simply had no ospreys after that until we erected these platforms several years ago. I get concerned when the structures lose too much nesting material to high winds during the winter. They're very exposed. In March Nancy and I always add some sticks, just to give the returning birds a welcome."

"Our birds are still recovering from a tragedy," Nancy took over. "The third year the platforms were up, Terp found a female lying headless on the ground. He asked a friend to scale the ladder and check the nest. The three chicks were in the same condition. Terp was so upset he had to leave town. Those birds were like his children. He'd watched them through the telescope upstairs."

"What caused it?" I asked.

"A great horned owl," Terp said. "The platform was obviously not far enough from the edge of the forest where the owl lived. The great horned, which is probably the osprey's most deadly aerial predator, took advantage of that. It eats only the hawk's head."

Terp reminded me of the Jimmy Stewart character in the Frank Capra movie *It's a Wonderful Life*. Having moved his ospreys into what he thought were ideal quarters, he wanted to shield them from mishap. Fortunately, he was able to watch a bird he hoped might be the bereaved male as it courted and won a new mate. He couldn't be sure it was the same bird, since male ospreys are hard to distinguish from the slightly larger, darker-breasted females and are almost impossible to distinguish from other males.

John Miller, a utility company employee who lives in East Lyme, is a fairly new initiate into the Order of the Osprey. Having obtained the state permit necessary for erecting a platform in a tidal wetland, he situated his structure in a small marsh across a river from an even smaller marina. The twiggy home the platform supports, which John visits during his lunch breaks, was relatively small and flat.

This inconspicuousness was fine with John, who had noticed a pair of swans nesting on a sandbar next to the marina's outermost dock. Boaters had noticed the swans, too, and seemed fascinated by the white giants' every move. The preoccupation diverted attention from the whistling raptors and, in John's estimate, helped to assure the ospreys' privacy.

John ferried Jerry and Dave and me across the river and led us on foot over several narrow ditches that snaked through the marsh. At the widest of these he made a bridge of Jerry's infamous ladder. Then, in a manner befitting a gentleman who has just covered a puddle with his coat, he gestured for us to cross.

Sooner or later these self-appointed fish-hawk godparents, along with many others, show up in state-sponsored newsletters. Rhode Island has a one-pager that comes out twice a summer. Connecticut's publication is a multipage affair that appears more often and reaches two hundred people. Coordinated by wildlife biologist Julie Victoria, it is called *Pandion Papers* after the osprey's Latin name. Here are excerpts from one issue.

Under the heading "Banding Efforts"—

> This is the seventh year that Greg Decker, of Northeast Utilities, has provided the [banding] team with an aerial lift to band the young at the Millstone Power Station in Waterford . . .

Under "New Platform Locations"—

> . . . six platform tops were donated to the Nonharvested Wildlife Program by the Woodworkers for Wildlife volunteer group . . .

Under "Disturbances and Mishaps"—

> A young bird that fledged near the filtration plant at Groton Utilities was electrocuted when it flew into power lines. An adult osprey was also found dead . . . below the power lines; it had been banded in 1988 as a nestling in the Black Point area of East Lyme.

Reports like these make it obvious that anyone with a shred of enthusiasm for ospreys eventually gets around to caring for them in some fashion. Yet the accounts are not just random notations. They constitute part of an ongoing diary that depicts the recent relationships between particular ospreys and certain human beings. Few other birds, large or small, can be said to engage us to this extent.

———

"No fence, no trespass sign, no warden is so effective [a preserver] as several miles of deep water . . . Of no less importance . . . is the possession and occupation of this fair land by but one family, its descendants and dependents, since Lion Gardiner purchased it from its red-skinned owners . . . Here, then, is the prime requisite of isolation rendered potent and continuous by sympathetic guardianship," wrote Frank Chapman in *Camps and Cruises of an Ornithologist* in 1908.

Gardiners Island, still a privately owned natural paradise off Long Island's eastern tip, hosts the most famous osprey colony in the world. An estimated three hundred nests were viable on the 3,300-acre land mass before DDT nearly obliterated the inhabitants in the middle of this century. By 1966 that unparalleled number had fallen to fewer than fifty, and only four chicks could be found. In 1980 the number of active nests totaled a tragic twenty-five.

The island birds, like the mainland ones, have recovered some of their losses, the number of active nests having stabilized around sixty-five. Next to the raised platforms some of the birds have separate perch poles as on Great Island. Others have shorter perches made of milled lumber fastened directly to the platform edges. From a distance they look like Christian crosses, their tall uprights angling out.

I observed the Gardiners Island nests on a late-summer day and found each of them a curiosity. One that spilled out over scaffolding suggested a lifeguard station. Another was built *au naturel* on the shell-strewn, wave-smacked shore. This virtually unsupported nest loomed enormous from my vantage point across a lagoon.

The size and variety of Gardiners Island nesting sites impresses every osprey fan who visits the island. Mike Scheibel, a wildlife biologist for New York State, has studied Bostwick Meadows on the island's north end ever since 1978. He noticed how the remnants of toppled red cedar trees had attracted the birds. "Two dozen osprey nests are built on the branchy rises," he told me. "The largest are nearly ten feet tall by ten feet wide." He also mentioned a big nest on a fifty-five-gallon oil drum in the area. The drum was a gift from the tides.

Environmental Defense Fund founder Dennis Puleston has focused on nests at the island's southern tip, which seems to attract ospreys with a minimalist bent. "These nests were right on the beaches of Cartwright Shoals," he notes. "They're little more than strands of seaweed, and they're likely to be washed away by winter storms. Wave action alters the topography of the shoals from year to year."

Puleston began banding the Gardiners Island ospreys in 1948, and he hasn't missed a year since. This undoubtedly qualifies him as the living naturalist who has the greatest continuity of experience with these birds. (The late LeRoy Wilcox banded an inordinate number.) Puleston's longstanding island association also makes him a particularly insightful student of pesticide-induced breeding defects. He is the person who drew attention to serious reproduction problems in the Gardiners Island birds of the 1950s and '60s. "Probably we will never see ospreys return to pre-DDT populations," he stated in a recent Environmental Defense Fund publication. "The seemingly inexhaustible food supply once found around our coasts no longer exists. But the osprey manages to cope."

If the talented Puleston had a Gardiners Island rival of

any sort, it would have to be one of the early-twentieth-century gentlemen-naturalists who recorded their observations in the formal photographs and fluid prose that characterized the era. My favorite such account comes from the earlier-quoted book by Frank Chapman, whose own ingenuity is equal to that of his subjects.

Chapman describes how a pair of Gardiners Island ospreys had constructed their home on the roof of a small, exposed outbuilding. He gives us a classic photo he took of himself standing concealed under the enormous nest. He's wearing a suit, tie, and bowler inside the small, open-sided edifice. "A camera was . . . erected some forty feet away," he writes, "and a rubber tubing, attached to a shutter, led to my hiding place . . . It required close attention to detect the sound of the bird's foot-fall on the floor above, but when assured of its return, I could stand boldly in the doorway and, with the aid of a bicycle pump, make an exposure at my leisure."

On Gardiners Island the osprey's unusual and often slapdash approach to nesting can seem uncharacteristic of the species. Yet this breeding group can get away with it, since, unlike the mainland, this island has no mammalian predators. There are no raccoons, foxes, red squirrels, minks, opossums, or even chipmunks. Nevertheless, animals such as gulls and night-herons pose their own threat to the eggs.

Gardiners Island ospreys seem unusual in other ways as well. They appear to have a sophisticated collector's gene. Though their nesting material includes the typical samplings of seaweed, whelk egg cases, and the like, in the late 1920s a certain Captain Knight found a book in one nest. *Lucille, Bringer of Joy* was the title. In another nest Knight found an intricate wood carving of a lion's head. Perhaps it had once held a place of honor in the quarters of some

Gardiner whose first, second, or even third name was, inevitably, Lion.

Knight was a Scotsman whose native land had been bereft of ospreys since 1916. Sportsmen and game hunters had systematically persecuted the birds until someone robbed the last Scottish egg from a small island in a loch in the dead of night. (Osprey eggs were sought after by professional and amateur egg collectors on both sides of the Atlantic.)

Knight did something truly remarkable, given the difficulties of international travel and other factors at the time. Having gained permission to remove two pairs of live birds from Gardiners Island, he took them home with him and released them onto the tiny, previously colonized loch in Inverness-shire. That was in July 1929.

A 1932 issue of *National Geographic* magazine features a splendid period piece, a photo of the natty-looking Knight back in Scotland supporting two of his quartet of recently transported birds. One hardly knows where to look first, at the man with the gloved hands and outstretched arms or at the birds with the incredible outstretched wings.

Yet Knight was not to prove the savior of Scotland's nesting ospreys in the long run. Knight's birds, having imprinted on their Gardiners Island environment, were at a loss when it came time to migrate to their winter home. They left Scotland and never returned. For various reasons ospreys were not able to establish themselves in Scotland until the late 1950s, when the Royal Society for the Protection of Birds succeeded in protecting a much celebrated nest on Loch Garten.

What Knight may have accomplished, at a time that would prove fortuitous, was to raise the consciousness of

National Geographic readers in the New World. If a Scotsman was so keen on re-establishing the osprey in Europe, then surely the bird was not to be taken for granted in North America.

———

"If I come out the front door and walk down to my mailbox . . . [the ospreys] don't say a thing," begins a quote by a boating gentleman in an essay by artist Julie Zickefoose. "But as soon as they see me put my boots on, they start yelling. I put my boots on 'way up by the front door, but they know that means I'm going to take the boat out. My boat is moored right next to their nest, and they don't like my messing around there."

If boots meant boats to ospreys, how would they interpret a long-billed, green-checked baseball cap sticking up like a knob and faucet from the middle of a Whaler? I'd worked out a low seat for myself near the stern end of the boat's central drainage trough. Periodic shifting of weight made my straight-legged position manageable for an hour or two of observation.

Snacking on red grapes that were as musky as the rich October day, I wondered how ospreys eat during their eighty-hour fall migration. The migrants utilize coastal updrafts and other external aids far less than most other birds of prey. Ospreys rely instead on their own strong flight, even over water and deserts. Nevertheless, they must eat en route.

Here is Alan Poole on how the birds approach mealtime: "Consider the problems an Osprey confronts when hunting. It must first decide where to hunt and how to get there, relying on memory or an ability to find productive new sites. It must also take into account such variables as weather, tides, and fish migrations." How can a migrating bird possibly do all this?

I was attempting to recap, somehow, the entire osprey season, and I hoped a bird would help me by landing on a tine of the dead-tree fork above my anchorage. The surrounding cordgrass had gone to amber, and a slight breeze stirred leaves that were turning red and orange and yellow and reflecting in the water. The ospreys that hunt over this area apparently had not yet headed south. One of them kept teasing me into picking up my camera, coming toward me a bit at a time from a long way away. I was poised for its closer approach.

Another bird whistled over me and looked down from a height of about thirty feet. Then it flew on past. The tantalizer traversed my line of vision again. This time it was just above some trees. With no warning at all, it transformed its soaring into a spin, and then another. The axis of its body was perpendicular to the water, and its head was down. The osprey looked like a huge wing nut being tightened, its white breast flashing toward me as it caught the light.

I think it was dancing. The non-nesters that fish around the mid-Sound coves and bays in summer are probably only three or four years old. Like nineteen-year-old human beings, they have energy to burn. This osprey seemed as overcome with the glorious autumn as I was. If so, it may have devised the pair of turns as an expression of that—an inverted pirouetting.

In the end it is the apparent joy of this bird that I love most. Ornithologist Arthur Cleveland Bent obviously loved it, too. He describes the osprey's courtship as encompassing "an expression of joy at homecoming . . . or an exhibition of exuberant spirits." He continues:

[It] consists mainly of aerial gymnastics in which both sexes indulge, chasing each other in swift pursuit-flight, soaring, scaling, circling, dodging with rapid turnings or quick dashes downward, as they sweep, now low, now high, in wide circles. Several pairs are often seen in the air together, and sometimes trios, all screaming their notes of love or excitement.

Witnessing this kind of ecstasy counters the increasingly mechanized character of late-twentieth-century life more than anything else I know. Even if we choose to downplay the osprey's emotional capabilities, the extent to which the bird commands the elements dazzles us, much as a wind-hover once dazzled the poet Gerard Manley Hopkins. Within a matter of weeks the osprey develops from a blunt, helpless youth to a lithesome flyer/hunter bridging water with sky. It touches the land lightly. And in the "hurl and gliding" before it throws back its wings and strikes the Sound, disappearing beneath white flames of spray, we cannot help but gasp—"The achieve of, the mastery of the thing!"

SHOREBIRDS

I think of them as birds of wind, as "wind birds."

—Peter Matthiessen
The Shorebirds of North America

MAY 18, 2:30 P.M.

I'm hunkered down in the lee of an old stone wall smack dab in the middle of suburbia. Some suburb, with its own salt marsh enhanced by the presence of my three excellent friends! One of them, Roland Clement, is our birding guru for the day. The other two, poet Amy Clampitt and photographer Elsie Wheeler, are knowledgeable enough to keep him honest.

Roland and I go back more than twenty-five years, to when he was a vice president at the National Audubon Society and I was a fledgling editor. He has always been generous with what he knows, having led scores of trips like this one. His impeccable eye and graceful verbal imagination characterize books he has written for a whole generation of naturalists and would-be naturalists.

Recently he's been trying his hand at watercolors. Terns, primarily. His face flushes with excitement as he watches a pair of least terns move closer and closer to us, plunging for fish. When they're aloft, they dip and soar and flit like butterflies. Roland's probably tracing their flight on a mental canvas.

We've timed this mid-May salt-marsh excursion to coincide with the spring migration of shorebirds en route to their Arctic breeding grounds. We're also in sync with the rising tide. The Greenwich Audubon Society's checklist of birds provides migration times for likely species here on the Atlantic flyway, but it takes an experienced shorebird fan like Roland to introduce us to the rising-tide trick.

Encroaching water drives birds from low areas onto high ground, where they can be seen massed in substantial numbers. Author Peter Matthiessen explains the process in *The Shorebirds of North America*: "A shorebird flock is best approached at the flood tide, when the feeding flats are covered over; the flock will then be concentrated on high beach or sand bar, and its individuals, until now scattered, will usually have sought out other members of their own species."

This Clement/Matthiessen logic seems reasonable, though I've taken the opposite approach with the large, solitary herons. Great and snowy egrets, for instance, feast at every stage of the tide. But I can't see their pale forms against the stones and grasses above high water as easily as I can against the dark tide line. By dead low tide, the birds dominate the fluid zone in which they've spaced themselves to feed.

We're not here for egrets, however. We're here in hopes of finding black-bellied plovers, which I've never seen before. Also ruddy turnstones and the smaller dunlins and maybe even some red knots. These sandpipers, plovers, and similar species make up the avian group known in America as shorebirds and in the British Isles as waders. They're closely related to gulls and terns and auks, yet distinctive enough that ornithologists have assigned them their own order, the Charadriiformes.

One of their unmistakable characteristics (which our white egrets may laugh at, as they stand out like beacons in the dark) is protective coloration. Roland illustrates this in his introduction to Henry Marion Hall's book *A Gathering of Shorebirds*, where a sketched plover and a sketched sandpiper are presented against two different backgrounds. The plain white paper of one background plays up the birds' plump silhouettes, while the mottled paper of the other background tends to make the same birds disappear. That mottling is mud and marsh now. And just as the book showed, the birds are the dickens to spot. In fact, now that we're quietly settled in, I'm beginning to feel we've kept a wrong appointment: I see no birds at all.

Then I look through the telescope we've lugged into this wet/dry world. Its 45-power magnification is so great that two dozen forms of similar size slide jerkily before and behind one another like glass in a kaleidoscope. I'm seeing only pieces—the necks and beaks and eyes and eyebrows of shorebirds.

Some of the birds (the plovers, I'm told) are picking small crustaceans and worms from holes in the spongy peat. Searching both the surface and the cavities beneath their toes, they spot potential morsels and rush to seize them before the water swamps both the prey and its home. Then, for a second, they relax.

The sandpipers are probing deep into the ground with their thinner bills, with such rhythm that Roland (like many ornithologists) compares the beaks to sewing machine needles and the activity to stitching. Dunlins are champs at this fast poking, which leaves strings of tiny holes. And it's dunlins I'm gradually recognizing among the other long-billed birds. Five of them are feeding at the outermost edges of the peat while a sixth wades in the shallows. I savor the rich coloring and almost toylike appeal of the little birds before I hand the scope to Amy.

Then I'm confused. I find myself squinting in an effort

to see creatures so well camouflaged they're invisible until they move. I've been here before. Elsie hands me her 7-power binoculars, and the birds return. The lower magnification melds their various parts into a smooth, neutral-and autumn-toned movie. A disrupted jet coloring tumbles sideways into chestnut. It's slashed with more jet above pure white. This jewelry is the neck and back of a ruddy turnstone, a medium-sized shorebird and the first I ever learned to recognize from pictures in the field guides. The turnstone takes its common name from its very specialized mode of feeding. It seems bound and determined to flip over seaweed, stones, shells, and other features of tidal mud flats and marshes. Then it swallows the animals it has exposed. The bird is so programmed to earn its living with its bill, in fact, that it turns stones almost incessantly.

Mark Catesby, the eighteenth-century painter and naturalist, played a practical joke of sorts on this beguiling creature, perhaps to test its compulsion. During one of his voyages Catesby captured a turnstone that flew onto his boat. The man obviously knew of the bird's habit and placed some rocks in its cage (from the collection of stones in his hold?). But he failed to supply food under them. The turnstone, of course, proceeded to turn over every rock until it frustrated itself literally to death, or simply starved.

Thinking about this has led me to understand something important here on the marsh: because the turnstone occupies a niche that eliminates it from competition with plovers and sandpipers, it has to contend only with others of its own species for access to stones and their substone treats. When rising tides bring more shorebirds to less land, as now, this limited competition may be nothing short of the turnstone's key to survival. Not quite the same as being the only redhead at the audition. But close.

As I pass the binoculars to Roland, something catches

the corner of my eye. Thinking it's my hair, I brush my hand across my forehead. But, for a second, the honey-toned strands remain. Then they reverse themselves and lighten to platinum as they fall upward. They reverse themselves again, and darken, only to flash like a dozen silver teardrops as they lift their wings and settle on their toes in front of the cordgrass. This is the first time I've seen a flock of shorebirds flying together, and I catch my breath at the quick perfection of it.

I'm looking at black-bellied plovers. They're speed kings among migrants, and—at just under twelve inches—virtual shorebird giants. They are also pawns of the moon: like other plovers, this one is thought to mimic tidal vibrations. It does this with its feet, in a sort of underwater wiggling of the toes usually referred to as "foot-trembling." As far as anyone can tell, this messing around with the bottom stirs up dinner.

I can't see if these recently arrived plovers are already engaged in such a ploy. But I can see two of them, among the now scattered individuals, standing in what must be a characteristic one-legged pose. Most likely they're waiting for the tide to turn, which it's beginning to do. Then they'll claim the newly bared land's outermost reaches.

Though black-bellied plovers are considered wary for shorebirds, their penchant for returning to favored high-tide roosts invited their deaths a century ago. Hunters learned to locate the roosts by reading the birds' footprints in the sand of exposed beaches. When the tide was out and the birds were away feeding, the hunters set up blinds in strategic places. Then they ensconced themselves and waited for the tide to return the birds to them in groups, at which they blasted away.

The U.S. Migratory Bird Treaty halted the slaughter of these and other shorebirds in 1918, in time to save most species from extinction. I'm grateful for this legislation. Yet some part of me wants to respond to these plovers and turnstones and dunlins in a form as definite as a shot. Not a shot, but something just as capable of bringing down a memento of the day. It took energy, gladly garnered, to reach this locale at the right migratory moment. At the best stage of the tide. In good weather. I need to place a stamp on this culmination of conditions. I puzzle over the longing as we pack to leave.

———

Milford Point, near Bridgeport, Connecticut, is the Janus of birding hot spots. In this segment of the Stewart B. Mc-Kinney National Wildlife Refuge a ridge divides a tidal marsh from the open waters of the Sound, commanding unobstructed views.

The marsh pushes inland toward a tonsure of greenery. A factory façade and three church towers finally halt it a mile away. There's no hint of I-95's megalopoliptic roar. The Sound stretches fifteen times farther in the other direction, its navy surface glinting in September light.

From an aerie-like platform straddling the ridge, the May shorebird party and two newcomers face the salt marsh as if it were a curtain about to rise. Instead, the high tide will fall, revealing mud flats rich in shorebird food. The scene attracts us because it represents tidal conditions that are exactly the opposite of our suburban spring excursion's. The emerging flats should attract the shorebird flocks we saw roosting on the Sound's high beaches as we made our way to this perch.

While we wait, nothing in front of us holds still. The wind is bright the way a musical tone can be bright. It touches every surface. Cumulus clouds are being dumped into chilly blue sky. Their tops balloon; their bottoms flatten and darken as they press toward the horizon. One cloud begs to be impaled on a needlelike steeple.

In the marsh itself, clumps of cordgrass throw their heads back each time a wave hits. From where we stand, layers of the assaulted clumps look stacked ten deep. The peristaltic ripple that begins in the front row of the marsh hopscotches its way to the rear.

Roland, who was once a weatherman, promised us brisk conditions. They result from the recent passage of a cold front. A shifting air mass pushed out the trough of warm moist air that had made the last few days sultry, and it ushered in a spanking northwest breeze. The shorebirds will probably wait till morning before they resume their southward migration.

A rattling call behind us announces not a shorebird but a belted kingfisher. We turn to follow the bird's erratic flight out over the marsh. Suddenly the animal jams on its brakes, and for a split second we can see the chestnut breast band that marks the female. Facing the wind, she hovers, her body vibrating as she gazes straight down. Kingfishers' eyes are adapted to minimize the water's glare, somewhat like a polarizing filter. This helps the birds spot surface-feeding fish from as high as fifty feet above the water.

Far in the distance, two American kestrels repeat the kingfisher's tactic as they hover over grass. A great blue heron rows through a slot of sky. Its slaty color and willowy motion reinvent the stingray. As the bird lands, a thick-bodied plane takes off from the Sikorsky plant to our left, its roar slitting the marsh. As if to mock the plane's noisy leadenness, five tiny birds zip past as one, from behind us. They're not ten feet overhead. *Cree-eet, cree-eet,* they cry thinly as they zigzag to the back of the marsh and disappear.

A second flock follows, tissue-light and so fast that I glimpse only their white south ends as the birds dip over the ridge. They flash, vanish, flash, and evaporate. "Least sandpipers," Roland says. "The smallest shorebirds. They require little space on the feeding flats, so come into the marsh as soon as the tide starts to recede."

Like hummingbirds, these diminutive creatures have an extremely high metabolic rate and need to eat constantly. Not only do they fit on the small patches of mud the tide has uncovered, they also start feeding as soon as they get there.

I spin around in time to see a third flock of sandpipers approach. I turn back. A fourth flock follows.

In the stillness of these birds' departure a white heron behind us fidgets next to the immobile silhouettes of two willets. At least we think they're willets. Even Roland is hard-pressed to confirm the identity of the two dark, back-lighted shorebirds without seeing the dramatic black-and-white patterning in their open wings.

The heron may also be a fooler, I learn. The juvenile little blue is just as white as the adults of some other heron species common to this region.

The insistent *Whee-e-ree* of black-bellied plovers draws me back to the marsh. Seven of the birds flying in a loose crescent catch up with their own repeated pipings twenty feet above our heads. I catch a glimpse of the black axillaries, jagged shapes that mark the white undersides of the birds' wings and bodies like painted-on armpits. They distinguish the species in every plumage.

Three more plover flocks hurtle over, crisscrossing.

Then each flock drops into the marsh in a unison so exact it suggests schooling fish.

No one understands how shorebirds coordinate these split-second maneuvers. Acoustic and visual signals seem improbable, the "flying-with-one-soul" school of thought too poetic, though tempting. Since flight plans alter instantaneously, signals must travel as fast as light. Electromagnetic communication may be the answer.

We're too far away from the plovers and other shorebirds on the mud to watch them feed, even through the scope. But we can still see the water recede. A slowly enlarging marine table fills the air with a briny perfume. Through some phenomenon of timing unknown to us and independent of daylight and dark, the tide has gathered southbound shorebirds from the Sound, sent them across the ridge in mercurial flocks, and treated them to a banquet.

The tide keeps falling and birds keep flying over us as the sun gradually moves overhead. We count ten flocks of shorebirds in all. The last of them is followed by a loner that I catch in silhouette. "Dowitcher!" I cry. Roland thinks I've said "Falcon," but I assure him I've gotten it right.

Though this identification isn't an enormous victory, it brings back another day I spent with Roland in this spot. He told me then that he was the person who'd discovered the short-billed dowitcher's nesting grounds in Labrador. Ever since, I've thought of the dowitcher as Roland's bird. To greet it now without hesitation gives me a special kind of pleasure, which floats above the scherzo of noon.

———

Somewhere between the Arctic tundra and the Sound's low, marshy islets many southbound shorebirds exchange their dramatic breeding plumages for somber autumn costumes. Each bird's clothes are custom-tailored, and even the best field guides can't entirely anticipate them. I thought I'd have a good view of the ensembles at Milford Point. But I saw mainly the birds' dramatic outlines and the marvelous coloring of breasts and of wings extended in synchronized flight, all from below. I want another crack at the shorebirds' fall regalia. And it's got to be soon, before the birds move on toward their wintering grounds in places as far away as South America.

Elsie and I pack our cameras in her boat and set out for a cove. We first approach a tiny island shaped like the profile of a tooth. With its root on our left we creep up on the more protruding of its two cusps. Not a shorebird in sight.

As we push along slowly, we look back to the shorter cusp. Three pairs of yellowlegs stand silhouetted on a stone against a pale wash of sky. Just in front of them is a single peep, a small sandpiper neither Elsie nor I can identify in the backlighting. A ledge of overhanging peat droops to become the top curve of a protective letter C until it frames the bird's plump little body with matching roundness. The peat looks like a wave that will never finish breaking.

The bird pokes repeatedly at the domed roof and curved wall of the special hollow in its tireless exploration. I can see a rhythm captured in feathers and feet, a rhythm drummed against the sun yet suggestive of domestic life, with soft edges and unhurried accomplishments. Author Charlton Ogburn's image of landed shorebirds as gentle homebodies drifts through my mind.

The view slowly fades as we motor toward the sunlit

Plovers and turnstones stand on the rocks

side of another islet. If we maneuver the boat well, the rising tide will take us within twenty feet of the shorebirds resting there. The buffer of cordgrass might buy us an even closer look.

As we approach, we can make out plovers and turnstones in various postures. Head-on, the dozen or so turnstones still look a little like Darth Vader. But the earlier Mardi Gras tones of their backs have given way to subtle mosaics, camouflaging the animals against the rocks. In the binoculars their orange legs look like toothpicks spearing nearly invisible canapes.

And the plovers! I can tell from their white rumps and tails that all of them are black-bellies. Yet their backs have molted into cloaks that look less like the reverse tux coats of spring and more like fatigues. One bird has lost so much darkness in the cheek that its head lacks color zones except for a hint of white that curves behind the eye. It's the last bird I single out.

As Elsie shifts her position for photographing, a glare bounces off her lens. Three plovers react with a cry as they lift off in front of us. The others materialize out of the stone. I watch them gather the turnstones on takeoff. They circle us once like a living wreath and are gone.

There. There I have it. The keepsake I yearned for in spring is the image of that flying wreath, that repetitive yet continuous travel, which like smoke has no clear beginning or end. The shorebirds' refueling stops on the tidal marshes of the Sound are essential. Yet one stop is no more important than any other.

I'd wanted to hold the birds. Of all creatures least needing to be held, they had confounded me with their self-sufficiency among the rocks and stars. As the wreath cancels my possessiveness, I see what breaks my heart. It's not the bird's departure. It's how long I've lived without their ephemeral magic. In retrospect I feel deprived, as if I'd learned only yesterday about sex. Or fried catfish.

There is a consolation. Owning the shorebirds' circle of flight as I do, I can close my eyes and return to the marsh from any taxi, any room. A brace of silver underwings skips in and out of sunlight. It flashes when I open the blinds of my eyes. It vanishes when I blink.

———

SHOREBIRD-WATCHING

To more than give names
to these random arrivals—
teeterings and dawdlings
of dunlin and turnstone,
blackbellied or golden
plover, all bound for

what may be construed as
a kind of avian Allthing
out on the Thingstead,
the unroofed synagogue
of the tundra—is already
to have begun to go wrong.

What calculus, what
tuning, what unparsed
telemetry behind the
retina, what overdrive
of hunger for the nightlong
daylight of the arctic,

are we voyeurs of? Our
bearings gone, we fumble
a welter of appearance,
of seasonal plumages
that go dim in winter:
these bright backs'

tweeded saffron, dark
underparts the relic
of what sibylline
descents, what harrowings?
Idiot savants, we've
brought into focus

such constellations,
such gamuts of
errantry, the very
terms we're condemned
to try to think in
turn into a trespass.

But Adam, drawn toward
that dark underside,
its mesmerizing
circumstantial thumbprint,
would already have
been aware of this.

—*Written by Amy Clampitt and sent to the author*
the summer after the spring shorebird excursion,
when it bore the title SHOREBIRDS IN SEASONAL
PLUMAGE OBSERVED THROUGH BINOCULARS

CORMORANTS

In spring, late summer, or autumn long flocks of dark birds larger than Black Ducks may be seen almost anywhere along the North Atlantic coast, flying 'in single file' close to the water with slow-flapping wings and outstretched necks. When seen passing diagonally at a distance close to the waves, the long wings of each seem to overlap those of the next in line, all rising and falling very nearly together. Often in the shimmering summer haze, which operates to deceive the eye, this spectacle will almost delude the credulous into the belief that they have seen the folds of a sea serpent rolling along the waves.

—Edward Howe Forbush
  Natural History of the Birds of Eastern and Central North America,
  from the passage on double-crested cormorants

The ancient archbishop rose for the blessing and began to stretch out his arms. Suddenly, as if possessed, he was seized with a movement so erratic that his entire body seemed to quake. His arms flapped repeatedly back and forth, and his black robes trailed them. The speed and violence of the gesture were tantrumlike, uncanny.

In seconds the old cleric was calm, as if he'd never undergone the spell. He spread his arms. His elbows angled up, and the hem of his dark vestments paralleled them into a pair of inverted, distorted Vs. The caped figure had the shape of a bat, or of someone who'd hung himself out to dry.

Cormorants, the big black birds of Long Island Sound,

are great mimes. This is their daft-bishop act, and it does allow the creatures to dry their less than waterproof wings by holding them open to the wind. But with what bizarre style! The birds give the impression of being bewitched and ponderous even when they're still. Their very posture suggests a hunchback determined to sit up straight. Legions of them perch on lighthouses and sit on the rungs of tall buoys circled by boaters. The scene has something of Rodin's *The Burghers of Calais* about it—like those noble burghers, cormorants take on dramatically different appearances from various angles.

It's curious how the birds react to tides. I've frequently seen three or four of them huddle on a small island until the imminent deluge forced a decision: swim or fly. Leisurely, they'd move to a spot only inches higher, where they were eventually joined by other cormorants. They kept up this tidal hopscotch until they were packed like feathered bowling pins onto the very tip of the last unswamped islet in the Sound.

Those birds that didn't then step into the soup did what weighty, gourd-shaped birds must do to leave the water and become airborne: they pattered with their feet and beat their wings against the surface. This gave them lift. It also made a sound like applause, well-deserved applause. A 747 doesn't face a tougher lift-off.

Audubon must have been aware of this odd drama. His painting of the Florida cormorant has a background showing clusters of birds in different stages of waiting, taking off, and swimming. The largest group consists of half a dozen cormorants on a shore at the painting's left. They appear to be debating whether it's time to go. Audubon even faced them toward a foursome that looks stranded on a rock in the middle of the water. Was the great artist playing?

Sometimes, at my telescope, I can catch what I think of as the cormorants' lima-bean trick. A bird that's crook-necked from preening its chest suddenly grows a beak on its back. The head to which that beak belongs sneaks into view, and finally the neck that holds the head. That neck starts to elongate and curve away in the opposite direction from the original one. Before long you've got magic out there on the guano—a two-headed creature looking like a dicotyledonous seed that's started to sprout. I know bet-ter. There are really two birds lined up, one behind the other. Yet I go along with the illusion.

The two start to separate, the rear bird angling forward till it's side by side with its clone. Their long necks horseshoe out even farther until one bird makes a perfect mirror image of the other, as if they were a pair of Thur-berish bookends. As they gradually increase the distance between them, they turn and regard each other like wary shmoos.

Given their exceptional entertainment value, shouldn't these birds be declared a national treasure? Depends on whom you ask. I'd say yes. But I'm in the luxurious po-sition of being charmed without needing to interact with the animals in any way. Their various postures are so dis-tanced from me by water and sky that the cormorants might well be shooting-gallery shapes. This perspective may make me a rare bird myself. Many people who have direct dealings with cormorants ARE NOT AMUSED. They find the creatures everything from "less than enchanting" to "downright revolting," for various reasons.

Although Native Americans are known to have eaten cormorants, in the early seventeenth century a European

Cormorants give the impression of being bewitched and ponderous

settler declared the bird's flesh "ranke and fishy." Audubon, that ultimate sampler of fowl, would probably have seconded the opinion. In fact, he said, "I have never eaten Cormorant's flesh, and I intend to refrain from tasting it until nothing better can be procured." Perhaps no bird with a reputation for such ghastly meat can ever win a warm spot in a nation's heart.

Bad flavor seemed only the beginning. For much of the nineteenth century the angling birds were seen as a threat to the fin-fish industry of Long Island Sound and other North American coastal waters. Consequently, they suffered severe human predation. This fact coupled with the devastating weakening of eggshells as a result of mid-twentieth-century DDT poisoning nearly wiped out both the great and the double-crested cormorant, the two dominant species on the Sound.

Today the birds are federally protected, and their numbers are soaring: cormorants are the most rapidly expanding group of colonial-nesting waterbirds on Long Island Sound, which attests to the quantities of menhaden and other fish available to support the creature's burgeoning populations.

"Nesting" is the key word here. Only since 1979 have cormorants nested in Connecticut, having gradually extended their range down the eastern coast of the continent from the Maritime Provinces and Newfoundland. Though the island-nesting birds move around, recently they've been constructing their stick nests on Goose Island near Madison, Connecticut, and on several of the islands in the western Sound, including East White Rock in the Norwalk Island chain.

The cormorants' expanded nesting range could become a serious problem. The birds are so large (nearly three feet in height) and so overbearing in their colonial habits that though they're not overtly aggressive toward other birds, their nests nevertheless crowd out those of roseate terns and even some gulls.

The nesters aren't exactly tidy, either, and often leave a trail of dead vegetation veneered with guano. In his life histories of birds Arthur Cleveland Bent has this rather vivid description of a cormorant nesting scene:

> The cormorant has not reached the point in evolution where sanitation and cleanliness about the dwelling place are considered important. A cormorant colony can be smelt from afar, and the vile, fishy odor clings to the clothes and remains long in the memory. Rocks, sticks,

bushes, nests, eggs, everything is daubed with the chalky, slimy excrement.

This makes you think. If cormorants eventually turn your favorite unsullied island into a reeking disaster, you may move the birds to the top of your avian hate list. In fact, you may do this even if you live far from the Sound.

————

Buckshot soil and gumbo are Dixie names for the dense, clayey dirt of the Mississippi Delta, where I was born. Catfish farmers love it. They bulldoze it into levees around squarish holes, then fill the holes with well water and stock them with fingerlings. The rich soil sticks together. And in a matter of weeks the scaleless adolescents it has corralled grow into grain-fed, pond-raised catfish.

Undoubtedly these cats have the sweetest, tenderest flesh in the world. It's subtle enough to blend with other flavors, yet assertive enough to stand alone as a culinary delicacy for the nineties. This adaptability has helped make catfish farming one of the hottest industries in the Deep South. It's the only industry with the marketing savvy and mystique to have all but replaced cotton as king of this traditionally agrarian economy.

But there's a hitch. In forming their shallow ponds the Southern farmers have inadvertently invited cormorants, which, after all, fish for a living. If the birds spoke our language, they might describe Mississippi's new soft-sided pools as bowls of catfish stew.

Yazoo City's Rodney Henderson is one of the new breed of aquaculturists and a former president of the Catfish Farmers of America. He agreed to spend a morning showing me the business and bemoaning the birds. Rodney's smart, having turned a consistent profit from the fish he grows on 100-plus acres. But by his own admission, cormorants are probably smarter. They discovered his ponds more than a decade ago, right after he began this venture, and their resourcefulness has given him nothing but grief ever since. He's even had to employ someone to patrol the levees on a four-wheeler during daylight hours to scare the birds off the water.

As we're surveying his ponds from the front seat of his car, Rodney holds his index fingers about six inches apart, to show me the length of a quarter-pound catfish. "Ideal eating," he says, "if you're a cormorant. From the air the birds can spot which ponds hold fish this big. Then they land—sometimes hundreds at once—and decimate the crop.

"I've even seen cormorants form a line and herd fingerlings into one end of a four-foot-deep pond," he continues. "The farmer's sole reliable defense is to stock larger fish exclusively just before the birds are expected to arrive for the winter."

In this first week of September I know that Rodney and his colleagues can enjoy only a few more days before the flocks reach the wide, flat land they've helped sculpt into a bumpy feasting place. It's a classic case of a monoculture attracting trouble. The big difference between this monoculture and cotton is that the boll weevil never had it this easy.

It couldn't have happened to a more qualified bird. The cormorant's fishing talent is the stuff of which tales are made. Like its relatives the pelican, the anhinga, and the booby, this animal has completely webbed feet that, under water, stroke in unison to shoot the cormorant along. On turns the wings can come into play. Few fish are able to outmaneuver something chasing it with this combination of submarine propulsion and adroitness.

Cormorants don't undertake the crazy aerial dives that pelicans do. Instead, they fish from the surface of the water, entering it headfirst with either a little leap or a simple and rather lazy-looking topple.

They sink quickly, thanks to heavy bones, limited buoyancy, and probably the weight of the small, smooth rocks the birds sometimes swallow. Cormorants can dive as deep as seventy-five feet without blinking. Make that *with* blinking: specialized eyelids let the birds keep their eyes open while they choose their lunch.

Usually a catch ends up crosswise in the cormorant's beak. The bird surfaces and repositions its trophy head-down, through tossing and nabbing moves that would make flapjack flippers envious. Then it swallows the fish whole. Sometimes it regurgitates into its near-pelicanesque pouch incompletely digested portions of fish as food for its young.

Audubon described a cormorant gone fishing like this:

> All of our Cormorants feed principally on various kinds of fish. If they seize one that is too large to swallow entire, they carry it to the shore or to a branch and there thrash or tear it to pieces. Sometimes the fish they have swallowed will discommode them, so that they shake their heads violently and disgorge it, or else manage to pass it downwards into the stomach. All the species are expert at tossing up a fish inconveniently caught—a foot or so above their heads—and receiving it into their open gullet, like the Man-o'-War bird.

Many fishermen exploit the cormorant's gifts of speedy hunting and easy catching. In the Far East, for instance, men still work as many as half a dozen cormorants at once. They place a collar—often made of leather—around each bird's neck to stop it from swallowing anything of size. Then they let the trained bird go diving. When it surfaces with a prize, they simply reach into the cormorant's mouth. *Voilà!* The bird's dinner becomes the man's.

The same fishing genius that Asians perceive as a positive trait, however, has driven other (pre-catfish) people to the brink of hysteria. The English may be the most damning. Their prejudice against cormorants dates back to medieval times or earlier. Chaucer lists "the hote cormeraunt of glotenye" (gluttony) in his *Parlement of Foules*. And Shakespeare echoes the idea of the cormorant's supposedly rapacious appetite in no fewer than four of his plays. In Act I of *Coriolanus* he refers to "the cormorant belly," and in *Troilus and Cressida* he has Priam speak of "this cormorant war."

According to Milan Bull, director of the Connecticut Audubon Center at Fairfield, cormorants are historically picked on not just because they're perceived as greedy but also because they're considered snake-like. They sneak around under water and are as secretive as bats, Bull says. "It's no wonder the poetic English dislike them. Cormorants are as far removed from the nightingale as you can get."

Ironically, cormorants may end up functioning as the Greek chorus of inland waters. Researchers near the Great Lakes are paying attention to the birds' frequent birth defects, which they think may result from high concentrations of aquatic PCBs. If cormorants are confirmed in reflecting PCB levels, they may eventually help advance the drama of conservation while providing a valuable commentary on it.

WATER

My mother cuts cake with a thread. Like a dentist preparing to floss a patient, she wraps the ends of a two-foot length of red mercerized around her index fingers. Then she pulls the thread taut, turns her palms down, and extends her arms straight out beyond the square blond layer on the cooling rack. Her forearms are spaced about a foot apart, and they whir as they hover about the cake. Jackknifing her body over the table, she peers back at the delicacy with upside-down eyes to judge where to position the thread: it should bisect the two-inch-high layer.

Mother stands up and starts to pull the thread toward her, keeping it parallel to the cake's upper surface. But she doesn't pull straight back. On either side of the cake she brings one hand and then the other toward her waist. She shimmies slowly like this for about a minute, releasing a macy aroma into the air .

What she ends up with is two inch-high layers in a stack that's screaming for icing. But you can't look at them and tell there's been a cut. The contrast of red thread against rich yellow is gone, and the crumbs that might have fallen along the edges didn't. The top layer settles onto its newly severed twin in such a smooth and subtle way that you'd swear the two had baked back together.

The horizon beyond the islands is this indefinite before a storm. In mist I look for a thread of demarcation. It's not there. A layer of sky rests on the Sound, and is separated from it by memory only.

BIVALVES AND BOATS

I heard the boat before I saw her. She announced herself in middle C, a half-spoken, half-glottal-stopped tone that drifted through my window in the early daylight of August. It continued for what I later learned was three-quarters of a spin in the water before the guttural engine cut out. Momentum carried the vessel the remaining quarter-spin into the current. I could hear the thick clang of the rising dredge and chains, a sound like a hiss of steam, silence, the motor again.

Dauntless motored parallel to the shore by the time I climbed out of bed and reached the telescope. Both her stacks spewed fidgety plumes. Silhouetted against the brilliant white of morning, the boat looked powerful, a tossing dragon. Except for the hot-orange color of the crew's work aprons, everything was shapes and sounds.

I studied the superstructure raked back from the bow. It was a conveyor belt. Beneath it on the vessel's port side stood a table. Smoke curled from a cigarette balanced on the table's rim, and over three wire baskets men appeared to be juggling eggs.

A beamy boat near *Dauntless* looked stranger. Her bow sported a tidy row of square cutouts below the gunwales, which lent a Victorian air to the whole scene. Yet they probably had the most utilitarian function imaginable, like draining the deck after the workboat got a bath. I could spot a crew of three: one dark, heavy-haired man on deck; one blond captain in the wheelhouse; and a black Labrador retriever. The two men were synchronized, and needed to be, since one of them was a window washer as well as a captain. The other man tended two braces of what looked like long string mops tapered on either end. Each of the eighteen mop heads hung from its own ring, and the rings all hung from a chain held horizontal by a series of pulleys.

The mop contraption was hoisted from the water whenever the mood seemed to strike the crew. After it cleared the deck, the mop heads were guided toward a rectangular vat along the gunwale. Before they were dipped into the steaming vat, the man on deck tossed some objects on them back into the water. He didn't remove the sea stars, huge numbers of which clung to the mops and got boiled.

Every time the brace of mop heads shifted position, the Lab chased around on deck and ran under the drippings. This was happening while the captain washed the windows, which he had to stop doing before he could redirect his attention to the levers that controlled the braces. Timing and Windex were critical.

Both *Dauntless* and the curious *Grace P. Lowndes* are owned by Tallmadge Brothers, Inc., Norwalk, Connecticut's well-known oyster and clam company. The latter boat, I discovered, drags her mops across oyster beds in order to pick up sea stars, or starfish. These echinoderms can send their stomachs into a bivalve's shell. They are such a serious threat to oysters that in his book *The Oyster* Robert Hedeen calls the starfish a "mortal enemy to be combatted with every means available."

The star boat's means are ingenious, but no more so than the countless moves Tallmadge owner Hillard Bloom has made on his way to becoming the largest independent shellfish operator in the country. He and his late twin brother, Norman, charted their now-legendary course in the 1940s, when they oystered in the historically mollusk-rich Sound. They worked from *Eaglet*, a sailboat not too different from the traditional Chesapeake skipjack.

Soon afterward oysters began to decline, for reasons no one fully understands. Perhaps a natural cycle was responsible. The ravages of hurricanes and the decimation of the bivalves by both sea stars and hungry seven-foot tapeworms didn't help. Nor did a noticeable lack of setting, the oysterman's term for the homesteading of oyster larvae. By the early 1960s Long Island Sound oysters were nearly gone.

Turning to clamming while taking a gamble on the oyster's recovery, the Blooms began buying older oyster companies and the boats that came with them. Most of the vessels were pockmarked wooden relics that required rebuilding. Some were actually chopped in two and given a new center section between the original bow and stern, an outrageous method of lengthening that nevertheless worked like a charm. Other purchases included two Delaware Bay schooners, a ferry, and a Coast Guard tender. While they required less drastic work than the oyster boats, they still had to be outfitted for modern mechanized shellfish harvesting. Like the fishing boats, they had wooden hulls, which can outlast steel ones if properly maintained.

The Blooms' faith and ingenuity paid off. In the 1970s and '80s oysters came back with a vengeance, and Tallmadge Brothers' fleet of twenty-two boats stood ready to bring them to market. Today the boats harvest the lion's share of Atlantic hard clams (*Mercenaria mercenaria*) and Eastern oysters (*Crassostrea virginica*) from beds between New Haven, Connecticut, and Delaware Bay. The Tallmadge oyster beds on Long Island Sound, which are among the world's most productive, deliver half a million bushels of oysters a year. At an average of $50 a bushel, this crop alone is worth $25 million annually. Tallmadge oysters and clams together represent 90 percent of the region's total shellfish crop.

Through a series of lucky events, I was granted permission to go out on a Bloom boat, though I hadn't met a Bloom and I didn't know ahead of time which boat I would board. She turned out to be the same *Dauntless* that had served as my warm-weather alarm clock. The Sound was choppy that autumn day and the sky a gray metal that I could taste on the edge of my tongue as I was hoisted from a tender onto the rocking vessel's high stern.

The long-legged steel sorting table I'd seen from afar seemed to glow in the intermittent sunlight. The only brighter objects were the crew's familiar orange aprons—which also blinked off and on with the sky—and Captain Jeff Yarde's hair. Even in the shade of the wheelhouse, Jeff had a head that shone legal-pad yellow.

At the age of twenty-three, Jeff's a ten-year veteran of commercial shellfishing. He began his career with the Blooms by helping out on deck during the summers of his Greenwich High School career. "There's no college for this kind of work," he told me. "You just do it, and if you like it, you hope you've got what it takes." What it takes is obviously more than a good brain and quick reflexes. It's a touchy-feely sort of thing, an inborn talent for dancing with submarine life that you can't even see. Clammers call it "bottom sensitivity."

If Jeff hadn't been encouraged by his employers to obtain information through his bones, he might have been standing comatose before a depth sounder as he spoke. Instead, he simply checked himself against his computerized equipment, which showed among other things the locations of the flagged bamboo stakes that mark the Tallmadge beds.

Jeff's deck crew hailed from Guatemala. Miguel was bearded and slender; Renaldo slightly stockier, with a perfect walrus mustache. Their English was a hundred times

Enormous black rubber work gloves balance on the rim
of the wire sorting basket

better than my Spanish would have been if I had lived in
their country for only a year. Yet they were shy of me,
probably of my blondness, my funny-looking leather vest.
Certainly of my camera.

To try to offset this, I asked at once if I could photograph
them at their table, the obvious focus of activity on deck.
Two pairs of enormous black rubber work gloves balanced
like mannequins' hands on the rims of the wire sorting
baskets. The gloves read SANITIZED in prominent letters.

The men pulled on the gloves as Jeff began to lift the
submerged clam dredge. It stayed to the inside of the circle
that *Dauntless* made during the drag, when Jeff controlled
it with a simple rope in the wheelhouse. Once the dredge
cleared the water and hung dripping beyond the deck,
however, it became the charge of the other two men.

This division of labor was necessary to keep the deck

crew from being accidentally doused by the pump hose mounted on the top of the metal dredge basket. When the dredge is on the bottom of the Sound, this hose shoots a jet of water slightly ahead of the basket's toothed lower rim. The jet dislodges the clams from mud or sand and makes it easy for the basket itself to follow along and pick up the shellfish. But the stream of water must be plugged once its job is done. (Because oystering requires no hose, which can get fouled as a boat turns, a captain can operate two oyster dredges simultaneously, one on either side of a vessel.)

Renaldo guided the dredge basket over the long table and emptied it by unlatching its bottom flap. *Whoossssssh,* long and loud, came the sound of clams hitting steel. And there on the surface was a microcosm of the Sound's foundation. Three squirming horseshoe crabs, a few oysters, one patch of sea lettuce, half a dozen gargantuan spider crabs, a couple of sea stars, and several bushels of clams lay like treasure from the deep. The organisms were interlocked, the legs of one partially inverted horseshoe crab playing a rhythm on the back of a spider crab struggling under the weight of shells. The clams glistened like round stones scooped up from a stream.

Miguel and Renaldo expertly untangled the extraneous animals and plants and tossed them back into the drink. Then they turned to sorting clams. In about a minute they had filled two baskets with the huge chowders, or quahogs, and a third basket with the smaller cherrystones. In another two minutes they had emptied all the clams into burlap bags. Finally, they bound the ends of the bags with twine and added their loads to one of the two mounting stacks of segregated mollusks. They hosed down the table and started over.

Oddly, there was no smell of any kind. I'd expected the boat to exude revolting odors, like a fish market down on its luck. But instead of being nauseated, I was impressed with nothing olfactory so much as—well, nothing olfactory. Certainly no decay.

Harvested Connecticut shellfish (oysters, clams, and mussels) remain alive for a long time under conditions that mimic their home. I'd just seen clams take a five-minute trip from Sound bottom to burlap. The bags, which shield the animals from the sun, were stacked close together. The temperature inside them would stay low. When *Dauntless* returned to the home port's refrigerated building at the end of the day, those clams would still be kicking.

Oysters, which are dredged in greater quantities, are not bagged on board. Instead, they are moved along a series of conveyor belts and deposited directly into steel cages near the boat's stern. Thus they are delivered loose to the cold house, usually within an hour or two of harvest. (The oyster boats make several runs a day in and out of the docks.) With this schedule also, the crop simply doesn't have time to die. In fact, oysters that are well harvested and well stored can last two weeks or longer, thanks in part to the seawater sealed inside their valves.

Jeff told me that Bloom's employees spend the Fourth of July or thereabouts hosing a year's worth of previously stored oyster shells from the decks of the workboats back into the Sound. This amounts to close to a million bushels. Clean, old shells on a clean bottom make the best cultch for the larval bivalves, he said. I scratched my head.

Oysters, he began explaining, can change sex from year to year. (The larger ones tend to be females.) In June the reproductive season starts. Before it's over about a month later, each spawning lady *Crassostrea* may have released as

many as half a billion eggs into the water, puffing intermittent clouds of them out of her shell. Only a fraction of
the eggs ever meet with sperm. After the larvae that result
pass a couple of weeks free-swimming, they settle to the
bottom and glue themselves to a surface, not unlike a barnacle.

But like the birds called martins and many other creatures, Jeff continued, the larvae have preferences we human
beings cannot understand. Though they like old oyster
shells, all cultch of this type is obviously not the same. The
tiny oyster larvae will, time and again, opt to call certain
locales home while they shun others that would seem, to
us, equally welcoming. This is fact A-1 for the oysterman;
he learns it in his very first season and never forgets it.

Having learned it, he is compensated. For once the larvae have begun to develop into spat (young oysters) and
have set, the oysterman begins to contemplate moving
them from bed to bed. The shifting controls the bivalves'
development, primarily by limiting environmental nutrients when growth must be slowed and increasing them
when the crop is ready to fatten for market. This manip-
ulation is possible primarily because oysters are filter feed-
ers. Being immobile, they depend on water currents to
bring them oxygen and the plankton on which they feed.
The richer the soup, the faster the growth.

A mature Eastern oyster filters as much as 100 gallons of
water each day. Translating this into human terms, writer
Eleanor Clark would have me swallow approximately half
the water in a large public swimming pool before I go to
sleep tonight. If one oyster behaves this thirstily, a large
population of the bivalves constantly pumping and filtering
is a godsend to the water quality of whole bays. In fact,
those areas of Long Island Sound with the densest blooms

of algae all summer long are often the ones that have no shellfish to crop the stuff off.

Tiny structures on an oyster's gills pull the huge amounts of water into the creature's mantle cavity, where the oyster does the molluskan equivalent of smacking its lips. (The mantle is the part of the oyster's body you see right after you part the shell's two valves. When the folds along the mantle's margin curl, your oyster stew is ready.) Chesapeake Bay author Tom Horton says the bivalve is indeed a real gourmand, a sort of Ph.D. of the palate. This is an amazing accolade for one of the world's best (human) foods.

In *Bay Country* Horton gives details when he writes that the oyster "is able to sample for size, digestibility, and, for lack of a better word, *taste*, virtually every one of the millions of particles of sediment and algae entering its mouth every hour it is feeding. Everything not to its liking is rejected out one side of its shell before digestion."

I read the passage by Horton on a cold January day just before I met Hillard Bloom. It must have stuck. For, preposterously, I noted *his* filter-feeding lifestyle. His office, the very opposite of the remote executive corner window, is a ground-floor corridor through which his employees pass in a steady stream. With most of them he exchanges greetings and information.

The room itself is small, dark, and narrow, yet physically and psychologically warm. It's furnished with a bank of old-style metal file cabinets, a couple of wooden desks placed at right angles along two walls, a hanging plaque mounted with oysters in six stages of growth, a squawk box that keeps Hillard in touch with his operation, and three straight chairs lined up just inside the front door. Soon after I arrived, I met Ashley, Misty, and Scampy, a trio of retrievers curled up in the chairs' seats. Their heads weighed on their paws in attitudes of total resignation to the downpour outside.

Much of Hillard's success is due to trusting the oyster-man's tradition, but not without first filtering out the "tradition for tradition's sake" attitude that impedes progress. The exterior of the building that houses the Tallmadge Brothers processing and refrigeration facilities in Norwalk Harbor is no low-slung, prefab affair but an exact replica of the 10,000-square-foot, four-story Radel Oyster Company, a shucking house. In the nineteenth century the original Radel stood within feet of current Tallmadge headquarters. In an effort to make sure no one misses the past represented in the headquarters' walls, Hillard rents the building's top floor to the Norwalk Seaport Association, which uses the space as a hands-on maritime learning center for children.

Tallmadge makes its own oyster dredges, or "drudges," as the word for the harvester is usually pronounced. The names for its various parts are fabulous if arcane: drudge blade, bale, frame. These parts are designed and assembled in much the same fashion that they were by the last generation of oystermen, from whom Hillard learned. "It's still the best way," he said.

"We make sure the drudge is properly hung, with the bag and doors set so they don't lie on the oysters during a drag. If you don't drudge 'em properly, you can bill 'em, just take the tops right off. If you see any damage on deck, there's a lot more on the bottom."

I'd guess Hillard Bloom knows where everything on a workboat comes from. Many of the captains he employs are family members who grew up in the business. And when I asked him about the history of the star boats, he said, "That goes way back. In the early thirties, when they had steamboats, they found out the steam would kill the starfish. We just carry it right on."

In spite of all this continuity, it wasn't history that impressed me most at Tallmadge Brothers. It was oysters. Like the visibly ecstatic woman in Jan Steen's seventeenth-century painting *The Oyster-eater,* I absolutely love this food. Being presented with a dozen oysters on the half shell is like being given a collection of edible, chilly soft sculptures, each of them unique. And because I'm never ready to eat such a gift right away, I invent small rituals that let me defer the pleasure.

Before I pick up the slender fork that lies across the bed of ice, I often note how snugly each oyster fits its nacreous manger, or the differences in the margins of the shells, or (on a no-color background) the exact color of the twelve off-center adductor muscle scars that stare up at me like eyes. Sometimes, if the presentation is fancy, I squirt juice from the cheesecloth-covered lemon half on one oyster and lift the cup-shaped left valve in which it's resting, as if to make a toast with it. But I don't make a toast. Instead, I run the index finger of my free hand over the outside of the valve, to try to feel the tiny holes that oyster drills have bored. As I tilt the cup toward my mouth and relish the exotic muskiness of the meat sliding down my throat, I thank the gods that made this exquisite stuff.

Hillard adds a dimension to the way I think of this gustatory wonder when he introduces me to his hoppers. Located on the second floor of his frigid processing building, the stainless-steel hoppers can hold 1,200 bushels of oysters apiece. A pair of them were nearly full when I saw them! Though the bivalves are clearly a cultivated crop, there was no way I could stand before these two mountains of gritty shells and think of oysters simply as products, objects comparable to Fritos. The creatures were barely out of their beds, hardly removed from lives of their own. I'd seen small numbers of oysters sticking out of the muck at low tide, but this was different. The sheer volume of them here, and their incomprehensible weight as they made the slow fall to the sorting floor below, brought me as close as I'll ever come to visiting them in their own city.

"Why is the Connecticut shore of Long Island Sound so full of good oysters?" I asked. Hillard markets nothing but bluepoints, which many people think of as the *crème de la crème* of American mollusks. Ironically, the name indicates merely a size (not a quality) to the professional shellfisherman, and it originated in the town of Blue Point, which is on the Sound's Long Island shore.

"I think it's the rivers coming into the Sound from the north," Hillard answered, "the mix of fresh and salt water. Connecticut has always had wonderful setting beds."

As we talked, he spread out a map of Long Island Sound's Milford shore. It showed his beds in neat parcels much as a map of the Midwest might show a farmer's fields. Hillard handled the document with respect, pointing out the names of the original oyster companies from which he'd purchased underwater plots. "Here's one of more than six hundred acres. It's still shown as the property of Long Island Oyster Farms," he said.

Hillard is generally optimistic about the water on which his livelihood depends. He praises the 1972 Clean Water Act for helping to control chemical pollution, saying, "At least the water in the Bridgeport area doesn't turn the oyster meats blue-green anymore. But now we have new problems, such as an increase in the populations of birds, mostly waterfowl and gulls. Their wastes raise the levels of bacteria in the Sound. Since shellfish hibernate in winter, there's no problem with our boats working inside the Norwalk Islands then. But in summer we try to stay farther out, away from the heaviest concentrations of birds.

"The state really watches us, and we want them to," he said. "In fact, state and local inspectors test regularly for water purity on the oyster beds. In addition, the shellfish are monitored at our packing plant after being tagged with the date and place of harvest. If someone gets sick from eating shellfish, we have the means to check out whole shipments. But nothing like this has been needed in a long time.

"Trouble usually stems from the way the shellfish are handled once they're purchased. You can't throw clams in a tub of cold, fresh water and have people dip their hands in there all afternoon without asking for problems. And please don't do what one customer of ours did. He bought a bag of clams on Thursday and set it behind his garage in ninety-degree heat until Sunday, when he served his friends. They weren't happy."

––––

The Eastern oyster has been shuttled between beds for nearly two centuries. When overharvesting or other factors made stocks of the bivalve insufficient for local demand in the late 1700s, shrewd Connecticut oystermen bought additional supplies from neighboring communities. By the 1920s those oystermen's descendants were purchasing from as far away as the Chesapeake. Though all this shifting didn't noticeably eclipse the mollusk's local flavor (a threat worse than having your Southern accent drilled out of you), it led to the term "bluepoint" being used generically.

To most food professionals this catchall now indicates any mild-tasting oyster from the Atlantic (though not the Gulf) coast.

In spite of such homogenization, bluepoints and other editions of the Eastern oyster have managed to keep some ties to the regions that originally made them famous. The names Chincoteague, Bristol, Cotuit, Indian River, Malpeque, Emerald Point, and others appear on the chalk boards of oyster bars from Prince Edward Island to Bayou LaBatre and beyond. All these names still mean *Crassostrea virginica*. Yet some of the oysters that go by these names begin life in ways that are very different from how the Tallmadge stock gets its natural start.

Dave Relyea is hatchery manager of Frank M. Flower and Sons in Oyster Bay, Long Island. The only oyster company in New York State, this is both a hatchery and a nursery for the bivalves, 60 million of them a year. When I went to visit Dave and asked him why a hatchery was needed, he said, "We don't get natural sets of *Crassostrea* around Oyster Bay anymore, the way they do up in Connecticut. That stopped in the sixties, when oysters all over the Sound nearly disappeared. While the Blooms went clamming as they waited for oysters to make a comeback, our company founder opted to give Mother Nature a nudge and create his own source of the mollusks."

A nudge! Flower brings adult male and female oysters into its facility as early as February and starts them spawning in warm water. They oblige off and on right through June, when their natural cycle ends. Then Dave begins overseeing larvae.

For their first two to three weeks the larvae swim in conical tanks that must seem as deep to them as the Grand Canyon would to us (four feet). The staff grades them every other day during this time, by returning to the conicals those hardy survivors that they collect on mesh-bottomed tins placed under the tips of the cones. These tins look exactly like metal tambourines minus the jingles. Dave and his crew are responsible for sifting and resifting the growing larvae through increasingly large-holed screens. I couldn't even see the minuscule openings in screens used to collect the youngest larvae, never mind finding the larvae themselves. Yet I was told that by the time they're twenty-four hours old, the larvae have begun to develop shells.

Oysters two to three weeks old are ready to metamorphose. Flower supplies them with a cultch of quarter-inch clamshell fragments and transfers them into the company's rich feeding tanks. These shallow containers are filled with a molluskan pabulum that the hatchery makes by inoculating nutrient-laden salt water with algae starter provided by various federal and university labs. The culture works like sourdough starter. Though the liquid oyster food reminded me of unset dirty Jell-O, it must have been a whole sea of Dom Pérignon to the bivalves.

Dave stuck his hand into a feeding tank and scraped his fingers along the screen bottom of a wooden-sided tray. The open palm he showed me was full of wedge-shaped, half-inch-long oysters that were a month old. In clusters of nine or ten they were stuck at odd angles onto every available surface of clamshell. The oysters brought to mind a large shipwrecked party hanging on to a small life raft, or ten Linuses and only one blanket.

Inside and out, everything except the huge, oyster-shaped Flower signs (bearing the founding date 1887) seemed to be on a reduced scale. The two main buildings were about the size of tall two-car garages. And the barges that slipped quietly in and out of the well-hosed, upper-level docks had the appeal of Huck Finn's raft. Their decks were just large enough for one or two sun-worshipping college students dressed in shorts and rubber boots to stand abreast with arms outstretched to the sky. Stacked next to them were trays of the little bivalves in four different stages of growth. The toy boats ran a hundred feet out to some floating planks, dropped their loads, picked up others, and ran back. (During the summer months oysters double in size every two weeks. That determines how often they need sorting.)

The floating planks in the bay were components of a system of culture. Oysters that had developed the knack of feeding themselves in the wild were transferred into this sopping kindergarten. Except for bimonthly trips to the sorting dock and back, this is where they stayed until they were ready for their own beds. At that point, usually when the animals were at least three months old and about an inch in diameter, they were considered seed oysters. This meant they were ready to be planted on the 2,000 under-water acres that Flower leases. After a total of two years on the bottom (oysters are thought to live ten to twelve years), they would be sold as market oysters to the Fulton Fish Market. Or to a customer in Virginia. Or to Tallmadge, if that company needed them to fill their daily orders.

———

Almost a year after I began paying attention to shellfish in the Sound, Jacquelyn came to visit. She was ten and full of invitations. "Let's go snarling," she said. Since she missed a beat in her usually breathless speech, I thought she made up the word as she said it. I accepted.

When we were beachbound, Jacquelyn explained that the goal of her game was to find as many snarls as possible, then to grade them. It was to be a cooperative venture— "not at all cutthroat"—and we should end up with a list. Printing in purple ink on unlined sketch paper, she showed me:

Snarls   Semisnarls   Supersnarls

Since I was embarrassed at being so slow to catch on, I wouldn't let myself ask her what in heaven's name a snarl was. Surely it would become clear.

She wanted to amass and somehow rank a collection of unnatural objects found in the Sound, snarls for sure. Since it was low tide, washed-up items counted.

Her left and right columns were quickly filled and not terribly interesting. Snarls included tide-line commonplaces such as mangled plastic juice containers. Supersnarls were one-of-a-kind wrecks—a Ninja turtle with an arm missing—and earned stars by their names if they had writing on them. But the center column—ahhh—the winners showed up here. These were items that, at first glance, weren't clearly this or that, natural or man-made. They demanded additional attention.

Jacquelyn thought a clear plastic, circular temperature dial looked like a jellyfish. She wrote "Jellyfish" in parentheses after the official entry "Round Dial." Some tangled catgut looked like hydroids, my scholarly contribution. Then we saw, simultaneously, the prize of all semisnarls, a piece of laminated something or other that in an earlier life must have been an oyster's flat upper valve. It was toffee-colored on one side and oyster-white on the other. The edges were notched, and the fragment was pointed like

Texas on one end to suggest an umbo, the starting point
of an oyster's shell. Even the size of the piece was astound-
ingly oysteresque. The only thing not quite right was the
straightness of one side where an oyster would have had
some sort of curve. In spite of this, if anything had suggested an adductor scar, Jacquelyn and I would have been
unnerved.

Quick, before the magic vanished, she printed the entry:

> Prize! Oyster
> shell lookalik
> layared plastic

The find focused my attention on the oyster's shell instead
of on the creature that makes it. (The oyster's mantle extracts various elements from the water and by means of a
nifty bit of alchemy secretes a shell that is primarily calcium
carbonate.) The valves that had washed up around us had
wildly varying shapes. Here were shells of picture-perfect
market bluepoint oysters. Thick and rounded, they had a
deeply scooped left valve. They also had aging ridges that
were as individual as an octogenarian's wrinkles. Since an
oyster increases the size of its shell by adding new material
along the edges, these crescents can be counted like tree
rings.

The not-so-perfect shells were a gourmet picnic,
mostly appetizers and desserts. Clusters of them were all
hooked together randomly, with the bottom valve of one
shell back-to-back with the bottom valve of another.
When their residents were alive, one must have lived on
the ceiling, like Fred Astaire dancing in the film *Royal
Wedding*.

Here was a five-inch-high left valve engaged in a permanent backbend, and another valve thickened by sinuous tunnels and overpasses built by the limy tube worm. Seeing the passageways from above was like peering down from a plane at the maddening complex of highways around Shea Stadium. A couple of valves looked so skinny and tall that I figured their inhabitants grew up in soft mud, with lots of close, hungry relatives. They probably had to stand at the mantel to eat instead of lying down like more pampered oysters do.

Except for the generally spiral configuration of many valves, the only constant I found in the shapes of oyster shells was the roundedness of spat attached to the shells of elders. For a long time I'd thought the spat were jingle shells trying to change their nomadic ways.

Scientist Paul Galtsoff finally set me straight on all this. On one page of his definitive work *The American Oyster* he shows the young *C. virginica* growing its shell from the umbo at a uniform rate. On the next page is a diagram of the adult oyster. The youngster from the previous page looks transposed to this second drawing's top section. But in the lower part of that second drawing all hell breaks loose. The shell margins careen across the paper, down unmarked lanes and through stop signs, all regard for law and order lost.

Galtsoff explains the erratic driving as follows:

> The principal axes of shells of *C. virginica* are not as permanent as they are in clams, scallops, and other bivalves in which the shape of the valves remains fairly constant and is less affected by environment than in the oyster. The plasticity of oysters of the species *Crassostrea* is so great that their shape cannot be determined geometrically.

C. virginica, then, is an obedient child, a model of decorum. But as it approaches adolescence and starts to establish its own identity, it strikes out in unpredictable ways. If it has to change bedrooms during this stage of its life, or if it gets moved to another town before it graduates, it literally gets bent out of shape. This has happened so often by now that "bent" has become the oyster's norm.

THE DOCK

"Sittin' on the dock o' the bay, wastin' time."

—"The Dock of the Bay," as sung by Otis Redding

I remember when Revlon promoted the lipstick color Fire and Ice—the *first* time. The paradoxical name was a stroke of marketing genius that must have raised erotic expectations across the country. Mississippi may have been among the regions most afflicted: that state's extreme heat made the possibility of ice irresistible. In 1995 Revlon reintroduced Fire and Ice with double-page spreads in the glossy fashion magazines, but the idea wasn't nearly so enticing the second time around. I was less impressionable, and in the intervening years a more intriguing cold fire had caught my imagination.

On moonless, late-summer nights the water near the floating dock where we keep our dinghy glows with luminescent organisms. Steve thought they looked like sparks flashing in the water when he was rowing the dinghy back toward the dock one evening. After he landed, he climbed out with an oar in his hand. Holding the shaft perpendicular like a giant swizzle stick, he lowered the blade into the water and traced a figure 8. A greenish glow followed the curves.

The next night, sitting in the tethered dink with Steve, I dipped a transparent cup over the side to see if I could capture a source of the light. Nothing. When I stirred up the water in the course of making several passes with the container, however, stars winked on in my arm's wake: the cup held a rounded glow that extinguished itself almost immediately. The beam of the flashlight through the cup gave a hint of something gelatinous, with rainbow colors showing faintly along its length. I waited a moment, and when nothing else happened, I poured out the water and its inhabitant.

Steve rocked the dinghy, and organisms near the dock flashed and faded. We climbed out, stood above them, and jumped up and down. Along most of the length of the platform, right where wood met water, what appeared to be a string of tiny, clear lights blinked into the liquid dark.

Bioluminescence, which means "living light," is a chemical reaction produced with such efficiency that there is no heat by-product. The phenomenon occurs in the presence of oxygen when the pigment known as luciferin combines with the enzyme known as luciferase. What's remarkable is that certain marine organisms capable of bioluminescing must be disturbed before they'll dance this radiant jig.

Marine animals are by no means the only ones that bioluminesce. Fireflies near the dock flash on and off by means of the same process. Unlike some marine bioluminescence, however, a firefly's display has a clear purpose: the insect blinks are mating signals. Each firefly species possesses its own pattern of illumination, with which the males of that species advertise for potential amours. Females of the same species respond in kind. Though the small marine crustaceans called ostracods and various fishes apparently also luminesce for sexual reasons, a similar purpose seems highly unlikely among marine organisms that reproduce asexually, which include many members of Long Island Sound's bioluminescent community.

Hundreds of genera of marine creatures are known to bioluminesce. They include certain squids as well as several species of jellyfish and tunicates. The latter are either individual small, bulbous or sac-shaped animals or colonies of creatures arranged in the fabulous shapes of stars and alphabet letters. The animal I captured turned out to be a comb jelly, or ctenophore, a non-stinging cousin of the jellyfish that's common near the docks of the Sound in the summertime. The ctenophore's rainbow colors, so indistinct at night, are often easier to see in daylight, when the eight rows of hairlike, iridescent comb plates that give the animal its common name appear to ripple through relatively clear, quiet shallows. Perhaps one day scientists will no longer have to wonder whether all organisms capable of turning themselves on do so in an effort to evade predators, find food, or survive through other means, and the mystique of cold fire will be gone. Until then, I'll liken the hyperbole of the ctenophore to the caroling of one brilliant note at a time into the darkest midnight.

———

I returned to the dock a day or two later, after a rain, to bail out the dinghy. Though her painter is twice as long as her stern line, the dinghy usually rides parallel to the floating dock. But the day's fluky wind kept pushing out her stern. Because I couldn't get close enough, I had to reach out awkwardly each time I filled and emptied the milk jug bailer. A lot of water had collected in the stern of the ten-foot craft, and I quickly tired.

To rest, I gave the stern a shove and sat up. I was still kneeling, with both elbows locked and my fingers curled over the board ends. With head and shoulders hanging out

The very concepts of animal or plant, motile or sessile, lose their meaning in the face of this phantasmagoric collection

above the triangle of water formed by the stern line, the dinghy, and the dock, I looked down at my reflected face. By leaning out just a little farther I could gaze back at that portion of the dock's base that Steve and I had set on fire when we jumped up and down that night. There were Nubian giraffes down there. And snow leopards. Or was it just their shrunken skins flapping? The largest was the size and shape of my tongue. The hides were patterned with tiny creatures arranged in stars, curvaceous capital D's, stretched O's, and a lazy V or two. A few of the letters were printed darkly on a field of light, by what tool I couldn't guess. But most were the reverse—pale yellows or champagne tones on charcoals and rich chestnut browns. Purple hides looked embroidered in gold.

In spite of color variations among the individual paisley forms, overall the dock's organic fringe had a restricted

palette of dark, velvety green and different values of cinnamon orange. An organism that led me to mouth the
words "dusky apricot smoke" trailed into nothingness beneath the wood. The wisps looked not only insubstantial
but also inverted. Small light-green hailstone mimics had
the same aura of reversal, as if the dock might have its own
laws of gravity.

At that time I recognized none of the organisms attached
there. I made my way home, donned a swimsuit, picked up
some snorkel equipment and a hand lens, and returned.
Then I climbed into our tender and slipped over her side.
The water was cold, and it clouded right away. Tiny bubbles played around my eyes and seemed to cloud them also.
Ripples set up by my paddling caused the whole band of
life in front of me to sway so violently that I couldn't keep
it in focus. Yet each time I stopped stroking and tried to
float, a foot or an elbow bumped a straggling part of the
mass. I must have dislodged half a bushel of tiny forms,
condemning them to the deep before I even knew what
they were.

Both discouraged and amused, I hoisted myself back into
the dinghy to plan another approach. With the hand lens
held out of the water just above the dock's base, I scanned
the growth in front of me. Game skins still swung slowly
above the apricot wisps and viscous-looking pale-green
balls. And I could see other forms of life. But I couldn't
sort any of it. Everything appeared to be living on top of,
or under, or clinging to, or trailing from something else;
and my eye simply wouldn't get down to the business of
drawing boundaries. The very concepts of animal or plant,
motile or sessile, lost their meanings in the face of this richly
interwoven, phantasmagoric collection.

After much prodding I recognized the hundreds of

skinny, heavily encrusted fingers reaching into the water: they were branching segments of the seaweed called Codium. In many places the fingers served as armatures for the tiny patterned hides. Some were incompletely concealed, however, extending through the star-studded material and exiting the other side. I thought of the Ragg wool gloves Steve sometimes wore in cool weather. Missing the fabric that covers the extreme digits in normal gloves, these specialized gloves were designed to leave the fingertips free for the intricacies of fiddling with boats.

I pinched off a Codium branch. The starry fabric that had swallowed its base was unexpectedly gelatinous. I stroked the clusters, feeling for some separation between them or some prickliness where the pattern looked raised. Neither was obvious. Instead, the jelly felt smooth and continuous enough to serve as a common matrix for the entire celestial colony embedded in it.

When I held the Codium up to the light, the amber-tinted gel looked speckled. Two Codium branchlets were bound by it. I pictured Steve's hand again. Somehow his index and middle fingers had ended up in the same truncated woolen tube of his glove.

The gelatinous organisms were so distinctive that they were easy to identify—*Botryllus schlosseri*, a form of tunicate sometimes called a star tunicate. Tunicates belong to a whole group of invertebrate marine animals exquisitely designed for filtering small particulate matter from the water. It seems somewhat surprising, then, that the adjective most often used to describe them is "degenerate." Scientists apply the word to organisms that have reverted to forms simpler than their earlier ones. Here is naturalist Jack Rudloe scolding tunicates in his book *The Erotic Ocean*:

The tunicates. Who would believe that these large, fleshy blobs resembling a sponge for all practical appearances are one of the most highly evolved of all marine invertebrates? In their adult form they are little more than a water pump, pumping water in through their vascular system, extracting nutrients and pumping the water out, but it is in their larval stage that the tunicates display the characteristics which make them part of the same chordate phylum to which all fish, birds, reptiles and mammals belong.

The tadpole larvae develop from union of sperm and egg, and they swim about freely as part of the great mass of planktonic life. They are strange-looking creatures, having a notochord, the rudiments of a backbone running the length of the body. Eventually the tunicate larvae get heavier and start to settle down. Some attach to wharf-pilings, others grow on shell, almost any hard surface. Then like a child prodigy that starts out doing something great and ends up driving a streetcar, the tadpole larva slowly absorbs its notochord much the way a tadpole absorbs its tail, only instead of growing limbs, it turns into a blob and takes on a very unexciting sponge-like existence.

I have a different, perhaps less sophisticated, perspective on these organisms, and particularly on *Botryllus*. My viewpoint is based on talents colonial tunicates have developed instead of wasted, and on one talent in particular—an ability to get organized.

This individual *Botryllus* organism—called a zooid—is one-sixteenth of an inch long and shaped like a teardrop. In the center of the drop's broad end is a tiny hole called an incurrent siphon. It functions as the creature's mouth. The zooid doesn't have an individual excurrent siphon for ridding itself of wastes and filtered water. Instead, a more ingenious waste-disposal structure has evolved. The slender ends of the zooids' bodies appear to meet and form a circle or an ellipse. (The configuration could be likened to an ingathering of the toes of synchronized swimmers floating on their backs with their arms locked.) In this center the animals' coats, or tunics, actually grow together. This results in a communal excurrent siphon for excreting and recycling.

The inexact aspect of the swimmer metaphor is that the zooid doesn't actually float on the surface of the gel in which it's embedded. It extends down into the gel, beneath a sort of ray. This ray is what's decked out in the marvelous hues I noticed initially. If a cross section of two zooids was drawn, it would resemble a pair of saddlebags. Each tiny pouch would be filled with a plump sieve, and the strap connecting the pouches would contain the shared excurrent siphon.

———

Except for this communal structure, the body plan of *Botryllus schlosseri* is similar to that of *Molgula manhattensis*, another tunicate on the dock. This solitary one is huge by comparison, approximately an inch wide. It often goes by the common name sea grape, though I'd thought of it as a flaccid hailstone before I knew its name.

After closely inspecting the little animal, I found both the white-grape image and the hailstone image limiting. While they convey the creature's roundness, they don't suggest its pair of siphons. Extended under water, these siphons make the tunicate look like the back of a pig's head, right down to the dirty, see-through skin. Furthermore, the pig's ears squirt. Sea squirt is the animal's other common name, and the one on which I settled. (Whoever thought up the tunicates' common names must have been ravenous. The group contains not only sea grapes but also sea peaches and sea pork!)

I tried to scrape away the amalgam of bryozoans and other organisms growing on a few of the squirts at the dock. I wanted to see what was inside the translucent coats. But this seemed impossible. Even a visit to the Hall of Invertebrates at the American Museum of Natural History frustrated me—the lifelike glass model of sea squirts was clean but represented a different species.

Steve came to my rescue. We hadn't sailed in about three weeks, and our sloop's outboard needed attention. On a weekend afternoon in autumn we made a hasty adjustment and got under way. About half a mile out Steve decided the engine needed further tinkering. The engine well is centrally situated, with the resting motor somewhat protected from wave agitation. When Steve opened the well cover to study the situation, he noticed a black nylon strap that had apparently drifted under the hull and hung up on the engine. It was covered with sea squirts. They looked as clean and attractive as sea squirts can.

We filled a small plastic bucket attached to the end of a line with Sound water, placed the strap in it, and nursed it for the rest of our six-hour outing. The animals' siphons contracted to nubbins each time we exposed the squirts to air while changing their liquid. If we could manage a quick, gentle squeeze before this happened, we were rewarded with tiny jets of liquid.

Technically *Molgula* have no sense organs, as Aristotle matter-of-factly noted in his *History of Animals* more than two thousand years ago. Each animal does have what biologist Donald Zinn calls "cells sensitive to touch and to chemicals on the internal and external surfaces of the siphons." Zinn continues: "When an animal is touched, or otherwise alarmed, the muscles lining the [tunic] contract and the water in the body is forced out of both siphons."

At midnight, after what had turned into a pumpkin-moon sail, we set the bucket of squirts on the kitchen counter. Backlighting them for each other, Steve and I spent half an hour trying to match the organs inside the slightly milky bodies with several publications' illustrations of those organs. The oldest picture showed a structure labeled "branchial sac," overprinted with the words "for straining food and aerating blood."

This sac, to which both siphons are connected, occupies the upper half of a sea squirt's body. It functions as both a food sieve and a gill-like respiratory organ not too different from our lungs. Along with the polliwog-like tunicate's disappearing notochord, the sac connects *Molgula* and all other tunicates to fishes, human beings, and other vertebrate animals.

In spite of possible overzealousness in my poking, I'd grown fond of the little animals by the time Steve and I had finished handling them and their gasoline-smelling trapeze. Their grubbiness and pudgy shape, their habit of squirting, even their size and stillness made them seem so utterly other than myself that I viewed the live water balloons almost as toys. Yet I was loath to dissect them. I returned them to the dock at daybreak, having no idea if they would survive their ordeal.

———

Polly tore her foot on a nail at the dock. Her dainty front toe pads, shaped almost like a deer's cloven hoof, printed her blood all over one of the wood-covered floats and along the top of the seawall. A few of the stains were still visible after a week.

I'm a bad influence on her, having shown her the best float from which to bark at great egrets, *Casmerodius albus*. The birds excite her beyond imagining, setting her trembling as they soar back and forth across the cove.

Her preoccupation with these creatures is nothing new. The first time I ever saw Polly, one late-spring afternoon, she was dancing with a great egret on the stone wall at a local beach. The tide was out, and the sun glinted off the water behind a white bird so large and elegant I could hardly believe what I was seeing. The egret had just landed on one end of the wall, in a characteristic last-minute shift of direction.

I saw Polly's black form chase across the entire length of the flat-topped structure, a distance of about forty feet. Just before she reached the egret, it lifted off, its legs dangling. The bird didn't hover. It hesitated. Then it arced over the prancing dog and repeated its unique landing in the exact spot Polly had occupied thirty seconds earlier.

In the summer and early autumn before she injured herself, Polly was again a coiled spring on egret days. Enormous numbers of the birds were themselves delirious with the plentiful food the lambent season had brought to the Sound. Weekend houseguests couldn't sleep. It was the energy level, they said, all that surging of fish in the cove.

Bluefish, also called choppers (for good reason), were after bunker, or menhaden. Our friends were mesmerized by the staccatoed feeding frenzies. *Paht . . . paht . . . paht . . . 105 . . . paht . . .* splashes in sixty seconds . . . *paht . . .* or slight-*paht*-ly more . . . *paht, paht . . .* than one and a half splashes per . . . *paht. . . .* second . . . Some of the panicked menhaden were flipping . . . *paht . . .* completely out of the water. One friend told us she'd picked up a few from on shore after she'd seen a school of about a hundred explode from the water in a ring.

There must have been five thousand fish in the forty feet between the cove's rocky shoreline and the floating dock where we all stood at high tide. After a while the syllable surfaced less frequently, until it was replaced altogether by the silent flash of fish schooling. Their submerged forms caught the light and bent it into crescents of tarnished silver that vanished as quickly as they had shone. Then the quick cracks of whips. And digestion's calm.

This was the circumstance in which I learned that the cool, svelte great egret isn't always cool and svelte. There's a prominent rock between the dock and the shore. I've seen it completely swamped only five or six times, during extreme tides. Usually its peak sticks up like the tip of an iceberg. Below this tip, which is often streaked with guano, the rock is surrounded by smaller stones. At slack tide rockweeds festoon the stones and float straight out from them like tutus, providing a foothold for the egrets' unwebbed feet.

At dead low tide the entire cluster of rocks measures about twelve feet across at the water line and rises nearly eight feet into the air. Though this is a lot of stone, it doesn't provide much space for five great egrets, birds whose wing span can exceed sixty inches. In the tight cove the egrets seem to prefer at least a ten-foot leeway on either side of them. When crowded, they start to establish whose rockweed is whose, a process that usually involves a banked aerial chase and several croaks, their signature warning sounds.

The days the bluefish drove the bunker wild, however, the only distress the fish-eating birds registered in the limited space near the stones was the occasional guttural noise one of them made as it traded places with another. Dip-necked, the egrets rowed back and forth through the air between rocks and shore and often stood only four feet apart. When lined up facing the sun, they angled their extended necks and heads, probably to minimize the glare. Three or four of them arranged like this—all listing to port—looked ridiculous, like golfers immobilized at the height of a swing.

After the extraordinary summer-long abundance of small food fish, some great egrets were feeding like gulls. Both in the cove that hosts the dock and along the shore of more open water I saw them beat their wings and hover briefly, then flop directly onto the surface (an egret's idea of a flop). This was a real departure from the norm, egrets being adapted to stand at attention on long legs.

One individual that I noticed seemed to hit upon the best feeding style of all. It hovered very low over fish near the surface, I suppose to check out their sizes. Then it settled into a spot on the nearby land, gathered its neck into an S, and waited. Soon a bunker shot onto the stones within inches of the big bird's toes. The egret picked up the squirming fish in its bill and swallowed it whole. I watched the extended neck twitch as the live food protested a downward course.

———

Two sections of eight-foot-wide wooden planking are joined lengthwise above floation to form part of the dock. A heavy iron rod runs through rings driven into the nearly abutting section ends. The contrivance keeps the identical floats spaced exactly four and a half inches apart. I think of the hiatus as "the slit."

I hadn't noticed what lived in the slit, or even that

there was a slit, until I happened to cross the planking at midday in September. The sun fell exactly between the two sections. It was reflected as a thin line of light that appeared to underscore a foot-long collection of submarine sculpture. Because the mustard-colored pieces extended from a board that was perpendicular to the water, I viewed their profiles. They imitated twist-ems in size and shape.

I flattened myself on my stomach with my eyes in the slit, to have a close look. My attention was drawn not to the mustard encrustation of eyed sponge but to a quintet of powder-puff anemones, *Metridium senile*. I had no idea anemones lived in the Sound, or in any other temperate waters, having met them previously only in tropical lagoons. These common East Coast specimens were a rich russet.

By dropping one arm between the two sections of dock, I could almost pet the largest anemone. It was fully extended, and its tentacles were so numerous and frilly that they called to mind a fabulous chrysanthemum instead of the simpler anemone bloom. The animal was the length of my index finger. Two other open ones were one-third that length, and squattily curved in the fashion of cooling towers at a nuclear plant. The littlest two, contracted, were mere blips on the wood.

I withdrew my arm long enough to pick up a pencil, which I manipulated slowly downward in the slit until its eraser gently nudged the king-sized animal. It shrank, collapsing its tentacles into the remnants of a soft crew cut and its body into a lump.

While I waited for the giant to reflower, I held the hand lens over the other two open anemones. Their hollow tentacles were the color of tapioca, and they moved so imperceptibly, in not-quite-unison, that I couldn't tell if the motion was willed or at the mercy of the slight current.

Metridium can bend a bit and can glide slowly on its single basal disk (it has no feet). But for all practical purposes it is rooted to the spot: the subtle waving is a dance of arms. It is also a dance of death. Specialized cells on the animal's tentacles possess a structure that contains a coiled tubular filament tipped with a barb. When potential prey organisms move within range of a feeding *Metridium*, the anemone discharges some of these mini-harpoons. They lodge in the victims and cause paralysis. The quarry is subsequently channeled into the center of the tentacles, where the anemone's mouth is located.

This mouth is a streamlined wonder, sweeping water laden with oxygen and captured food into the body cavity directly beneath it. The mouth then reverses itself and sweeps out the wastes. Adapted grooves and hairlike forms actually implement the directional switch. (Tunicates, of course, must call on both an incurrent siphon and an excurrent one to accomplish the same functions.)

It wasn't the mouth's efficiency, however, that held me facedown on the dock. Even with the hand lens I couldn't see the anemones feeding. But I could appreciate their sophistication. Here is a radially symmetrical invertebrate that is basically a hollow tube. It has no head or central nervous system. It can't travel. Though it possesses chemoreceptors for taste and smell and mechanoreceptors sensitive to touch, it can neither see nor hear. Nor does it undergo true circulation, excretion, or respiration. As a member of the phylum Cnidaria it is classified fairly low in the scheme of things. Yet it appears to have been compensated for all this by

a talent for harvesting its food as ferociously and beau-
tifully as anything I could imagine. Why?

I don't know. I can't quite take the whole thing in. I
witness the chilling dreaminess of the hunt, the slow, undulating rhythm of cream-colored tentacles above a body
styled like a tree trunk. It's a spellbinding sight. Yet I'm
disquieted by the extreme contrast between this seemingly
languorous motion and the quick, spiky deaths that power
it.

———

If I were to uproot an anemone, invert it, then set it drifting
and swimming with tentacles trailing, I would devise a jellyfish. This familiar invertebrate is the anemone's relative,
and it functions in basically the same way. What distinguishes it most clearly from anemones and other polyp-
bodied members of the phylum Cnidaria is its bell-like
saucer, also called the medusa.

Common moon jellies (*Aurelia* spp.) use their tentacle-
fringed bells to pump themselves through the cove's quiet
waters. It's a slow way to get about, alternating jet propulsion with a glide. When strong currents or a turbulent
surface prevail, the jellies get tossed around like any other
planktonic form.

This seemingly erratic mode of travel did me a favor.
Unlike a fish's darting motions, the moon jelly's drifts and
pulses gave my eye time to wander. And in wandering it
was often idly led to that part of the dock toward which
the jellyfish was heading. Eventually I realized that *Aurelia*
had become my guide, calling my attention to many organisms I'd overlooked.

Near a sunny corner were three slipper shells piled into

a lopsided stack. It appeared that one good flick of my finger could wreck their little arrangement. But I knew how hard these mollusks cling, and I didn't test them. The jellyfish nudged some sea lettuce once or twice. This is the bright-green seaweed I'd heard cygnets crop noisily between high-pitched squeals. They always left it in rags on the wood.

The most dramatic dock community *Aurelia* showed me looked as if it had been dreamed up by Hieronymus Bosch on one of his less judgmental days. Shapes that suggested castle crenellations turned out to be sponges, and the castle guards, amphipods. These are shrimp-like invertebrates that seem to show up in any dockside water I stare into long enough. The Bosch ones were shaped like bananas, and battalions of them drifted up and down in the water between binges at table.

Of all the dockside organisms, however, the worms surprised me the most. I've never been enamored of these invertebrates. My Southern childhood buffered me from exposure to many of them, through a practice I've seen referred to in print as "princess fishing." This is an indulgent method of angling that grants a girl's father or uncle sole authority over the baiting of hooks and the removal of catches, should both be necessary. The credit for what happens between these two activities goes to the maiden, who can gloat over the bream she caught without ever having handled the worm it swallowed.

In my Mississippi summers this "worm" was most often called a catalpa worm, though it's really the larva of a sphinx moth. It comes in two color phases, green and brown. Chances are that it was plucked from a catalpa tree leaf just before chewing that leaf into oblivion.

The Southern catalpa has wonderfully smooth and

rounded autumn seedpods. They are brown, measure about a foot long, and rattle as they dangle in profusion from leafless branches all winter long. As if to deny the very act of using live animals as bait, my sheltered self invented the notion that these pods were the infamous worms. Hearing of catalpa worms' periodic abundance on the trees, I expected legions of the leathery "animals" to rain down on any passerby who so much as inched a toe under the plant's spreading limbs. I felt both disappointed and amazed to learn later that real catalpa worms, far from dropping down the collars of timid children, seemed quite content to remain on the huge heart-shaped leaves that succored them.

Decades after the last recurrence of my catalpa worm fantasy I read of *Nereis (Neanthes) virens*, an animal I have yet to get to know well. This bristled, free-swimming marine worm, also known as the clam worm, is as popular for bait in the Northeast as the bald catalpa larva is in the South. And it really does reach a foot or more in length! Though it never lives above anyone's head, it whips its body through quiet waters in a luminescent ritual performed after warm and moonless midnights. Donald Zinn elaborates: "The nocturnal habit of *Nereis* swimming together in large numbers and in characteristic undulations presumably is connected with seasonal reproductive activity."

Apart from being acquainted with historical and literary references to worms, many of which seem harsh even to me, the only other in-depth association I've had with the animals has been in the garden. Earthworms as thick as my little finger are a sign of rich soil, on which I pride myself. So I cultivate not just hellebores but also the worms that aerate those plants' roots. Now and then my trowel accidentally slices through the segmented body of an oversized earthworm, or flips a smaller sample of the slick creature onto my arm along with a shower of dirt. I shiver, and the tormented worm convulses. Then it vanishes back into the ground.

The worms I first noticed at the dock are nothing like this. In addition to having great beauty, they are infinitely more veiled and private. Many of them expose their typically tubular abodes to full view but show their bodies from the neck up only. They cannot do otherwise. They are permanently attached to the homeplace and withdraw into it when I try to touch them.

My favorite marine-worm homes are calcareous tubes about an eighth of an inch in diameter. Chalky white next to the pastel sponges on the wood, the tubes twist and turn and double back on themselves lavishly. After two or three inches of this they head toward the surface of the water, their open ends facing straight up. This makes it easy for me to peer down and spot the plumes on the extruded heads of the inhabitants, some of which are known as fan worms and feather dusters.

Each set of plumes on these worms forms a jewel-toned funnel, one per head. I saw a purple one, a bright-orange one, and two yellow ones side by side. They are the animals' filter-feeding mechanism and are wonderfully adapted to their purpose. When open in the water, the plumes create currents that direct planktonic food toward the worm's mouth. The procedure is a study in beckoning one's sustenance, and many affixed marine invertebrates do something like it. When the worm stops feeding and retreats into its tubular residence, it plugs the opening with a tentacle adapted to function like a wine cork.

I was probing more than just these particular worms,

however. A vast and unsuspected world of worms awaited me in the water, a fact of which I was unaware until I ran across the following sentence in a field guide. It appears after the heading Marine Segmented Worms, Class Polychaeta. "Of approximately 9,000 described species of segmented worms, two thirds live in the sea."

The book, *Harper and Row's Complete Field Guide to North American Wildlife*, goes on to mention a handful of the polychaetes. The enticing appellations alone are worth the read: sea mouse, lugworm, blood worm. Other books go into great detail about the bristles that characterize the bodies of most members of the huge polychaete tribe. And still others play up whether the worms are stuck at home like my fan worms, or whether they can venture out for a swim, in which case they're immediately dubbed "errant."

I will never wax rhapsodic about worms. Yet the discovery of the huge cosmopolitan populations of certain marine species has softened my prejudice. I can't simply write off a group of animals as widespread as these. Furthermore, I find the polychaetes' varied lifestyles remarkable, particularly the inch-long journeys that the attached tube worms make all day. Their situation is comparable to my own on muddled Mondays, when I find myself going more than once to the market around the corner. If the fierce-looking *Nereis* someday forces me to reinstitute my habit of fishing like a princess, I would like to think the palace dock had attracted a few bright heads to fan the water.

HORSESHOE CRABS

"There is . . . only sand and sea and moon, and these dark, helmeted creatures . . ."

—Tom Horton, "Baiting the Blue Bloods,"
Audubon magazine, May–June 1996

California boasts of grunions, round-bodied silver fish herded onto beaches by spring tides. As the adults spawn in the sand at night, they make prime hand catches for fishermen who watch the local papers in anticipation of the event.

The Atlantic coast has its herring. *Alosa pseudoharengus* returns to its natal tributary in many river systems every year to lay eggs. Drawn by a potent organic signature unique to each finger of creek water, this fish also arrives to the wide welcome of local anglers.

Then there's Delaware Bay, home of the largest population of North America's horseshoe crabs. This arthropod's mating season is greeted not by anglers smacking their lips but by migrating shorebirds hungry for horseshoe crab eggs. Also by researchers who value the crab for its important medicinal and commercial properties, by fishermen who bait their eel pots with crabs that they quarter, and by a well-organized army of volunteers prepared to tag at least fifty to a hundred thousand crabs of those that ride a single full-moon tide to shore from who-knows-where. These folks hope to find out. They have about two hours in which to work.

Functioning almost as a footnote to Delaware Bay is Long Island Sound, with its less imposing beaches, smaller

One enormous shed—a female's—hangs on the wall

concentrations of crabs, and less professional chases. And me.

I'm fascinated by the age of this animal. At 360 million years, it makes youngsters of dinosaurs, which it outlived with its adaptability. Bavaria has limestone quarries that still turn up horseshoe crab remains alongside those of archaeopteryx, the feathered reptilian ancestor of birds. And here this fossil is swimming off my shore.

Its physique also gets me. What other animal has a mouth in the midst of twelve legs, no nose, four eyes on its back, and only one bite of really juicy meat on its entire form—near its rear? What's more, as many as seventeen times in a life span of perhaps that many years, the crab packs up all this paraphernalia and leaves home. By the front door. The exit slit in its abandoned shell seems to close without a trace.

I'd seen these uninhabited shells along the beaches when I first moved to the Sound. But I hadn't known then that most of them were sheds, like snakeskins. I'd assumed dead giants, their pleated limbs intact.

In warm weather the carapaces (and the carcasses) float tail down like dolls' barques on the waves. Occasionally one gets sidetracked into an eddy and bobs around the cordgrass at high tide. Winter waves and ice pulverize this grass into floating tan mats and try to grind the horseshoe crab shells along with it. But they succeed only in separating the two main shell segments. When they churn those segments into the litter of the strand line, the appendages are the next to go.

Once matching shell segments are disconnected, they're Humpty-Dumpty to reunite. As puzzling as egret bones: a femur here on the beach, a toe digit beyond the cut at the seawall. It would take a forensic lab to put either animal back together.

Steve and I tried to take some of the complete sheds home by their tails but quickly discovered the folly in this: the weight of a shell held upside down causes the structure to fall away in pieces. We switched to carrying the sheds by the V at the front of the ventral surface. The index and middle finger of an upward-facing hand can easily be placed on either side of this point. Then a shell, even a heavy one, can be lifted and moved.

One enormous shed—a female's—hangs on our wall.

Steve very cleverly invented a technique that uses rubber bands to suspend the structure from the V. After a few months of this duty the bands grew tired, and the shell fell to the hardwood floor at midnight. It awakened us with a sound like the clatter of crockery flung against stone. But the shell didn't even crack. We rehung it with thread and a good bit of awe.

I like looking at this chitinous wall art. Yet it isn't very instructive about living horseshoe crabs. I was, after all, simply hanging up the clothes the animals had stepped out of on their way to some new phase. I decided I'd have to tag along with the crabs, preferably during their mating season. It extends from the middle of May to July in the Sound and promises easy access to the animals, which move from deep waters onto sand beaches to spawn. The stages of the tide are critical then, the night spring tides facilitating the climax of an annual rite I had to see.

———

On May 23 I met my naturalist friend John Campbell at his boat club in a warm drizzle. It was 10 p.m. High tide was listed for 10:58.

A wide, railed deck runs around three sides of the clubhouse. If you stand on it and look down, the spotlights mounted on the building's roof help you pick out forms moving in the shallows.

John and I stood silently next to each other for a good five minutes, leaning our slickered elbows on the railing and staring into the murk. We were the only people there except for Peter, the night guard. He wandered over to ask what was up.

"Horseshoe crabs?" he said. "They're here. I've seen the

couples swimming hooked together for the last week or
so. You'll get some if you wait." He ambled off.

We held our pose about ten more minutes before John
saw a double shadow move through the water next to a
piling. It was a pair of the crabs. The large, dark female led
them along the bottom, in what John called a meander.
This pair crossed casually in front of us twice before we
spotted two other pairs swimming with the same leisurely
motion. Their saunters looked well coordinated once the
rhythm became established. But one of the pairs had trouble getting into gear and looked as tentatively joined as
teenagers on a ballroom dance floor. The male became
separated twice and had to scramble to regrasp the female
from behind. Two nearby bachelor males could have
picked up the female's pheromone during the lapses. But
this didn't appear to happen, probably because the season
was just getting under way.

One pair of crabs stopped moving for a moment and
released a string of bubbles into the water. The little spheres
rose to the surface and floated along in a mass. Confused
by the water's haziness, we couldn't tell how the bubbles
had actually been produced. John hung over the deck and
tried to gather some. But there was a rip in the discarded
newspaper wrapper he was using for collection. The crabs'
activities slowed after the tide crested, and around midnight
we left.

I was back by myself exactly twelve hours later, just before the noon high tide of a partly cloudy day. I'd brought
a bucket for the bubbles, just in case. But I saw no crabs.
However, a different boathouse guard, with Paul New-
man's eyes, told me he'd recently observed crows and bait
fish eating what he assumed were horseshoe crab eggs,
from depressions made in the sand along the tide line. The
depressions were under water.

———

On May 26 Steve used a derelict oyster rake to fish a dead horseshoe crab out of a cove for me. It was a male that had lost one of his two club claws. The males develop these bulbous front appendages for the reproductive season only. Pimpled in two or three places, each claw gives rise to a short stem. That stem, in turn, shifts direction ninety degrees to become a not very crooked hook. The slot between the knobbed part of the claw and this hook is what the shell of the female slips into when the male grasps her from the rear. An altogether ingenious if somewhat eccentric system of coupling. And cruising.

Never having seen the swollen appendage before, I decided to hang on to the male for a while. But this involved the daunting prospect of trying to de-smell it.

In an emergency move I placed the crab corpse in a maple tree far from the house, to air. After five days I could approach it on a run. After seven I could stroll under it. And in nine days I could carry my crab around in a bucket and marvel at its sexy, fat claw.

———

Toward the end of this period I went to the town hall for a beach permit. Patiently I filled out the requisite forms, only to be told I needed an extra piece of documentation.

"Fine. But what about tonight?" I said earnestly. "There's going to be an extremely high tide around nine. I have to be on the sand beach before then, to watch the horseshoe crabs mate."

The look the fresh young employee gave me had nothing to do with municipal beach regulations. It was a back-off stare, the kind you see in movies about found-out voyeurs ten minutes before the credits appear.

I spoke slowly. "Look. You're welcome to join me. I need to stay just about an hour. But it has to be on either side of high tide. At least that's what I think."

She placed one perfectly manicured nail—coral—squarely in the center of her right cheek as she said, "Beach permits aren't required until after Memorial Day."

I was dismissed.

————

From the phone: "My beach is crawling with crabs. Come over." It was Elsie, who'd heard about my crab watch. In previous years she'd pointed out the coupled mobile horseshoes to her children in an effort to further sex education. Not bad thinking, overall.

By the time I reached her house it was twilight. Seven o'clock, to be exact, two and a half hours after high tide on May 29. Elsie met me on her seawall to show me a barnacle-burdened mated pair, huge, swimming in the two feet of water we could fathom during the chilly rainstorm that was drenching us both. Then she got permission for me to visit two neighbors' beaches before she left me to explore on my own.

Elsie grew up on the Sound, and it shows. Her generous nature is mirrored in the openness of water. This water, in particular. This cove, with its tattered coastline and well-groomed yards and houses, its small islands and long beaches, its mud flats and spines of engine-wrecking rocks across from embankments and bridges that lead over inlets to sand.

I crossed one of these bridges onto a platform that floated in a protected thumb of backwater. Several single crabs patrolled the fifty-foot shoreline in front of me. Two more lay upside down farther up the sand, one of them kicking the air periodically. It was enormous, probably a female that had become stranded by a receding tide. I resisted an impulse to wade through the muck and right her.

Das Rheingold's opening scene is simplistic compared to what I saw next. Almost simultaneously two horseshoe crab couples began to bury themselves—one duo in a mixture of mud and stones, the other in sand. Apparently this was no game of hide-and-seek but the immediate preamble to egg laying and fertilizing. I paid attention.

The mud couple worked the broad, silty bottom directly beneath the platform. I could look down on the female's encrusted shell and the lighter male's smooth one. He seemed to be riding her bareback into the mud, though in terms of control he was the horse and she the rider.

The other pair was engaged in the same disappearing act, but on a slant. The sand beach rose gently before a copse met it some thirty feet away. The crabs had left half a broad arch in the slope right above the receding tide. Extending no more than two feet up the sand now, it would become a depression after the crabs and the wave action finished with it.

I looked back down at the mud couple, which continued to churn up clouds of silt as they shoved themselves deeper into the bottom. When they were about two-thirds buried, the male began to push directly on the female's shell, or so it appeared. The next thing I knew, she was bent double, like the back of my hand when I make a fist. Just as my knuckles stick up then, the place where the two parts of her carapace were hinged made a sort of ridge. From beneath the flanges that angle out from her forward shell, huge numbers of bubbles began to issue. They were identical to the ones John and I had seen at the boat club. The bubbles gradually rose to the surface of the water, where they floated in spitlike masses. They were, I learned later, foam generated in spawning, gas bubbles, or a combination of both.

I switched back to watching the sand beach pair. They were engaged in exactly the same motion, the female contracted at her midpoint. In fact, the female had already developed a right-angled body, which made her look like a dowager hump. This pair seemed less of a bubble machine, though my distance from them and the angle made it hard to see. When they'd completed their most strenuous pushing and the spawning was over, the female pulled the fertilizing male's still attached body over her nest of thousands of eggs. Then they crawled down the wet bank and back into the water, where they vanished.

I looked at the slope they'd just left. The semiarch of sand that marked their upward climb now had its other half. And right at the top of the completed arc, like a keystone in the slanted sculpture, a curlicue made by one leg that the female had used for digging the eggs into moisture marked the climax of the pair's spring mandate.

I studied the sand all along the water line and saw no fewer than three other arches of similar size and shape, although none with the delicate top ornament. Two were surrounded by random lines and jabs in the sand, probably hieroglyphs written with tails and the big hind, pusher legs. Viewed altogether, the arches looked like tire marks some amphibious vehicle had left. In half a day they'd be gone.

———

Naturalist Alison Beall serves as chief curator of the Marshlands Conservancy in Rye, New York. On June 2 she led a salt-marsh walk for ten avowed curiosity seekers, including Elsie and me.

The walk answered two questions about the crabs: Exactly what did the famous depressions look like after they were no longer fresh? And how could someone identify the eggs?

The depressions at Marshlands looked, in fact, like yawning volcanoes fit for Lilliput. In their centers, where Alison knew to dig, were spherical horseshoe crab eggs no bigger than shot. She showed us the balls—some light green, some tan—and then replaced them carefully in their moist, sandy cones. If undisturbed, they would lose their hue in a few days.

Each egg's opaque covering would soon be sloughed off and replaced by a clear membrane, "through which the embryo can be seen doing somersaults," Alison said. Shifting sands would rupture this round window, probably on the next spring tide. And while the adult crabs were mating, whole nests of the poppy-seed-sized larvae would ride the water table to the surface of the sand and set themselves adrift as infant plankton.

In the meantime, I intended to find my own eggs, and luckily, on the new-moon night of June 3, I got an eleven o'clock call from Elsie. She had a hunch about timing. We set out in her Whaler for the beach just across the inlet, where I'd watched the pair of spawning crabs leave their trademark in the sand.

Elsie was right about the crabs and the tides. Right like only this beach and Mont-St.-Michel can be right. Right like perfect. After she poled us over, she kept the moon at a ninety-degree angle to the grainy slope. Along the water line, in three different places, crabs were milling about in moonlight so bright that it illuminated their shells. The brown, leathery animals had changed to pods of quicksilver. We didn't need our flashlights.

She rowed us to within a foot of the largest group, which consisted of about a dozen males and one female. They didn't respond to us at all. We maneuvered the boat's stern directly over them and even reached down into the shallows to touch the backs of three males. Still no response. Overcurious, we were crashing their orgy. Yet they were so focused on their own high-tide mission that they didn't even seem to notice. Only the odd spear-shaped tail breaking the surface of the water in slow motion told us our presence might have registered.

This large-group energy was a new wrinkle. It made the two pairs of crabs I'd seen here last week look like old married couples. The bachelors may have been still revving their seasonal engines then. Or simply engaged elsewhere. Or both. Whatever the explanation, Elsie and I were bowled over by the single-mindedness of the animals we were watching. Also a little ashamed at having tried to break up the party, which disbanded on its own after seven or eight minutes.

We debarked between the other two groups of crabs and searched the depressions onshore for eggs. In the one farthest from us Elsie found a few sand-colored ones. In fact, at first we weren't sure we hadn't mistaken sand for the little globes we cupped in our hands, somersaults to come.

INTERTIDAL ZONE

*A*s if frightened of waves, the thin-footed least sandpiper keeps from getting its feet wet. Or tries to. Its rounded profile moves on legs that are the written sign for kisses: XXXXX. My pen cannot draw the marks as fast as the legs can cross.

The bird surprises me by seeming unafraid. We share the spring rain. In its view I am a giant stillness, perhaps a tree, given my standing height and open green umbrella. I was planted before it flew onto the sloping sand ten feet away from me.

We are both here because we need something: the bundles of living and dead tidal fragments that have washed over the low seawall and onto the beach behind two side pockets of salt marsh. Drying now, the bundles form several sets of erratic peaks and dips, like suspect EKGs placed one above the other. Seen as a panorama, they repeat the crescent shape of the shoreward push of water and suggest an amphitheater's curved seats. For me the tidal arcs are undeciphered scripts that may contain some clue to this marginal place. For the peep, they hold food. The bird chases along and picks among the tidbits with its bill.

The tide is rising. Broad fingers of water gently lift the scallops of debris nearest the Sound, move them up the incline a fraction of an inch, and withdraw. They leave behind undulating, fibrous ridges. Above them, a previous tide left contoured clusters of shells and of marine algae that now look broiled by the sun to a rich *maroon. Segmented, hollow stalks of a plant reminiscent of bamboo make up the shallow arc farthest from the water.*

I glance down. The peep cannot ride a surge to shore, but falters in the same wave that drowns my shoes. These repeating crescents necklace the intertidal zone.

The oars fight the swift water. I cannot control the slant of their blades beyond the gunwale or the speed with which salty liquid . pours off the blade ends after each hard stroke. The drops blend back into the Housatonic River beside the marsh called Nells Island. I cannot tell where the river stops and starts.

Neither can I fathom the tall cordgrass plants that live along this vague boundary. A single stem appears to thrive in every element but fire, and often in three at once.

I guide the dinghy into a thumb of quieter water. All around me, the strong current stretches the completely submerged plants into pale-green flames, transforming the stems into underwater lightning that zigzags and flickers. It bends and tugs lower portions of amphibious clumps as if they were handfuls of long hair. The exposed parts of those clumps are a farmer's field of leaves. I reach out and touch the pointed tips above August's rising tide.

Still farther in, entire stands of the grass breathe air. Water

covers only the roots. Some stems culminate in steeples of tiny
blond flowers that rise higher than my head. The plants return
tapered reflections, dark on the silver-backed brine.

I cannot yet explain why some plants swim in place while
others like them wade. I only know this pliancy contains the marsh.

The red swimming trunks of a man and the aquamarine bottle
tilted to a woman's lips provide the only real color in my view of
a distant island. It is the week prior to Memorial Day, not quite
the Season. Yet the temperature is 80 degrees. In my telescope
the couple walk barefoot, through heat waves, on the sand and
the dun stones.

I scan the island's breadth. Near the water irregularly cantile-
vered ledges of brown overhang the dark sand, which toward the
upland lightens to biscuit. The ledges' top surfaces want to be
green. But they are not. From this distance they still seem a non-
descript hue, a retarded stepchild of the sweet-smelling and al-
ready twice-mown grass beneath my feet.

The tide is falling. For a moment the shadow of a cloud cloaks
the island in winter light, and even the subtle hues flatten. The
surrounding water goes to slate. As the sun begins to saunter
around a point, a wide band of blue-mussel-shell blue shows its
cool tint. This island cummerbund is new, probably the legacy of

last winter's pushy ice. Growing through it, or appearing to, is a line of green leaves. I judge them to be a foot tall. Behind the interwoven midden, single stems of last year's reed grass bend their tan plumes in the wind.

To the west an American oystercatcher in three-quarter profile—one, not the more usual pair—stands motionless as the sun returns the shock of hot orange to its beak. The island transcends this wait in time and light.

SALT MARSHES

Behind the open coastal waters of the Sound, where love-sick ducks called goldeneyes snap and stretch their white necks toward April and oldsquaws outcroon one another in rising inflections—"Ah, Alouette . . . Ah, Alouette"—behind such fitful dazzle lies a more subtle world. It is strung together from its various parts, not all of which necessarily exist in any one place. Like the children in T. S. Eliot's apple-tree, this world is frequently "Not known because not looked for." Yet it is often manipulated, more often ignored and maligned. It is the world of the salt marsh, and it takes me by surprise.

Well inland in this world a tidal creek slips through mud. The shallow banks that contain it rise thirty feet apart. Yet at dead low tide they hold a mere trickle of water that meanders and switches around in the curved bowl's bottom. Never completely vanishing, it merely shrinks to this dark string of S's that relieves the whiteness of broad, snow-covered slopes.

Black ducks swim up the creek in a businesslike single file unless a thick crust of ice impedes them. During extremely low tides their wide bodies fit the trough with little room to spare. When the birds reach the end, they turn around and begin to dabble for mollusks and other winter fare. As they paddle along, I can sometimes hear the slush-slush of their bills straining food. If I am not looking when one of them stops to rest in the muddy basin, I can mistake the duck for a stone.

Scientists refer to this mud as muck. It is a dark, viscid madness of wet dirt in which organic material is thoroughly decomposed and oxygen so scant as to be almost absent. One Northeasterner I know calls the sticky stuff black mayonnaise, often preceding the phrase with an expletive: "Once the . . . black mayonnaise sucked hard on my boots and wouldn't turn loose. Had to walk home barefoot."

Author John Casey takes a different view of the mud. He celebrates it as a bond and a catalyst for transformation in the most rambunctious love scene of his prize-winning novel *Spartina*. The maturation of the book's crusty protagonist, Dick Pierce, is gauged by the character's growing resemblance to various aspects of the New England salt marsh in which he grew up. In the night love scene, he and the woman who shares his passion for the marsh rise from its primordial ooze like humankind emerging from the sea. But not before they've painted each other invisible with the slick black mud. "It spread like very thick paint, thick as toothpaste but black, even by starlight you could see it was black." The athletic sexiness of their coated bodies stays with me: mud is erotic stuff, as spa owners and other professional mud merchants well know.

Muck is central to the salt marsh. Though self-contained, it is also literally the marsh's main floor, one that is covered with a cushiony linoleum of bacteria, fungi, and algae. Most of these life-forms are microscopic and therefore invisible to me as individual organisms. Yet they are essential to the salt-marsh food chain.

The algae occupy the lowest position in this food chain. Even in the cold marsh muds of the Northeast algae photosynthesize year-round, converting sunlight and oxygen into food that's tasty to the mollusks the ducks eat as well as to fish and other creek creatures. A plant's manufacture of food is a magical process. It operates inside the cells of the large marine algae we call seaweed, in oak leaves, and

anywhere else in the natural world that chlorophyll exists.
When photosynthesis occurs under winter's gray skies in
mud organisms so tiny that I take their presence on faith,
I am humbled.

I have accidentally discovered other things that occur
above the busy mud. Early last spring I took a leisurely
walk along creek banks that spilled me out onto a tidal
slope near the Sound. The tide was out. The land that it
would later cover hosted a sparse patch of vascular plants
three inches high. Shaped like upwelling fountains, the
green organisms were homesteaded in the mud farthest
from the water, about ten feet back from the low-tide line.
Their roots had bound so much sand washed from the
nearby beaches that the mud was actually a mud and sand
mix. It supported my weight.

Leaf particles, shiny fragments of blue-mussel shells, bits
of stiff, blackened seaweed once supple and floating free,
and other organic materials brought in on the tides were
caught on the plants' stems and lower leaves. When I
leaned over and gently poked beneath all this with a stick,
dozens of small, dark amphipods—"bugs" that really belong to the crustacean tribe—exploded from the soil and
crisscrossed in the air under my nose.

The twenty-foot-wide shore that supports this tangled
neighborhood is full of stones and man-made trash. It is
tucked behind a rocky headland. A cliff hems it in from
the landward side. The narrow hodgepodge hardly con-
forms to the impression of a wetland as an expanse of soggy
terrain. Nevertheless, as I knelt there on that cool April
day, I saw evidence of what I had run across in my reading:
the tentative accretion with which I toyed was peat in a
very early stage of development. I had found the start of
peat above mud and sand, which meant that I had found

a young salt marsh, perhaps the most malleable and elusive wetland of all.

Salt marshes are communities of particular kinds of plants, animals, and soils that thrive in the transitional zone between low water and consistently dry land, or upland. They differ from more recognizable rocky or sandy intertidal zones, as well as from bogs, swamps, fens, freshwater marshes, and other types of wetlands, in part by virtue of what binds their various elements together: a certain type of peat. Peat as young as the parcel I found suggests a building's unfinished second floor, one still full of nail holes and littered with half-sawed beams. As the specialized soil ages and accumulates more and more trapped organic material, it eventually becomes thick, dense, springy. Pit it and water oozes.

Salt-marsh peat that is well established along a somewhat exposed leeward shore often suggests a mezzanine more than it does the second tier of a building. Frequently undercut by waves in this situation, the soil layer develops pouty lips that overhang caving vertical edges, as in my island view prior to Memorial Day. If waves and tides continue to gnaw at the drooping peat long enough, they cause it to collapse in one place after another.

This peat is nothing like gardeners' peat moss. Salt-marsh peat develops only at the level of mid-tide and only where shallow waters move slowly enough to allow the particulate and suspended organic matter they carry to settle out. The sedimentation that results provides rootholds for plants capable of catching even more material. Eventually (and ideally) a marsh pushes out into the water this way until it fills what once may have been all creek or cove.

Along the margins of Long Island Sound, as elsewhere, waters quiet enough to allow the development of salt marshes typically flow near the mouths of rivers—the Housatonic, the Connecticut. Here sediments from upstream wash down and join the greater volume of sediments brought in on the tides. Quiet waters also lap the leeward side of sand spits, headlands, and boulders as well as the backs of larger land formations such as barrier beaches.

The prime example of a barricade protecting the Sound, of course, is Long Island itself. Its 110-mile length serves as a buffer for the entire waterway, shielding it from the kind of constant heavy wave action that the Island's south-facing beaches endure. Long Island's coddling of the Sound has encouraged the ongoing development of salt marshes along that island's more or less continuous northern shore. It has also permitted marshes to develop and persist along the more indented coastline of Connecticut. With few exceptions, smallness is the rule among salt marshes in this New England state. Not that size matters much—large and small marshes work exactly the same.

Only one genus of plants (which includes those three-inch shoots I found) is adapted to perform the actual peat-making function. The genus contains what are, in fact, the definitive organisms of every salt marsh in the Northeast. More than the tides' partner in marsh development, these plants are the marsh's mother. *Spartina* is their Latin name.

———

Salt-marsh cordgrass, *Spartina alterniflora*, is one of the most common grasses of the New England salt marsh, the type of marsh found from Long Island to Canada's Bay of Fundy. Cordgrass typically reaches four to five feet in height and is actually a land plant, a true grass. It is the species that deserves credit for pioneering the marsh. This *Spartina*, according to scientists William and Stephen Amos, "has successfully invaded a marine habitat and, in doing so, has created an entirely new ecosystem." Along the Sound its invasion began as recently as 3,000 years ago, when rapid post-glacial sea level rise, due to melting, began to stabilize.

Spartina's dual nature is still evident. Like a kid dangling legs from a dock, the plant thinks it must keep its feet wet half the time. It manages this by restricting its range to the low marsh, that area submerged by each high tide. In spring, summer, and fall an established cordgrass plant expresses its terrestrial personality by trapping debris in its leaves and stems. Also by using its roots and rhizomes to stabilize the same peaty soil it has helped to create. In winter it takes on other roles, including that of creating soil by contributing its own tissue. Here is John Casey's description of how mature cordgrass went about that work one imagined November. "The dead spartina broke, blew off, wrapped onto the next stalks, and sank under the rains down to the live roots, mixing into the blackness. It was useful death."

I, too, have watched this gradual demise well into winter and beyond. In the most protected New England marshes shearing and blending appear minimal. Brown mats of more or less intact grass stalks rest or float atop the parent plants, to which they are usually still attached. In more exposed marshes, storm waves and winds begin an incremental sacrifice. First they snap the stiff four-foot-tall *Spartina* stems. The plants' still attached heads—on long, thin necks—all bow in the same direction. They form a monkish procession of 7's.

Soon these heads are felled, adding to the carnage that

an increasingly mean season leaves on the shore. As the plants dry in the harsh winter sun and are buffeted by more wind and waves, they break again. And again. By New Year's, two- to three-foot-long fragments of the grass stalks are a constant fixture in the marshes of the Sound's northern border. When not floating in high water, they lie end to end across the tops of narrow cuts in the rock. They snake over riprap and coastal terrain all tumbled together into what look like the messy blond braids of a giant. Further churning and tangling reduce some palomino straws to the length of cigarette butts that freeze into the milky ice of tide pools, or that lie under fallen dominoes of ice.

What is left of the rooted *Spartina* plants after most of their stalks have been clipped away can only be described as stubble. In February 1994 the stubble that remained on my twenty-foot-wide marsh extended a mere two inches above the peaty ground. It felt rough and brittle when I ran my palm across it. The low winter sun backlighting the dried, truncated tubes turned them a translucent apricot. This color, so unexpected in winter, emphasized the relative darkness of soil newly exposed by the merciless shearing above it.

The ice that came still later in that harsh winter scoured the marshes clean of cordgrass stumps along my stretch of the Sound. Floes and ice cakes wide as a mattress and twice as thick gouged away even the shortest of the growth, or flattened the fibrous segments into meek stars. For ten days, off and on, a mini-glacier rode my tiny marsh like a horse, leaving the marsh's backbone one minute, only to slam down on it relentlessly with the next hard wave.

In late March I checked on another swath of salt marsh. Though broader and more exposed than the small one, it, too, lies behind stone. The cordgrass stems that had risen from it like spears six months earlier were evident only in infrequent, squat, dry cylinders the ice sheets had missed. The surface of the now tawny peat had been buffed to a high gloss.

As I looked out over this marsh, I had the sense of being in an Escher-like setting, where shapes I know as fish might metamorphose into the negative spaces between birds. Though the tide was out, dips in the peat's surface still held water. Some of these shallow pools narrowed to runnels that drained slowly, but most were level and static, reflecting the blue of the sky. Water had sculpted and rounded every one of the peaty edges until nothing but soft, organic contours framed the pools.

I twisted the polarizing lens of my camera ninety degrees. The still water vanished, and the peat itself dominated what I saw through the lens. From among all the soil shapes there emerged a sinuous six-foot-long one that looked like a giant hare. With hindquarters extended, it tried to escape. On either side of the hare's long ears and across a moatlike channel from them pranced the feet of a horse. The channel repeated the outline of ears and feet, yet held a shape of its own. I snapped the shutter.

I walked across a land bridge that was a bear. Peat and stone had intermarried to form it. The bear's bulbous head was water-haloed and supported me while I made another exposure.

In every direction I looked, land and water echoed each other in these animal-like silhouettes. I realized then that the two elements were the two parts of a single pattern, that the environment created by stripped peaty soil exhibited a unity of figure and ground.

Seeing this helped me begin to comprehend the salt marsh. It was, at that moment, a recumbent golden zoo

Water sculpts and rounds the peaty edges until nothing but soft, organic contours frame the pools

born of plants and water and a brutal winter. Ice had not destroyed all the *Spartina* and other living things. It had revealed them in their least dressed-up mode. Like many things reduced to basics, the simple shapes radiated a beauty and connectedness invisible beneath the fire of summer's rich green leaves.

In addition to scrubbing the peat nearly bald, the persistent ice had actually shifted large segments of the soil, then shoved or dragged them across the underlying mud and sand. I found one block of peat that had been moved and apparently abandoned. Perched on a high rocky outcrop, it was thirty yards from any semblance of marsh. The peat was the size of a large box of laundry detergent, and still heavy with water. When I tried to turn it over, it split in two. One section of the block flipped upside down, exposing roots and rhizomes that looked like clumps of supine insects, their pale legs futilely protesting the air. I struggled to put the segment back in place.

When the ice melted and the marshes once again advertised their characteristic smell, and when green *Spartina* shoots began thrusting through the peaty soil, I realized what had been happening even during the coldest months. As I walked toward the water on the slanting beach, several arcs of cordgrass fragments and other matter—remnants dropped by the tides—became increasingly fine. The dark particles stood out against the beige sand. The dried grass and other organisms of which these were the mere leftovers had been so thoroughly clipped and tumbled and churned and pulverized by ice and storms, and so completely broken down by decomposers, that they and the algae associated with them had turned to soup. Or more precisely, to a chocolate-colored batter of vegetable particles. This was the decomposing product of *Spartina*, algae, and other organisms—detritus. Perhaps even more than the algae alone, this detritus with its rich store of microbes is the universal sustenance of the salt marsh, and ultimately of the entire estuarine food web. This was cordgrass nursing the world to which it had given birth . . .

———

I step toward the seawall slowly, but not slowly enough. Over the rock rim I glimpse the lateral sprint of a disturbed fiddler crab, a smoke-colored creature with a body smaller than an ivy leaf and almost as flat. Frantic to escape the sudden shadow of my head, it scurries down a hole in this finger of muddy sand, where sparse stems of cordgrass aspire to begin a marsh.

A second fiddler, a self-absorbed male, choreographs what artist Walter Anderson once called the animal's hymn to the sun. This crab, however, has his back to me and the midday light. He cuts a lone figure as he partners only his shadow, rising as far as he can on permanently bowed legs while opening and raising the large front claw that is the mark of his gender. It is a restrained move with something of Elizabeth II's wave about it. Several times the fiddler repeats the gesture, which is used for both courtship and defense. Then he folds the oversized and relatively harmless appendage in close to his carapace and lowers himself to a tuck: a crouched shape, arm in a sling.

Holding his low position, the fiddler shivers for a moment, an additional sign that he is hungry for a mate. With his other and much smaller front claw he begins to scoop up balls of the muddy material that surrounds him, detrital material that no doubt contains sediments, some algae, probably specks of decaying vegetation with its attendant microbes. His body rhythms quicken. Suddenly it is mealtime at low tide on an early-summer day, and the little claw's repeated trips to the mouth confirm an appetite even more compelling now than sex. As I watch, the fiddler continues to harvest from the same rich ragout through which he and some of the rest of his colony—about thirty individuals in all—may soon be sidling along.

These crustaceans are not indiscriminate in their tastes. Their specialized mouthparts, which are actually modified legs, isolate the various dishes that will make up lunch. Different fiddler species have mouth structures adapted to work over either sand, the mud in the top zones of tidal creeks and mud flats, or the soil components of brackish marshes, those less salty than this one. Usually a given crab cannot deal with all three types of soil, an adaptation that decreases the likelihood of territorial spats and is one of the main characteristics scientists use to distinguish the species. The crabs before me are the sand-loving *Uca pugilator*.

What stirs me most about fiddler crab behavior is the sophistication of their food-sorting process. First the animals place the materials they reject into specialized sorting chambers. When the chambers fill up, the fiddlers spit the materials into their chelipeds, or front claws, thereby treating those appendages as attached miniature spittoons.

Whenever a spittoon fills up, the fiddler does the equivalent of taking out the trash: the crab deposits the package of rejected material (called pseudofeces) back onto the marshy soil. The animal also leaves behind pellets of its own nitrogen-rich body wastes. Bacteria and other microbes that break these materials down further help to enhance their nutritive value. The enriched materials may even be assessed and used by the same fiddler that produced them, in an elegant instance of recycling that can continue almost indefinitely.

The next high tide picks up enriched organics and churns them back into the detrital mix. When that tide falls, it leaves behind yet another set of culinary options from which not only fiddler crabs but also some snails and other consumers of detritus (organisms called detritivores) can choose their meals. Every tidal cycle helps redesign the already-worked-over marsh menu this same way. Clearly the complex detrital food web, though still incompletely understood by science, is like no other on earth.

I eventually settle cross-legged on the seawall, hoping not to disturb the small fiddler colony more than I already have. But I fail. What the crabs must perceive as the rocking of a dark behemoth triggers a frenzy and, a moment later, stillness. The animals that were near their burrow holes before I loomed have dashed into them. Those farther away have simply stopped, frozen.

The fiddler crabs' rapid spurts of motion may serve to confuse potential enemies. Clapper rails and other marsh birds relish the flavor of fiddlers. The crabs' ability to sprint and then disappear into immobility seems to help keep the threat at bay.

I remain still for three or four more minutes, during which the crabs start to adopt a cruising mode. Those who reached home a few moments ago begin, very warily, to surface. Those who froze start to move about again. Feeding soon resumes, along with intermittent male posturing.

With some difficulty I single out a female. She is a much smaller creature, almost uniformly dark in contrast to the male, whose big claw is typically light in color. She has a distinct advantage over him: she eats with two hands. She gathers detrital bits with one front claw, delivers them to her mouthparts, then immediately begins foraging with the opposite claw. She finds more delectable morsels, practically throws them in, and sets the first claw back in mechanical motion. Were she not so efficient, she would be a caricature of herself. Female fiddlers can afford to lose a small claw, a not uncommon fate among crustaceans in general. While both sexes can regenerate this lost member, the fiddler male, lacking a viable spare, may starve to death before he completes the process.

While the sun is still high, I decide to reverse my perspective. At the far edge of the soil I look back at the wall on which I'd been sitting, and I see what I missed earlier.

Mud balls with the light behind them make shadows on the surface of the marsh. Some of the half-inch-wide spheres are clustered into what look like children's snowball forts, only black. Others are more loosely grouped. Most rest near the crab burrows' entrance holes, which appear to be about the same diameter as the balls themselves.

Fiddlers excavated these dirt balls in the process of making home repairs. Years ago I absently watched some fiddlers coax balls like these out of their burrows. I remember the movement as suggesting Sisyphus rolling his impossible stone. But as these crabs at the base of the seawall repeatedly enter and exit their slanted burrow ramps, I am struck with how unencumbered by their earthen plugs they appear. The crabs practically dance with their globes, in a sort of traveling side step that uses the legs like arms, overhanded. I watch a female, *en pointe*, scrape soil particles along until they accumulate into a sphere that fills her leggy hollow, and I wish I could do something like it.

A bigger difference between *Uca* and me than our legs, however, is that fiddlers love mud and what washes over it even more than I do. Fiddlers eat mud throughout their lives, not just as toddlers. They model it like clay. They live in burrows of mud, sand, and peat, usually within or near the interlocking roots of *Spartina*. These rounded dwellings fit the crabs' bodies like gloves and put the animals in contact with mud the minute they reach home. Fiddlers walk on marsh mud. They run there. They court there. They are the supreme mud babies, which is one reason scientists consider them among the few quintessential salt-marsh creatures.

Though fiddlers have a toylike appeal to human beings, they play a crucial role in the life of the marsh. Like the earthworms in my garden, their infatuation with mud leads them not only to utilize the stuff for their own purposes but to aerate and drain it, thereby speeding the decomposition of subterranean material. In doing this they help turn the top layers of otherwise anaerobic marsh soils into livable habitat for the cordgrass and themselves. In certain circumstances, in fact, the denser the fiddlers become in the soil, the more lush the cordgrass grows above it—clear evidence of the reciprocity these two key forms of marsh life enjoy.

———

I spent the better part of a summer tracking fiddlers. Their home in the cordgrass at the far end of Black Duck Creek (as I called it) became my favorite muddy haunt. It was a meandering quarter mile from the nearest cove, and the resultant quiet made the place feel like a world apart. Whenever my Whaler rounded the creek's final turn toward the fiddler colony, I became as calm as the mirrorlike surface I was interrupting.

The tides wash in and out gently in this remote backwater. A few trees and houses overlook the creek from afar. But for the most part, the place in summer belongs to the crabs, a few mosquitoes, and the one or two great egrets often found here feeding on small fish.

It also belongs to the thickest fringe of *Spartina* I know. High-water marks of beige or silver accessorize the bordering stands of tall grass like tiers of painted-on cuffs. The markings are precise, as if a housepainter had cut them in. In late summer the markings' neutral colors are topped off with more vibrant ones—the sparkling green of the grasses' upper leaves, above which panicles of creamy flowers sway in the slightest wind. These fresh greens and pale yellows are evident only above the uppermost limit of the tide, which falls and rises like a slow curtain on the most marginal environment on earth.

Next to the channel that defines this creek, a few individual blades of *Spartina* bend their tips to meet the water. The upper leaf surfaces are white with a covering of salt. The lower surfaces look almost black. Paired with their reflections the blades form irregular ovals, Oriental in their elegant simplicity. I touch the tip of my bent index finger to the end of the thumb on the same hand, to try to replicate the shape.

The small movement, which I make almost instinctively now, doesn't seem to faze the creek's fiddler crabs. They are intent on ferocity and love when they're not absorbed by eating. Perhaps the isolation and somnolence of their homeplace makes these fiddlers trusting, or maybe it simply makes them slow. Whatever the explanation, if I douse my motor and drift down on the colony, or even if I pole toward it by quietly thrusting in an oar, I can inch the Whaler up next to shore and nudge the fiddlers' living rooms. Then I quickly flatten myself across the bow and wait. In a minute or two the crabs recover from their jolt and start to surface right at boat-eye level.

What I see in this situation is essentially always the same. It is what I saw from the seawall. And it is what I see when I look straight down on a third colony of fiddlers, animals that make their home near the foot of a low-slung bridge: the big-clawed males bluff and tussle over female affections; the two sexes eat their respective amounts of fluid earth; and burrow keeping proceeds apace.

Yet what I see is also different each time, every marsh having a different rhythm from every other, and even the same marsh changing from one moment to the next. From the bridge I once watched a male fiddler use the torn corner of a glossy magazine page as a makeshift patio. The paper, obviously delivered by the tides, was white, with a partial capital letter *B* printed in yellow. The crab was stacking dark mud balls on the sheet's light background as deliberately and methodically as some people stack firewood. Furthermore, he was doing it under water, which told me his name was *Uca pugnax*. Committed to burrowing in soil that doesn't collapse easily, this Long Island Sound fiddler is the only species who doesn't rush to beat a rising tide to the door of his abode.

I did discover one fiddler crab colony that defies comparison with all the rest. Their home measures ten feet or more from top to bottom, an extraordinary dimension. Except at extreme flood tides, at least half the peaty structure rises higher than my head when I am seated in my boat.

The multifamily dwelling looks like a dark Mesa Verde. In summer, well after the one hundred or more fiddler residents have emerged from hibernation, layers of irregular holes beneath the tide line become festooned with bright-green seaweed. The plants' individual strands and clumps resemble strips of wet crepe paper and lend a festive air to what could be a terraced moonscape.

The interior must be a catacomb. Male bluffing games seem to go on without recess, as hordes of the crabs emerge from inside the habitation onto one of the several levels of peat. Invariably the males follow their own light-colored claws into cartwheels that land them on a lower level. As I watched these seemingly unattached claws roll downhill, I realized I had developed crab eyes, the ability to spot a fiddler male from afar simply by locating his pale lure.

———

Directly below this layer-cake warren the tide rolls back to expose hundred-foot-wide mud flats. They are soft and fragrant with sulfur on a hot summer afternoon. Steve and I allowed ourselves to get stranded here once, then felt conspicuous and somehow vulnerable as the only vertical objects at the bottom of a shallow and seemingly unvegetated tureen of slip. It was too late to change our minds. The Whaler, which normally registers shifts of movement, sat stymied by a tide that had yanked all but an inch of water from under her hull and glued her in place.

I leaned over and peered down. Hundreds of gray-brown, oval mud snails glided along in the shallows very slowly, almost as if they were skating tedious school figures. They left behind them a system of highways the width of their bodies, about half an inch. Several of these roads ran more or less parallel with one another. Others wound into loose cloverleaves. The roads dead-ended, of course, with the snails themselves, which appeared to follow along behind their antennae-like intake tubes (for respiratory water).

The snail, an *Ilyarassa* species, is typical of the mud flats. In fact, another snail, known as the common periwinkle, which was introduced to the Northeast from Europe in the latter half of the nineteenth century, has become so prolific here that it has more or less restricted *Ilyarassa* to this kind of muddy habitat. Since the floors of tide flats are unstable, they cannot support the weight of heavy grazers, as most people think of them. Here, then, instead of a cow or a horse, was a grazer of marshland proportions. I was watching a snail herd, hoping for a stampede.

Ilyarassa is typical of gastropods (mollusks with single, uncoiled shells) in the way that it feeds: it scrapes along the bottom with a specialized file-like tongue, or radula.

Sometimes it detects carrion through a heightened sense of smell and turns scavenger. It also forages for bottom deposits, particularly algae.

In a bare space between snails I reached out and sank my hand into the shallow water, letting an index finger rake through the top three inches of mud. The texture of the soil was soft and silky, its tenacity unparalleled. It clung like a second skin. I brought my arm back into the boat and passed my hand near my nose. It would take the greater part of a week for me to get my hand and nail odor-free.

The trough that my finger left in the soil was slow to fill with water. Curiously, it was two-toned. A slick bronze top layer about an inch deep showed along the impression's edges. The soil beneath it was charcoal gray in the bright sun. There was nothing fainthearted about the duo of colors.

The bronzing on the surface was caused by diatoms. These are the same microscopic, silica-bodied algae that sustain life in tidal creeks. I must have pulled my finger through millions of the plants. They move up and down through the uppermost mud according to the stage of the tides. Since diatoms must trap sunlight in order to make food, they require an open exposure. Yet the extreme heat of a low tide in midsummer can fry them if they are unprotected. In such critical conditions the tiny plants must keep their depth judgments ahead of temperature changes.

Tiny animals also make migrations of sorts in this place (as do plankton in the water). When the tide turned and water began flowing slowly over the mud, hermit crabs tripped through the shallows in their leased shells. Segmented worms popped their heads in and out of conical homes that extended above the marsh floor. The skinny worms I took for threadworms gyrated almost completely free of the muddy coverlet before retreating to safety, and briefly entombed mud snails twisted themselves about as if self-basting. In a patch of mud no bigger than a coaster, three mystifying, softly colored invertebrates raised one after the other of the appendages that edged their bodies like mucousy fringe.

Stuck here in the Whaler, Steve and I were guests at a wiggly Mardi Gras of the mud too small to see. We sat not only at the bottom of a bronzed punch bowl but also at the bottom of a broad-based food chain. The small celebrants whose bodies blended with the color of the mud were gulping plant plankton and detrital bits and each other, and who knows what else, in invisible snatch after snatch.

My eye moved upward to where mud gave way to peat, then peat to the green of cordgrass. The terminal floral clusters of the cordgrass looked white against the bare middle branches of a woody plant called marsh elder. Like the cordgrass, the marsh elder grew within one horizontal zone parallel to the water line, the zone stated in the plant's more common name—high-tide bush. Apparently cordgrass is easily outcompeted in that upper region. Nor will high-tide bush survive farther down toward the water.

The more I looked around me, the more I saw how the placement of all salt-marsh plants follows some unwritten hierarchical code. The grass called salt hay, *Spartina patens*, constitutes a thin layer of this particular marsh cake. Yet it forms extensive meadows in some New England marshes. The thin slice was difficult to see from my boat, this plant being much shorter than its pioneering cousin and growing farther back from shore. If I looked closely, however, I could discern the cowlicky swirls of stems that distinguish its infrequently flooded zone above the cordgrass and be-

low the woody plants. Sprigs of sea lavender waiting to
bloom rose here and there within that zone.

There is little leeway in what determines the vertical
placement of these and other types of true marsh vegetation. Each species can tolerate being submerged in salty
water for just so long. Some species tolerate anoxic soils
and higher soil salinities better than others. Far from giving
any clue as to how carefully regulated their lives really are,
the marsh plants around me appeared studiedly casual as
they arranged themselves above the biggest mud pie I ever
hope to encounter.

———

With its narrow creeks and wide, slick mud flats, its fixed
tides and shifting nutrient broth, its unrelenting hierarchy
of plants large as huts, small as glassy skeletal dreams—this
seemingly contradictory salt marsh demands specialized ad-
aptations of every living thing that calls it home. Few species can meet the demands full-time.

But there is another way to enter the marsh—as if entering a temporary haven instead of a permanent residence.
Migratory birds rely on the habitat during their arduous
annual journeys from north to south and back again. The
marsh offers them a chance to regroup, to feed, to rest. I,
too, have found it a place of respite. It provides a chance
for me to relinquish thoughts of schedules and lists and
replace them with the natural rhythms of water meeting
what is never quite land.

The spotted sandpiper, the shorebird that ranges over
more of North America than any other, seems to visit the
marsh as if it were a spa. Or perhaps a neighborhood bistro,
one that the food critics have yet to discover.

In the last week of July, the full moon gave a nine-foot tidal bath to the marshes. I caught the flood in a small pocket of cordgrass eager to bloom. A sea breeze that rustled the dense plants and urged the waves onto shore masked the morning heat and humidity. I settled cross-legged on a stone far back from the water, in the shade of what I was surprised to realize was a scruffy ailanthus tree.

I had just had time to adjust my sunglasses and writing pad when a hoisted sail's red triangular tip, then its lower white and blue diagonal stripes, appeared over the low headland that set apart my world. Preoccupied with watching the sail colors flap and fold, I didn't notice when a spotted sandpiper landed on a rock slope that leads into the little marsh. When I shifted my gaze, the shorebird was suddenly there, its white breast cleanly rounded against the veined and mottled bedrock of the cut. Its back was the color of thunder. Along the leading edge of the bird's folded wing, a small irregular patch almost like a fringed epaulet sutured gray to beige. The solid colors told me that the creature was either a juvenile or an adult who had only recently lost the spots of its spring breeding plumage.

This robin-sized sandpiper cannot hold still for long. It seems to be powered by two engines that work independently of each other. One operates the body; the other works the area where the neck joins the head. The rear engine apparently can be programmed for automatic and regular forward tilting. The front engine is less sophisticated, being capable only of jerking the rounded head out and up on its feathered stem and pulling it back in. When both motors are engaged, which they usually are, the effect is of an indecisive person with a tic. Yet the animal manages to make its separate bobbing rhythms look graceful and natural.

Early sunlight was filtering through the leaves of trees that grow across the marsh from where I sat. Hardwoods and pines rooted on a high rock ledge dispatch their trunks to the sky there. Along the ledge's flank, at my eye level, are lichens in wonderful shapes above a dark stain that marks the tide line. On this particular morning every one of these surfaces was dappled in a pale light. The sandpiper seemed drawn toward it, as if knowing its own muted colors would blend with the pied tones to provide a camouflage.

A nearby band of old marsh wash-up must have contained the worms, mollusks, and other invertebrates these sandpipers love. The bird began to pick through these offerings with its needle-like bill. It took a break from its unhurried foraging to duck beneath a bridge made by a foot-long curve of branch, one end of which was propped on a stone.

I was still for a long time in my watchful shade and suddenly realized that my limbs were numb. In slow motion, so as not to alarm the bird, I wriggled and shook. All the while I kept my eye on the sandpiper, who wandered on the far side of a four-foot-high clump of grass directly in front of me.

I had seen this green mass only as a buffer between some of the cordgrass and myself. Now the bird was framed under one of its leaf blades, which formed a soft, blowing arch I then studied. It was the highest leaf on the stem, and an eight-inch-long terminal sheath was beginning to flower above it. This was panic grass, *Panicum*. No other plant has quite its loose habit, and its placement along the high margin of the sloping habitat confirmed its identity. The plant is a signpost of sorts, since it marks the uppermost limit of true marsh. What grows above

Panicum belongs to the upland, having little or no use for salt water or spray.

I turned my head back downslope toward the wet-footed cordgrass. Like *Panicum*, it had some arching leaves. By comparison, however, they looked as if they were with-holding something of themselves, as if they were unable to afford *Panicum*'s easy surrender to air. The sun landed on one down-curved blade of cordgrass, glinted for the brief-est moment, and flew back to heaven—a curious, wet shining.

For the next hour or so the sandpiper alternately foraged and rested, and I adjusted with it. After each of its reposes the bird stood and, as if turning itself on, began the separate movements of its attempt at syncopation. When the sand-piper reached the base of the shear that faced me, it spread its wings and flew almost straight up to the lowest of several natural stone stairs, a distance of some six feet. It did not take the steps but paused briefly before gripping with its feet to scale the rest of the cliff as a veteran human climber would. The openness and ease with which it did this seemed to signal some new stage in our mutual tolerance, or our pretense of not seeing each other, whichever was our understanding.

I expected the bird to fly in its alternately fluttering and gliding, arc-winged fashion toward a nearby series of flat rocks that stand up and overlap one another like mountains in a stage-set range. They are part of the promontory that permitted this marsh to develop in its lee. Instead, the sand-piper continued walking uphill and down as surefootedly as a mountain goat until it reached this same fanned-out set of stones.

As the bird stood still in perfect silhouette on the highest peak, I heard the faraway pounding of some piece of heavy machinery. It had a rhythm regular as a clock's. The sand-piper appeared to match its body bounce to the distant beat. I knew it wasn't so. The fantasy was my way of smiling at the outrageousness of a gavotte played on an air hammer and stepped off by an out-of-sync shorebird in cleated shoes. Nevertheless, the beat and the bowing continued long enough to cement my warm feeling for this creature with whom I shared what I had heretofore regarded as my own private mini-marsh.

The angle of the sun changed noticeably during the time of my self-imposed immobility. It exposed the brightness of my white T-shirt and yellow writing pad. I was afraid the glare would drive the bird away. But the creature continued unperturbed. It picked its way back along the route it had come, passing near me once again on its way to a small isolated pool high above the rock where I had first seen it. Indulging in a bath, it showed me the tip of its moving tail over the natural tub's stone rim and the top of a bobbing head bearing eyes that could fix me in spurts of time.

I returned three days later, when the tide was in the same stage that it had been before—two hours short of the flood. The sandpiper's elevated bathing pool, to which I'd paid little notice earlier, teemed with mosquito larvae. The quiet, dark strands, about an inch in length, were vertically suspended just below the water's surface. There was a bumper crop of the slender immatures; within weeks the pool and everything in it would be indicted as part of the most mosquito-y Long Island Sound summer in recent memory.

Stooping over the shallow pool, which was only two feet long, I wriggled my thumb to cast a moving shadow. Pandemonium! Dozens of larvae contracted and flipped tortuously downward toward the brownness of decaying oak leaves. The vegetation had given the pool its color of strong tea and had apparently also caused it to function as a hatchery, by stagnating the water to perfection. The disturbed larvae sifted between the layered foliage on the bottom and disappeared. Even as they escaped the mock danger, new and braver larvae used their breathing tubes to hang themselves up from the water's skin.

The salinity in such a place varies dramatically, depending on how near the tide-splash zone a pool like this is situated, on how recently rain has fallen, and on other factors. The pool may have already undergone considerable evaporation. Unless moisture replenishes it soon, it will become a mere crusting of salt around the rim of a rock basin.

I've seen Polly drink from pools like this. She's taught me a lot about saline levels. I've even watched her wade into a marsh-edged lagoon formed by a seawall and drink from the top layer of the water in which she stood. The first time I saw her do this I thought she must be lapping at the waves, which flirt with her on occasion. But she was drinking, drinking water that was fresh enough to float on top of the saltier and consequently heavier water beneath it. Pools and lagoons all along the estuary mirror its salinity this way.

As smart as Polly may be, her intelligence concerning salinity pales next to that of the cordgrass I'd come back here to see. As John Casey notes in *Spartina*'s second paragraph, it is "Smart grass." "Only the spartinas thrived in the salt flood, shut themselves against the salt but drank the water," he writes.

I followed the rock slope down into the cut, where I curled my toes inside my sneakers to keep from falling face-first onto the same slick incline where the spotted sandpiper had materialized. I reached far into the center of the four- and five-foot-tall cordgrass stems, toward where I had seen the sun gleam off an arched leaf three days before. I pulled on a blade and wrapped its outermost portion over the top of my index finger. After I sawed at it with my thumb for a while, its end portion finally snapped off. This left me holding a two-foot length of the coarse, parallel-veined leaf. At its widest it measured less than an inch across.

I carefully drew the top surface of the blade end across my tongue. Salt. The glistening I'd seen previously was light catching saline crystals. Unlike the salt that can rim shrinking mosquito-filled pools, these crystals are not a coating left by simple evaporation. The salt I licked came from inside the cells of *Spartina*. Dissolved in seawater earlier, it had traveled through the plant's xylem tissues all the way up the stem, still in solution. Finally, it was expelled as a dense brine through highly adapted glands on the leaves. The water evaporated, leaving the salt in crystalline form where I found it. Smart grass indeed.

Another amazing capability is the cordgrass's importing of oxygen, which its roots require for vital processes. Rather than merely competing at ground level with the bacteria, algae, and other organisms of the practically anoxic marsh mud, *Spartina* (like mosquito larvae) harvests oxygen from the air. It begins the process in its foliage. Scientists John and Margaret Teal elaborate:

A set of hollow tubes runs from the leaves down into hollow spaces within the roots. All of these spaces are filled with air and are open to the air through the stomata on the leaves. This provides oxygen by a direct pipeline from the air, in through the stomata, down the leaves, through the stems and rhizomes, and into the roots.

I twisted off a stem of cordgrass and peered down its length. I saw a cluster of cylindrical sheaths. The outer ones encased the next slightly smaller ones like Russian dolls pregnant with more Russian dolls. I peeled away the increasingly tender green tubes of one segment until I reached—what?—a hollowness, a nothingness bounded on either end by a partition. The stem walls house the oxygen and water pathways, which my unaided eye cannot see.

I ambled over to the stone from which I had watched the spotted sandpiper, and I placed the stem across my lap and looked at its topmost segment. As if frozen in the very process of being born, tight flowers were enveloped in an oval casing at the tip. The floral tissue was not yet fully differentiated, and I saw the coming blossoms through a green veil, half imagining them and half really seeing them. I tried to sketch their form, but the drawing eluded me even as the stem had mystified me. I was left merely fingering a thin almond of suggestion and hope.

In the sky above me I saw the MetLife blimp with a painted, goggled Snoopy on its nose. Humming softly to itself, it swam above the open water beyond the cut. Its paired anchor lines billowed like the whiskers of a satisfied catfish. From somewhere across the water came a boat engine's whine. And from the land behind me, the monotones of grass blowers and insect noise swelled the air in waves. No single noise dominated. Everything seemed far away, like the wilderness calls of birds.

Taking all this in at once along with the omnipresent marshy aroma and the occasional soft slam of water against stone, I was caught up in a moment of sheer sensory pleasure. I closed my eyes and let my head fall back. When I looked around again, the sky had the same hazy glare it had had when I arrived. The water still returned Gustav Klimt reflections. The stones around me still radiated heat. And there, on one of them, was my bird.

It teetered for a moment and then began to follow the identical route it had followed three days earlier—down the incline past the cordgrass and into the tide zone, then across the higher marsh very gradually to the rock wall at the far side of the cut. It knew this place much better than I. Knew to walk instead of fly to the overlapping stones of the headland, knew to let the fingers of tidal water rising around the stems of the grasses stock its hunting shelves anew. It knew to bathe in one of these fingers and fluff itself dry, and to cease bobbing long enough to sink into the grayness of the stones until it merged with its own shadow. It even knew to wait for the noisy chickadees overhead to grow tired of flitting among the cones of the pine that grew next to the ailanthus. After it had done all these things, for who knows how many times, the sandpiper marched back to the elevated bathtub full of mosquito larvae, took a drink, and flew away.

————

In 1878 Southern poet Sidney Lanier penned the line "The sea and the marsh are one." The sentence rounds out a stanza of his paean to the Georgia salt marshes, a work called "The Marshes of Glynn" after the state's coastal Glynn County. Relatively unknown today, this poem or certain parts of it were required memorization for high-school students in the Deep South of the 1950s.

I was one of those students. Though I don't remember

learning or reciting the sentence in question, I must have done so. As I reread the entire poem not long ago, those seven words "The sea and the marsh are one" echoed down the longest hall of my memory.

Lanier was a thoroughgoing romantic, a musician-poet without elaborate scientific training. Yet he seemed to know in his bones what science would need nearly a century to catch up to: the tide-bathed marsh creeks and grasses appeared to welcome high water. ". . . the sea/ Pours fast: full soon the time of the flood-tide must be:/ Look how the grace of the sea doth go/About and about through the intricate channels that flow/Here and there,/ Everywhere . . ." Lanier perceived that the entire marsh-land-tidewater ecosystem is the moist yin and yang of a process as well as a place, a mutual embrace and interchange.

Many of the substantiating details of how the embrace occurs and what the interchange provides were worked out, interestingly enough, within a few miles of where Lanier had waxed eloquent and not far down the coast from where Pat Conroy would later set his marsh-rich novel *The Prince of Tides*—at the Sapelo Island Marine Institute of the University of Georgia. Beginning in the mid-1950s, Dr. Eugene Odum and other scientists conducted ground-breaking research there in an effort to determine what a salt marsh really is.

As John and Mildred Teal's popular 1969 book, *Life and Death of a Salt Marsh*, explains, a salt marsh is a self-sustaining garden productive enough to support an incredible amount of life on land and in the water. In a volume entitled *Guale, the Golden Coast of Georgia*, Odum explains marsh productivity in slightly different terms. "The notion came to us," he realized in a boat moving between mud banks, ". . . that we were in the arteries of a remarkable energy-absorbing natural system whose heart was the pumping action of the tides. The entire tideland complex of barrier islands, marshes, creeks, and river mouths was a single operational unit linked together by the tide." The possibility of having begun to understand what could be a "naturally subsidized ecosystem" guided the researchers for the next fifteen years.

In the course of their investigations the Sapelo Island team quantified the productivity of the Georgia salt marsh. One acre of it produces as much as ten tons of detritus and other organic matter a year. The figure for Long Island Sound's annual salt-marsh production is lower—between three and seven tons per acre. The difference reflects the fact that, in the Southeast, salt-marsh grasses can grow year-round.

Even with this geographic difference taken into account, the annual detrital output of a salt marsh is astonishing. The heavily fertilized wheat fields of the American Midwest yield only a single ton of aboveground biomass per acre. Even the tropical rain forest produces only about six tons per acre.

What the impressive figures associated with the salt marsh actually mean to those of us who live along the Sound may best be expressed in terms of human food. Unlike fiddler crabs, we cannot eat the "product" in the catchall phrase "salt-marsh productivity." Even if we could metabolize detrital particles, they are typically too small and too hard on our digestive tracts to be harvested for our use. Herein lies part of the reason that marshes have been considered worthless to the modern fast-food lifestyle.

Construct a slightly more imaginative human food web, however, and the picture changes. Estuarine residents such as clams, oysters, and mussels feed by filtering detrital particles from the water. Small fish such as the mummichogs that sometimes swim near fiddlers nibble tiny marsh plant parts and diatoms in the mud. These animals are direct, or primary, consumers of the marsh's "product."

Larger fish also abound in or near the marsh. As adults they consume the smaller fish in enormous quantities, perhaps having already swum alongside them while using the marsh as a nursery, a place in which to grow. Some experts estimate that as much as 40 percent of all commercial fin fish caught along the Eastern Seaboard spend at least some portion of their lives in this environment. The large fish are considered secondary consumers, being one step removed from the producers of the marsh's food.

Our place in this scheme makes for complexity in both syntax and dining. But it doesn't obscure the notion that to take away the salt marsh is to eliminate, eventually, the source of much of our own seafood. As Edward Weeks wrote of Massachusetts' marshes in *The Atlantic* more than thirty years ago: "At the eleventh hour it is realized that these salt marshes . . . must be either saved or lost—and if lost, the fish are lost too."

———

On a dank Saturday morning in spring I am in Stamford, Connecticut, attending a meeting organized by longtime Sound advocate Art Glowka. Thirty avid recreational fin fishermen of all ages, many in flannel work shirts, gather for what became one of the last of these annual events for a while. Our room at the headquarters of Save the Sound, formerly the Long Island Sound Taskforce, is peppered with old-fashioned wooden desks, the kind you slide into under writing arms shaped like meat cleavers. Steam rises from well-balanced mugs of coffee as participants settle in the seats. They exchange nods or a few words squeezed from the early hour as from a flat tube of toothpaste.

Most of these men work the western Sound, which has a heavily developed shoreline. Wetlands that once fringed Stamford's coast are victims of the past half century of suburban expansion. The simple metal headquarters building of Save the Sound, like much of the adjacent commercial waterfront, sits atop marsh that has been dredged and filled. The way this once fluid area has been subsumed into a more "necessary" fixed landscape suggests some of the region's better-known former salt marshes—New York's LaGuardia Airport, Connecticut's Sherwood Island State Park.

The numbers of fish harvested from western and other regions of the Sound have been low the past few seasons. Everyone here knows this. Yet it seems necessary to read and try to comprehend, once again, the litany of losses. It is an act of honor. From the podium Art begins on an upbeat note.

"Okay, let's go into a quick survey . . . Are the mackerel gone offshore, or what?"

A muffled response from the front of the room.

"Seals. Has anyone heard anything about seals? . . . Al?"

Al counters with a question about the marine mammal's prey. "What happened to the Atlantic herring fishing this year? Last year it was so great. This year, nothin'."

"Two years ago you had great herring fishing. Right, Al?"

"They had a good run for about two weeks . . ."

"Who wants to talk about bluefish?" Art continues.

"Down." Murmurs of assent from across the room . . . "Goin' down."

"What are they feeding on? Homer, you know. You guys are lookin' at stomachs."

"We found a lot of green crabs . . . grass shrimp. A lot of grass shrimp."

"Striped bass?"

"Up."

"We had a blitz this fall like we'd never seen before. Right?"

The communal "Yup" provides only a hint of the bass's strength, in terms of numbers and health. Stripers are an unqualified success, the only one on the roll call.

"Weakfish?"

Answers that surface in the course of the disjointed discussion include "Nonexistent," "Weakfish catches on the south shore of Long Island were significantly higher last year," and "I don't even hear of an occasional catch."

"Sand eels . . . Sand eels?"

Inconclusive.

"Blowfish?"

A definitive "Nothin' " from the man sitting next to me.

"Winter flounder?"

"Lots of small ones and a few very large ones. Nothin' in between."

"Spearing, whitebait? . . . Alewives, smelt? Anyone seen any smelt at all in fifteen years? . . . Sea bass?"

"A few here and there."

"Blackfish?"

Another "Nothin' " and some murmurs.

Art draws laughs with the mention of spider crabs and starfish, both of which are apparently out there in force.

Buoyed on by this dubious success, he announces, "Mike said we're gonna be up to our ears in squid."

But the mention of porpoises darkens the mood again.

"Spanish mackerel?"

"There were little Spanish mackerel around the docks . . ."

"That's right, there were mullet, too," Art interrupts almost enthusiastically. Someone interjects that Port Jeff has some catchable ones.

"Mantis shrimp?"

And then it's on to gulls and other unscaled creatures.

Earlier, several biologists whose work is connected with the Sound were asked to explain their current reseach projects. I'd heard them assert that the Long Island Sound Study contains no up-to-date live habitat studies—or in the words of one of them, "There's no touchy-feely stuff."

"The study is based on mathematical modeling, which has replaced habitat studies as the way to arrive at estimated numbers of fish in the water," said Mike Ludwig of the National Oceanic and Atmospheric Administration. "No specific habitat studies have been done here for more than two decades. Mortality models have been used to determine stock health. Canadian fisheries crashed several years ago. That mortality modeling was overly optimistic."

The Long Island Sound Study is the mammoth diagnostic tool that government agencies and individual investigators developed in an attempt to understand and remedy the estuary's most pressing problems. The study took eight years to complete and cost $16 million. Though the management plan that grew out of it is not yet fully implemented, the study has already made major contributions to our understanding of the estuary, shedding light on the massive fish kills that sometimes plague the western Sound.

According to Dr. Gerard Capriulo of the State University
of New York at Purchase, who would like to have seen a
greater emphasis on biological data in the study, the study's
physics data are good—the way the water mixes, the tides,
the currents, the winds. These all interact in complex ways
in the Sound, and the study reflects this.

Gerry's expertise lies in understanding plankton, the billions and billions of tiny floating organisms that have been
credited with forming the basis of the marine/estuarine
food chain. In the Sound, he told me, "we're somehow
changing the entire food-web complex—from the bottom
up. We don't know exactly how."

Gerry does know that the presence and relative amounts
of certain nutrients in the water determine, for the most
part, what species live there. In the western Sound nitrogen
levels are often high, due to concentrations of effluent from
waste water treatment facilities. Nitrogen encourages the
growth of phytoplankton (plant plankton). When the
plankton die, they sink to the bottom of the estuary, and
marine bacteria and other microbes break down their remains. In doing this work the microbes use up oxygen that
would otherwise be available to fish. In extreme situations
this pattern of decomposition can lead to hypoxia, a low
level of dissolved oxygen in the water. The Long Island
Sound Study calls this summertime condition (which is
responsible for the fish kills) the most serious problem facing the estuary.

In a later phone conversation Gerry told me he thinks
effluent-induced hypoxia is not the principal cause of the
fish population problem. "I can imagine solving the hypoxia dilemma and finding that the fish are still not there,"
he said.

Drawing on patterns of decomposition that occur in the

natural salt marsh, he continued, the director of Stamford's waste water treatment facility recently developed a method of reducing nitrogen levels in effluent discharged into the Sound. This could eventually save significant tax dollars, since it may eliminate the need for more elaborate tertiary sewage treatment.

But, Gerry said, managing waste water to limit nitrogen without also managing to limit phosphorus is asking for trouble. The Japanese tried a nitrogen-only strategy, he continued. They experienced shellfish poisoning caused by red tides, which are masses of a planktonic organism called a dinoflagellate. The organism "flourishes in phosphorus-rich water. Salt marshes help maintain the balance between nitrogen and phosphorus. But in the western Sound we have few of those left."

Over the phone I heard Gerry take a deep breath. Then he told me he thought the high nitrogen levels may be doing something like enhancing the growth of those phytoplankton that support elevated concentrations of copepods. "Copepods, which are tiny crustaceans, are a favorite food of larval fish," he said.

A new crop of copepods is in the water now. "The irony may be," Gerry said, "that these very organisms the young fish favor are out there in such huge numbers that, when they die, their decomposition robs adult fish of oxygen." Then adult fish die, too. "I'm doing a study concerned with such possibilities," he concluded. "Its results suggest . . . that the two most basic causes of the fish [population] problem may be the loss of critical habitat and overfishing. The former translates into 'not enough coastal wetlands.' "

———

To the extent that science has begun to glimpse the intricacies of salt marshes just as these places are on the verge of disappearing, the habitat has become our rain forest. And there is no simple explanation for the myopia that led to this state of affairs.

Native Americans apparently appreciated wetlands in their unaltered condition, having harvested much of their food from fish weirs erected in them. In the sixteenth and seventeenth centuries Europeans arrived on these shores carrying the baggage of certain negative wetlands mythologies, including the fen-dwelling monster Grendel of the thousand-year-old Anglo-Saxon epic *Beowulf* and echoes of the phrase "Slough of Despond" from Bunyan's widely read seventeenth-century allegory *Pilgrim's Progress*. In spite of this, the settlers, like the native Americans, prized the marshes, particularly the high marsh with its salt hay unique to the New England region. They harvested the hay for pasturage, for mulch, and for many other uses.

By the mid-1700s New Englanders could purchase imported hay from Canada more reasonably than they could buy salt hay from the marsh next door. A century later so many colonists and their descendants had homesteaded along the Northeastern coastline that there was a perceived need for more land to accommodate them and their land-based farming. Since many of these newer Americans were of English and Dutch heritage, they sought solutions to the land-use problem using the same wetlands technologies that had worked for their forebears back home—draining and diking. A crazy quilt of national legislation usually referred to as the Swamp Lands Acts encouraged this by deeding some 65 to 70 million acres of wetlands to fifteen different states. The understanding was that such presumably worthless habitat would somehow be transformed into "useful" land.

Almost an entire century after that—in the mid-1900s—
the government was still promoting development of the
nation's wetlands. In the meantime, the Northeast's coastal
economy was shifting from an agricultural one to that of a
suburban bedroom community. Once this happened and
the majority of the people who lived along the shore no
longer depended on its bounty for their livelihood, the
perceived importance of wetlands faded, and sheer indifference set in. Salt marshes had become invisible to all but
the few people who sought them out for recreation and
rest.

Not all of what has replaced the lost marshes can be
considered "civilized" in the way we normally use that
word. We have no shortage of marinas and sodded lawns,
to be sure. But we also have no shortage of huge former
marshlands that, if we think of these tracts at all, strike us
as a sort of intermediate environment, one that (literally
and figuratively) is neither fish nor fowl.

One sees such a neverland in the Bronx between Interstate 95 and the Sound. Driving north slowly over the
Whitestone Bridge last February, I noticed that deep in the
parcel's heart of tall reeds a helmeted figure on a dirt bike
followed a serpentine path toward a large white truck. The
back of the truck was open. A ramp led into it. Two more
bikes leaned against the truck's flanks. As I watched, the
rider threaded his way closer and closer to the vehicle that
had apparently disgorged him. He was a couple of twists
from his goal when I had to move on.

Still elevated on the bridge's ramp, I could look down
into other pockets among the long stems. Rusting and
burned cars filled them. As I entered the toll plaza, I saw
even more of the twelve-foot-tall plants, which are reed
grass, *Phragmites australis*. Yard after yard of them looked
uniform in their ragged brown headdresses, a far cry from

the way mud, peat, and other salt-marsh features grade in and out of one another inch by inch.

A fat bundle of *Phragmites* is stuffed into a raku vase that sits on a pedestal in the corner of my living room. It's been there so long I don't remember where I gathered it, though I am sure it was somewhere close to home. As I walked into the house after my drive, I stared hard at the awkwardly placed stalks, really seeing them for the first time in a long time. This is the plant that displaces salt-marsh plant species, I realized, the same plant I had just tried to outrun. Clearly I didn't have to go to the Bronx to find it growing in significant numbers.

I have heard people who are interested in wetlands preservation refer to *Phragmites* as a tall, bad plant that overruns the marsh. Though I take issue with their use of the word "bad," I cannot disagree that the plant appears to be taking the marsh world by storm. But we invite it to proliferate. According to scientists at Connecticut College, *Phragmites* is a native, a natural and integral part of the wetlands environment. In fact, it is adapted to survive in different types of marshes. In the salt marsh it grows along the upland, where it can regulate its numbers as well as *Panicum* and high-tide bush can. Tidal restriction trips the switch that causes it to behave otherwise.

There is unmistakable evidence of this at Great Meadows, a 500-plus-acre salt marsh in Stratford, Connecticut. This is the largest marsh in the state that was not ditched for mosquito control back in the 1920s and '30s. Unemployed laborers were engaged then to "improve" the state's marshes by digging wide gashes through them. Instead of helping to reduce the number of mosquitoes, however, ditching ultimately had the opposite effect. Great Meadows has been Connecticut's "most controversial piece of real estate," according to the Nature Conservancy's David Sutherland. The question to whom does the classic marsh rightfully belong, the state of Connecticut or private owners, was debated for almost a quarter of a century.

My Great Meadows guide is a veteran birder named Charlie Barnard. He is the fourth person I've asked to take me into this area. The other three apparently relish the notion of getting caught here even less than he does. Although we are in territory that Charlie has birded for twenty years, we are trespassing. The same Great Meadows that was described as "the premier bird habitat in the entire greater metropolitan New York region" in the 1920s has been in the hands of private developers since 1951. The owners don't seem to like binoculared folks skulking around on their land. It's a hard point for anyone trying to get past the well-guarded entrance to miss, though it wasn't until we were coming out of the marsh that Charlie and I actually saw a man's silhouette in the open door of a strategically placed trailer. We had slipped in early on a Sunday morning and followed a route that Charlie knew well.

In Connecticut the continued private ownership of large tracts of wetlands like this one is no surprise. Even if the developers had not acquired the property when they did, before the state's 1969 tidal wetlands legislation was enacted, there is nothing illegal about their claiming it. (No blanket federal wetlands legislation exists.) In Connecticut, where individual citizens can own the land above mean high water, as much as 90 percent of the state's tidal wetlands is in private hands. Some landowners pay dearly for tiny patches of salt marsh that help buffer their lawns from storms that hit coves and bays along the Sound.

Similarly, there is nothing illegal about the current condition of Great Meadows, unless Charlie and I can be considered petty criminals for being here. Yet something feels terribly wrong. Open, layered-looking sweeps of *Spartina* and other true marsh grasses should be turning September gold around my knees. Instead, terminal tan seed bundles like those on my living room stems meet above my head. They keep the life-giving sunlight out and make walking here a march under a reed-domed path. Charlie reflexively snaps the brittle stems as we pass through them. I hear the crunch of boots on solid ground instead of the suck of mud.

This path doesn't belong here any more than we do. It runs along the top of a bermlike serpent of earth, earth that was dredged from the Housatonic River just to the east of us. This is only one in a whole maze of berms built to stop the flow of tidal water into the more inland sections of what was once all marsh. Berming, Charlie tells me, is a common way to begin killing a wetland, since it cuts the marsh off from tide-borne nutrients and halts the development of peat. The part of Great Meadows that is closest to the Sound has not been separated from what forms it and is therefore still more or less intact. But I catch only glimpses of that untouched segment beyond the growth that encloses us.

Charlie and I eventually arrive at a divide along the reed-topped ridge. A fence denies access to the marsh beyond it. The divide is actually a strip of sparsely vegetated fill that overlays and surrounds a conduit pipe some four feet in diameter. Water from a channeled creek at our backs runs through the pipe beneath where we stand and trickles down a creek in front of us. To my surprise the creek is bordered on the right by the omnipresent tall plants atop not just a ridge but an entire mesa created from fill. The vegetation stretches as far as I can see and blocks the view.

On the left side of the creek that we straddle, marsh grasses appear to emerge from peat in the normal way. Some overhang the edge of the waterway so dramatically that anything beneath their graceful curved blades is hard to see. This is my first real look at the open coastal marsh. It is a managed view, the only view allotted me so far, and is neither impressive nor unimpressive.

Identical linked raised paths take us from vista to vista of marshland in the same way that a construction site's fence with peepholes leads from one view to the next. One glimpse reveals not just a single creek but the confluence of three. Every inch of the low-tide mud flats is covered with snails. I've seen long-legged birds stand and pick snails from mud like this. They looked as if they were plucking bonbons. Today the snails go unconsumed.

For two sultry miles Charlie and I continue to wind in and out of the live tubing atop the berms. Twice, when open vistas are few, we lose our way and are forced to double back through the undifferentiated stalks. "I never got lost here before," Charlie fumes. "This whole section used to be brackish marsh dotted with places I knew— ponds where gadwalls nested . . . and spotted sandpipers."

Finally, dripping perspiration, we find that the reed grass peters out and lets us step down into the natural tidal marsh. Over the scent of useless insecticide it smells rich and wonderfully pungent. The sky is unfettered. I relax.

Charlie motions toward a marsh hawk, or northern harrier. The raptor is quartering the grasses, low—probably hunting for mice. I watch it rise and settle several times. Its slowly beating wings are so long that they seem to bridge earth and air near the tidal inlet called Lewis Gut.

The sighting is precious to me. Fewer than 1,500 marsh hawks migrate through Connecticut each fall, the females and juveniles near the coast and the adult males most probably inland (few males are seen). The birds' general southward movement is as deliberate as the rhythm of their wings: the hawks pause for a day, a week, in what's left of the network of marshes on their route. Any parcel that's missing may tax them beyond their limits.

These magnificent raptors once bred in Connecticut's salt marshes. But their numbers, even as migrants, have declined dramatically as more and more of the state's coastal wetlands have been drained, and Connecticut now lists the bird as endangered.

As soon as Charlie and I turn around, the tall screen of vegetation once again obstructs our view. I can no longer pretend there are only patches of this plant blocking the Real Thing of the marsh. *This* seems to be the real thing. The thickety stuff demands to be reckoned with.

Phragmites can be handsome when the wind blows through it. At the edge of go-on-forever stands of it—the kind I can't begin to walk through—I've seen the plant's terminal flowering and fruiting clusters in several distinct color phases at once, as if spring, summer, and fall coexisted. Some of the young plumes are a sumptuous aubergine: when touched by the sun, their blossoms show an iridescent gloss like an eggplant's skin.

But reed grass can gallop through soil. Especially, it seems, through fill. Once the rhizomes establish themselves in material brought in from outside the marsh and dumped above the tides, neither fire nor mower blades nor ordinary chemicals can halt the plant's spread for long. Soon the growth extends over entire impounded or tidally restricted marshes. (Large acreages of Connecticut's *Spartina* marshes have been converted to *Phragmites* by tide gates used to prevent flooding.) A symptom of our earth-shifting time, the rampant growth reminds us graphically of what was underneath it, hence of what we have destroyed.

If I look very closely, I see that the reeds are not entirely jealous of their space on the berm. Borders of pure *Phragmites* give way here and there to other types of plant life as Charlie and I start to move along again. Low-growing herbaceous plants such as the delicate marsh pink appear. Single stems of the plants are discreetly tucked at the base of the reed-grass stems, where their soft pastel blossoms call little attention to themselves. The bolder goldenrod is everywhere, even in the center of our raised path. And the tufted, small white fruits of groundsel tree, a woody plant almost as tall as the *Phragmites*, peer from behind the reedy monoculture as if around a shoulder. These herbs and shrubs which are part of the upper-salt-marsh environment look healthy if timorous.

Charlie and I move out into the coastal marsh for a second time. From somewhere behind the tall reeds we've just left, an engine starts up and accelerates to a deafening whine. The sound rises as it comes toward us. A red-and-white model airplane clears the tops of the grasses and goes into two double flips and a roll as it circles far out over the marsh. It skirts the harrier's hunting ground. Two more models follow. One is bright yellow, the other red and gray. All of them suggest nervous, overgrown insects as they buzz by. Ah yes—Sunday.

I look at Charlie. He cocks his head and starts walking. With the drone of the planes blocking conversation, we step out of the marshy habitat into a pocket of woody brush left standing along the perimeter of an enormous oval of hard-packed earth. Someone is driving a semi's cab toward us down the straightaway. We wait. After the truck makes

A broad, classic marsh in early autumn looks both ordered and spontaneous

a turn, we see a big red-and-blue sign bearing a phone number and these words:

> Learn to Drive
> Tractor Trailers
> Educational Training

———

Charlie and I are standing on the sandy ridge called Long Beach. It is the more eastern segment of the barrier behind which Great Meadows developed. The town of Stratford owns it. Like the coastal marsh we just left and which we now face, Long Beach is slated for inclusion in the Stewart B. McKinney National Wildlife Refuge, if money becomes available and acceptable terms can be reached.

The top of this ridge, Charlie tells me, attracts the federally threatened piping plover and the state-threatened least tern. It is a significant nesting spot for both birds.

The leeward side of Long Beach is studded with goldenrod. Its chubby fingers of bloom bleed their primary yellow into the broad foreground of my view. Beyond the goldenrod, at the slope's base, last year's cordgrass fragments lie in an uninterrupted raft some fifty feet long and ten feet across. I have no idea how many tides have lifted and dropped the straws that compose this mat. Perhaps a score. Each buoying and subsequent draining has swirled the khaki tubes into new interlocking roundnesses. Now they appear homogenized into this canal of identical ghosts, this rug. It forms a clear demarcation between the barrier beach and the plants of the living marsh.

Beyond the raft lies gold—not a uniform gold, which comes later. This is a marsh gold that rides comfortably just below the very tips of the *Spartina* plants. In this broad, classic marsh these grasses must number in the millions, and this mellow aura is the ribbon that ties them loosely together. Spiking across it in some places, drifting over it in others, are the ecru hangers-on of blossoms loath to depart.

The lower portion of every cordgrass stalk has managed to hold on to summer or leap into autumn on its own schedule. The stems shade from Granny Smith green into olive and ocher and russet in a soft, lineless manner. Yet there's the slightest hint of a second color band, of green.

Below all this, the brown of the tide line has drawn a vague horizontal across the stems' base. The mark is nothing like the precise ones left on *Spartina* along the edges of protected marsh creeks. More than anything else it is a clue. A thread of incandescence in a color I cannot even name weaves through the stems above the basal darkening.

This intricate tapestry is visible throughout every inch of the pristine marsh. Brown is always nearest the water, then green, the burnished tones, and a light brushstroke of cream. The colors weave in and out of one another in this spontaneous yet ordered way until they meet the sky. Distant shadowy tufts and hummocks participate in the waves of rich hues and break up the marsh as if they were small, humpbacked mammals snuffling through it.

I think of the contrast between the varied colors of this healthy marsh today and the uniformity of the nearby—and also healthy—Nells Island marsh just a few weeks ago. At its peak of bloom Nells Island was a uniform stretch of green with a top dressing of pale-yellow blossoms. The flowers formed an uninterrupted line that reached from the mouth of the Housatonic River all the way to the Washington Street Bridge, a distance of at least a mile. When the wind blew, it tousled the slender flower clusters, placing them in bold relief against the stems' consistent verdancy. This visual world was a simple, two-toned declarative statement.

The autumn marsh, by contrast, has a Faulknerian syntax. The benign slashes and splatters of bronze that infiltrate it permit me to hear, perhaps this one day only, how model planes and other wetland dissonances can resolve themselves into color chords of astonishing beauty.

———

Shortly after Charlie and I made our furtive expedition into Great Meadows, the most critical portion of that marsh was saved and designated for inclusion in the McKinney Refuge. The nominal savior was the United States Fish and Wildlife Service, which signed the first of four options to purchase the coastal wetlands from the Stratford Development Company for $2.28 million. A second parcel was purchased soon after, leaving the future of fifty-eight acres that could still be developed hanging in the balance. A decade of restoration, it was estimated, will allow the currently bermed "marsh" to heal significantly. Eventually the site may once again provide cover and other benefits to wildlife, though it will never be as valuable to any living thing as it was in its original state.

The *Connecticut Post* carried this chapter of the Great Meadows story on its front page under the headline WETLANDS A SHORE THING. Reportedly, people who had participated in the negotiations were ecstatic. They deserved to be. The agreement, which was reached with the help of the Nature Conservancy, the Connecticut Department of Environmental Protection, and several other like-minded organizations, represented the culmination of years of work and set a precedent for how wetlands preservation can be achieved. It was a thrilling moment.

We who live along the Sound can look forward to more victories like this. We know we can reclaim at least some of the salt marshes we've altered. For more than a decade, in fact, the state of Connecticut has been a leader in the field of marsh restoration and creation, and it now works in partnership with wetlands guru Dr. William Niering and his colleagues at Connecticut College. Though Connecticut has lost 30 percent of its salt marshes since the turn of the century, Saybrook Point Marsh in Stonington, the municipally managed Pine Creek Marsh in Fairfield, and other of its altered sites are making comebacks.

Yet even with these technological advances, ironies persist. So long as only a fraction of the people who live along the Sound recognize the significance of tidal marshes, that fraction will continue to have to fight for what is really everyone's wetlands heritage—nurseries and feeding grounds for commercial fish and other forms of marine life, nesting areas and stopovers for a great variety of birds, storm buffers, incredible productivity amid remarkable scenery, even a model for the chemical interactions necessary to upgrade effluent from the forty-five sewage-treatment facilities that empty into the estuary. The challenge is in battling indifference to wetlands, so that more than a handful of people may appreciate the magic. The political will and savvy will follow.

Any hope we have of accomplishing this ultimately rests in admitting wetlands not only to our thinking about the nation's water resources but also to our lexicon of wilderness. The salt marshes of the Sound, which are the only types of wetlands that directly fringe the estuary, are also the only natural coastal spaces left that require significant planning to reach. At low tide Windsurfers, jet skis, and large motorboats and sailboats cannot approach them. This means that canoeists, kayakers, clammers with their crusty boots and rakes, serious maritime students, birders, and a few of what I call true "muck nuts" may have learned the best way in, since they can visit marshes almost anytime. What these people say to the rest of us is that there is beauty to be discovered in this waterscape, beauty that can renew us like mountains and contain us like the sea.

I myself can never go to the salt marsh in quite the same way that I go to other places along the Sound. It is an open yet private world—part prairie, part water—with much of its life bound up in particles too small to notice or too quick to catch. The best that I can hope for is that the marsh may come to me, its power flooding my senses and enlarging my scope.

Though the habitat may be my civilization's last frontier, it is also the parent I have known forever. Its mood is both noisy and quiet, moving and still, comfortable and as alien as space. For the marsh is never one simple thing. It is the home of a glory I can see only from shifting angles, and of an alchemy that changes it from one instant to the next.

If I try to peel it back, to stir it or lay it bare in a straight-forward motion, I meet the ultimate paradox: more than any other estuarine environment the salt marsh, in addition to being a place and a process, is a metaphor for a state of mind. An ambiguity itself, it is a model for the human tolerance of ambiguities.

BARNACLES

In an 1849 letter Charles Darwin referred to his "beloved Barnacles." In 1852 he wrote: "I hate a Barnacle as no man ever did before."

In October 1968 U.S. pole vaulter Bob Seagren competed in the Mexico City Olympics. His run, his planting of the fiberglass pole, and his takeoff and swing propelled him across the bar feetfirst, in top form on his way to winning the gold. Seagren landed in the pit on his back, his feet once again in the air.

Earlier that same year an almond-shaped barnacle larva with a pair of rodlike feelers near its forward point drifted onto a boat hull in Long Island Sound. It planted the feelers on the vessel's fiberglass surface. The attachment up-ended the little animal, which shot its feet free and flipped its body over in stages. The larva slowly landed on its back near thousands of identical youngsters known as *Balanus balanoides*.

I love to breakfast with these barnacles on crisp fall days at the shore. The new adults have hit their stride by then, and the colonies' midsummer Grey Poupon tones have darkened to a warm maroon, thanks to blanketing algae. Often I sit on a south-facing boulder by a cove and savor the band of new color while I hug my knees to my chest through my father's old brown suede jacket. It holds the sun's warmth, which magnifies the mingled fragrance of briny backwater and my herbal shampoo. Out of habit I

Where do they come from, these barnacle houses like tide-zone dots?

tuck my nose inside the stand-up collar for a minute. Then I raise my head, bring a muffin to my mouth, and take a bite.

If the tide's in, the thousands of acorn barnacles stuck to the rocks around me use their feet to hustle more varied meals. Each hidden, shrimp-like animal lies upside down in its own limey tepee and pushes six pairs of jointed appendages through a valved hole and into the water. The feet repeatedly open and close in unison as if they were the fingers of a twelve-digit hand. This silent, come-hither motion sets up mini-currents, which deliver all manner of planktonic delicacies to the homes of the sessile crustaceans. The feet are reflected in the name of the subclass to which barnacles are assigned—Cirripedia. "Ped" means foot, and "cirri" means curl. Cirrus clouds take their name from the same Latin root.

When the tide recedes, the barnacles escape being fried and dried by sealing themselves inside the calcium-carbonate dwellings they've built. Like snowflakes, the half-inch-wide, nearly conical structures are all slightly different, though each has walls constructed of six plates. These toy building slabs intrigue me when I look down through a hand lens on their magnified forms. They could be stone petals set in a ring.

The plates also intrigued Charles Darwin, who, in the middle of the nineteenth century, devoted eight years—yes, eight—to the study of barnacles and barnacle residences. The writing that grew out of this research is still among the standard reference materials on the subject.

Darwin states emphatically that the highly variable plates are not reliable for identification purposes. "The discrimination of the species in most of the genera, offers very great difficulties," Darwin says. "I cannot too strongly impress on any one intending to study this class, not to trust to external characters."

No kidding. As I focus the lens carefully on several encrustations of padlocked houses, the plates appear as customized as handmade bricks. The ones that make up the crowded barnacle high-rises resemble jagged teeth. They're dramatically different from the broad, smooth plates of the ranch-style dwellings built by another species near the top of the splash zone.

And the numbers of homes around me! An easy million barnacle dwellings pave the entrance to this cove alone, in colonies that look more tightly packed than cells in a honeycomb. Yet the clusters seem to sprout from the stones at random. Where do they come from, these houses like tidezone dots? Did some would-be pointillist of the shore paint them into place?

The grown-up barnacles will never tell me. They unanimously slam their doors with a hiss whenever I come too near. No, the infant creatures hold the key to the origins of these tiny, chalky abodes. These larvae end an early planktonic lifestyle with their vaulting dance upon the rocks. Once they plant their poles, they're home to stay, in houses that metamorphose as magically as butterflies.

———

I spent last spring chasing barnacle babies, not exactly a daunting task until you consider the equipment required. The most important item was a microscope, which I hadn't used since college days with lab frogs. Tired of hearing me mirate over the joys and sorrows of barnacle life as the textbooks report it, a friend loaned me an ancient but perfectly adequate monocular model. "To see the little buggers for yourself."

Bob Bachand showed me how to get started. A former Norwalk dentist, Bob is also a writer and publisher, a diver, a daddy of saltwater aquariums, an architect of programming at both Save the Sound and The Maritime Aquarium at Norwalk. He is also a connoisseur of cereal bowls.

"This one's shaped best to hold what you want to see," he told me, fingering a shallow, heart-shaped glass bowl from my kitchen cabinet. It was actually part of a set of delicate ice cream dishes that had been passed down through my family. I doubt it had ever experienced mud pies being concocted in its vicinity, much less anything so crusty as experiments with barnacle larvae.

Billions of the larvae are hatched into Long Island Sound about mid-January, when life on land is still dormant except in the great horned owl's nest and the buds of pussy willow. The timing is no accident. It is coordinated with an early bloom of plant plankton (the larvae's food source), which sustains the drifting little creatures through six complete molts.

While I'm still stoking the fire and wrapping myself in blankets on the Ides of March, the naked larvae (called nauplii) are preparing to colonize the shoreline. In their final, pre-adult—or cyprid—stage they are, preposterously, less than one-twenty-fifth of an inch long. Fasting as they drop farther down in the water, they begin to wash in untold numbers onto anything hard—rocks, boat bottoms, and propellers, concrete breakwaters, wooden docks, mature barnacles—you name it. Nobody needs to tell yacht owners about their mass attachment.

I wanted to locate at least one cyprid in the act of gluing itself to a surface for life. Then I'd watch it grow up. That appeared straightforward enough, easier than training a puppy and a whole lot quicker, since the maturation from attachment to pinhead-sized adult takes only about twenty-four hours.

Bob and I gathered a blue mussel and some small stones from the lower intertidal zone and placed the mussel in the ice cream dish on the microscope's stage. We scotched it with two imported olive shells and used my bulb baster to transfer a little Sound water from a bucket into the dish.

I held the flashlight on the magnified bivalve while Bob

searched its surface. He spotted two live cyprids. But by the time he could show me how to zero in on their apricot translucence, the mussel was tossing and turning in its bowl. When I pushed back from the eyepiece, I could see its byssal threads, with which it was attaching itself to the olives that flanked it.

I tried enlarging the life on a dark stone, where cream-colored barnacle abodes stood out in contrast. Half a dozen well-housed adults could have passed for breathing volcanoes each time they opened and closed their valves in the water to feed. I could see only portions of them at once as their cirri swept across my circle of vision like overlapping snowstorms, soft and beautiful in their rhythmic advance and retreat.

The areas of the stone not colonized by the adults suggested battlefields strewn with bodies. Parched amber cyprids lay scattered on the slopes of miniature peaks like scabs.

As I rotated the ice cream dish, a series of quick, jerky motions came into focus. I'd found a live larva, one that was poking at the ruins of a limey house with the two antennae at the front of its body. Six pairs of short legs thrust out behind it worked almost like fish fins to propel the nosy little creature. There was the barest hint of internal organs—a white dorsal dot that moved in tandem with the busybusy feet.

The larva rushed and jabbed at the house in a frenzy until it dislodged the dwelling from its base and sent the six plates, still hooked together, flapping through the water. Since *B. balanoides* obviously prefers living close to others of its kind, this cyprid may have been responding to a homing call from the limestone, to the chemical command "Settle here!"

The particulars of their homesteading fascinate scientists.

They paint slates with the boiled extracts of various barnacle species and test who's attracted to what goo. In 1975 two European researchers found that "cyprids of *B. balanoides* settled in greater numbers on their own extract in the ratio 2:1."

Rachel Carson comments on the barnacle as finicky real estate client in *The Edge of the Sea*.

> The settling down of a barnacle larva is not a haphazard process, but is performed only after a period of seeming deliberation. Biologists who have observed the act in the laboratory say the larvae "walk" about on the substratum for as long as an hour, pulling themselves along by the adhesive tips of the antennae, testing and rejecting many possible sites before they make a final choice. In nature they probably drift along in the currents for many days, coming down, examining the bottom at hand, then drifting on to another.

Once it finally chooses an address (who really knows how?), the barnacle begins its lifelong athletic feat. The larva glues itself down by releasing cement, in peristaltic waves, through the front feelers. I actually saw a cyprid go through this. It held its neat little form almost straight up and down, like a swollen exclamation mark; then it pulsed in place.

I was afraid to risk concentrating on this single cyprid while I ignored all the others. Yet I couldn't find a barnacle in the next stage, when the attached larva starts to flatten itself and really hug its stone. The stages that I did see were impossible to sequence. That amorphous blob rocking itself awake on its slightly milky base—was it older or younger than the lighter-colored blob next to it? Both resembled the profile of an asymmetrical, fleshy sombrero. Something underneath jostled the hats a little.

Once, a brim was lifted just enough to tease me about what was going on inside. But the heads that wore these live sombreros were the stones themselves. I'd have to move inside those stones and look out in order to see the post-attachment sleight-of-hand.

"Glass," posited Eric Lazo-Wasem of Yale's Peabody Museum of Natural History. "Get the cyprids to stick to glass instead of to stone. Perhaps you can turn the glass over and see what's happening inside the little creatures."

Of course.

A local plate-glass company graciously supplied me with some four-inch glass squares, which I wedged into crevices between barnacle-encrusted stones at low tide. Then I waited for the cyprids to swim aboard.

Two complete tidal cycles and an irrepressible optimism sent me and my sloshing bucket back up the hill with enough barnacle-coated glass to fill days of flashlight-held, elbow-padded observation. As before, I located several gelatinous, freshly battened-down larvae, which I examined from above and below.

But the joke was on me. *Balanus* are the ultimate introverts, becoming opaque soon after they attach, so that even a bottoms-up view reveals no more than slightly oval closed shops. One cloudy membranous base was laced with what I presume was cement oozing in both directions from a common point. The two ends bypassed, and the center began to fill, in a pattern that resembled a jagged coastline. And that was that.

On the flip side of the glass an orange broth bubbled between two undifferentiated ridges of ruddy pink. I was looking straight down through the developing doors of a barnacle's house, doors that would calcify while I was off brushing my teeth or combing my hair. For now, however, there was only this full-lipped peephole, beyond which I could see not a single change in the adult that was imminent. The tiny sign nearby read POSTED.

———

Years ago a friend told me that she admired the survival instincts of the cockroaches that took over her Manhattan kitchen at night. She rose early and often found the insects making off with her sugar, her cheese. She didn't try to stop them. She simply watched. From my well-scrubbed, perfumed lair I thought, How strange!

Now I hear her. Barnacles are no cinch to love, either. I try to pry their remains from odd angles on my boat hull with scrapers and the heaviest screwdriver I own, sorry I've let another winter go by without purchasing some shares of Band-Aid.

Like roaches, these animals are here to stay, washing ashore as fragile larvae and then moving onto their backs for three to five years, maybe longer, in the hard houses I cannot see them build. The hermaphroditic youths have long penises that can bend like hospital straws. They send these members out the open doors of their own abodes and into their neighbors' chambers. Then they bear fragile larvae of their own. Two springs from now, awestruck, I'll drop my jaw on a hundred grandchildren at once.

Barnacles are the smallest units of intertidal life I can see. I need my 8x loupe and a greater gift for winking just to make them out during the few weeks of their spring shore wash. It's not until mid-May that the rosy-green cast they lend the stones can be broken down into separate items I note with my naked eye. They're on the cusp, these creatures, between the visible and invisible worlds, a unique reminder of all the dancing matter that makes up the cosmos.

Yet the tiny adult, which in some ways resembles a soggy Rice Krispie, is very intricately formed. It has a brain and photoreceptive organs and a well-developed digestive system and a circulatory system (though not a heart!). That such a lot of perfectly differentiated matter comes wrapped in a tiny package strikes me as nothing short of miraculous. Thoreau said nature "spends her whole genius on the least work." And I respond, What better least work than this to bespeak the detailed mystery that lies at the very heart of things?

I've undergone some major changes in my life. But proportionately, none seems as profound as the culmination of a barnacle's routine metamorphosis. No change has stopped me in my tracks forever, transforming me from a gypsy into a permanent resident. None has altered the very posture from which I operate in the world, or given me the means to secrete my own home, or taught me how to harvest food with the limbs I'd used for walking. It's the magnitude of the change that grabs me. I think it always will.

ISLANDS

"Whether for diversion of thought or for the easing of the physical body, men demand mental periods, points of reference, islands fixed in the turbulence of giant waters, or, if eluding the compass, still haunting the mind."

—Loren Eiseley
from the introduction to
Galápagos: The Flow of Wildness

"Island." The very word is magic. Silent *s*. Accentuated *I*. Accentuated "eye," a magnifying glass placed over a parcel of earth removed from the mainland as a dot above the letter *i* is separated from a word. "Aye" to the islands of the Sound, which are small enough to sustain the illusion of being comprehensible: *I*-lands.

The estuary's islands are found primarily along the north shore. The three prominent chains are the Captain, Norwalk, and Thimble Islands, all off Connecticut. The first two of these support colonies of herons and other large birds, which relocate as conditions change. In 1993, for instance, raccoons inexplicably showed up on Norwalk's Chimon Island, which is only one-tenth of a square mile; and the birds began moving elsewhere to nest without the harassment. Some colony members went to Cockenoe, another island in the Norwalk chain. Others headed west and took up residence on Great Captain Island, off Greenwich. Since then many of Chimon's raccoons have been trapped and released elsewhere. In another year or two the interior of Chimon will probably be predator-free again. Then it can host thousands of nesting colonial waterbirds, as it did formerly.

In addition to these chains, about two dozen individual, named islands span the estuary's length. They include Hart and City Islands close to New York's buzz, and Pea, Huckleberry, Glen, and Davids Islands, a little farther to the northeast. Falkner Island and Mason Island lie nearer the eastern end of the Sound. At a mile and a half long and half a mile wide, Mason is the largest separate island near the upper shore, save for nearby Fishers and Great Gull Islands, which constitute segments of the Sound's boundary.

This smattering of islands doesn't take into account the numerous intertidal rocks that cartographers note but that inexperienced boaters often ignore until they slam into them at mid-tide. A nameless drumstick of land in front of my house is one of these. At all hours it produces sudden, loud complaints—primarily the scrape of metal and wood across an unforgiving plane, though occasionally also invectives that carry across the water into my living room.

Like the estuary itself, the Sound's islands and would-be islands are extremely varied. The Norwalk and Captain chains as well as Falkner Island are glacial in origin, and their unstable margins seem to shift with each rise and fall of the tides. The Thimbles, off Branford, are made up predominantly of pink granite. The Statue of Liberty, in fact, stands on granite quarried from the area. The archipelago of three small islands known as The Fish possesses both glacial and bedrock characteristics. It attracts me most, not only because it's close to home, but also because the variety of its physical features seems to be mirrored in other aspects of the place. The Fish represents one extreme of island life in the Sound.

Bedrock like that of the mainland shapes The Fish's contours. This bedrock *was* the mainland before a rising sea level separated it from the current shore. Since then, the stone has trapped so many pockets of sand that the outcrops look like elbows poking through the holes of old sweater arms.

Some of The Fish's fringes have developed fragile marshes with hip-high peat, and I'm careful where I walk. In spring the soil sends up spiky *Spartina* and the spatulate leaves of sea lavender. On the island farthest from shore are basswood trees. Their height serves to identify this small island cluster from afar.

The stone, sand, marshes, pools, and trees of The Fish all grade in and out of one another like watercolors left in the rain. They create such a diversity of outdoor spaces that the place attracts practically everyone—children and kayakers and small-craft sailors, genial picnickers (the regulars) who treat The Fish's sandy beaches as their own front porch, and unrepentant lazybones who lather up in sunscreen and doze in anchored speedboats. All take the salt breeze right along with the gulls and egrets. And all seem oblivious to the tombstone-like marker that reads:

PRIVATE

PROPERTY

NO TRESPASSING

NO FIRES   NO HUNTING

NO CAMPING

NO LITTERING

VIOLATORS MAY BE PROSECUTED

NO

DOGS

OWNER

1995–6

But today it is quiet, and I am both spectator and character in The Fish's ongoing show. From where Steve and I sit in the Whaler, I spot an oversized, slightly faded baby-blue umbrella with its fluted edges turned inside out by the wind. It clashes with the blue-green haze of sky. Someone has driven the umbrella's long shaft at an angle into a hollow of sand near stones, shells, and peat. Three hours after flood tide this island still glistens.

Beneath the umbrella sit two adjacent beach chairs vertically striped in navy and purple; a towel stark in its whiteness is draped across the four arms. Two large black dogs with plumes for tails chase nearby. Their owners, a man and a woman who have been rearranging items in a large ice chest, squint and wave to us. "Nice day." They smile through teeth as they start to saunter toward the island's far side. We watch their knees and waists, then their bare shoulders and heads, disappear over a ridge.

We've been anchored in this water for an hour and, in a falling tide, are now ten feet from the closest spot of land. We've breakfasted on cereal and fruit. Between us we've read five sections of the Sunday *Times*. We've let out several feet of line to avoid nudging the rocks that are becoming increasingly exposed close to shore. We're getting hot.

Steve dips a black coffee mug over the side, lifts two tiny crabs and some water from near the Sound's surface, and tilts the miniature pool to see if the crabs will stop swimming around its rim. They do. When he holds the mug level again, the crabs, which are only half an inch wide, sally from one ceramic side to the opposite one, then appear to ricochet off the curved surface in between. One of them soon resumes its many-legged dance inside the circumference. The other seems disoriented. Steve returns the

The islands of the Sound are small enough to sustain the illusion of being comprehensible

crabs to the water, then peers into the darkness of the mug to see if, in fact, both are gone.

Four American oystercatchers, apparently agitated over the dogs' presence in their rightful territory, have been wheeling and piping around us. Their separate, high-pitched *Peek, peek, eek, eek, eek*'s gather and accelerate until a torrent of sound, then another and another, pours from the circling foursome. Much smaller birds had flown in earlier. And in the process of starting to land, a snowy egret had chased fish, apparently without making a catch. The bird's feet were in water no longer than thirty seconds before the snowy lifted off, ephemeral and lithe.

I settle with a cushion at my back, my face to the sun. What were the tips of rocks an hour ago have now become islands to two dozen herring gulls. Like us, each of the gulls has claimed a particular spot. On an islet just fifty yards from our anchor one gull turns itself inside out with preening. Another flies along a length of land to a point, pinches its bill around a blue mussel, and returns in our direction. It drops the shell onto the island's hard spine—*thwock*. The shell fails to crack. The gull, who floats down after it, rises with it once again. Four drops accompanied by four solid sounds are required to break the bivalve open. The bird gobbles up the flesh inside.

When I first moved to the Sound, I was surprised by whole or partial bivalve shells lying on lawns that extend to the water. Also by the warty carapaces of spider crabs on rocks along the shore, and by the crabs' jointed legs. The soft internal tissue of these prey animals had long since dried or been plucked, until all I saw were dining tables littered with hard remains. (Herring gulls don't usually drop spider crabs to break them open, but pick them up by one leg and then another until they shake the creatures apart.)

The gulls' shell-cracking habits are keenly refined. The birds make their drops from heights determined by the size of the hard surface beneath them. Above parking lots, for instance, gulls fly high and release the shells where they will. Above small areas of stone such as those around us, where they can't risk losing their treasures, the birds fly quite low. Seldom have I seen a herring gull abandon a bivalve it has found, though I am still not sure why some shells end up on cushiony lawns. (One expert offers the explanation that it takes gulls a long time to learn to drop on hard surfaces.)

The Sunday activity seems leisurely for quite some time. Once I look up to try to match a soft cluck with its owner, only to realize I am hearing human voices drift out over the peat and grasses. Yet somewhere in the seemingly calm narrative a curious subplot is unfolding. A dust-brown gull, its neck hunched into its bullet body, is pecking the bill of another, less-submissive-looking bird. The creature has all the appeal of an ogre, and the white-and-gray gull it pesters is trying to ignore it. But the ogre persists as it stands within the widening band of seaweed that camouflages it. It repeats its urgent, plaintive call—*Klee-ee, klee-ee, klee-ee.*

In all probability, the dark gull is the sullen child of the mature bird, and hungry. Only a few months old, it is in the awkward position of still needing to beg for food. Interestingly, its shrill pleadings are almost identical to those emitted by female herring gulls as they solicit food from potential mates. The ritualized feeding between consenting adults helps to cement the pair bond.

Earlier in the century Dutch naturalist Niko Tinbergen discovered that newly hatched herring gulls demand food by pecking at the red spot on their parents' yellow bill. The parent responds by regurgitating semidigested fish, mollusks, and carrion, though urban gulls may feed their young from landfills, which are diminishing in this region. The culinary interchanges continue until well after the young have fledged and begun to assume the demeanor of this whining adolescent, when the parents often lose patience with the entire procedure. Then the chicks (if such overgrown birds can still be called chicks) are forced to begin finding food on their own. It is a critical transition for the inexperienced gulls, and about a third of them don't survive.

This particular beggar, meeting no sympathy, soon

abandons its imploring song and posture in favor of a stroll
into the shallows. It sinks its head beneath the surface and
tips its body straight up, like a mallard. When it rights itself,
it has a large clamshell in its beak and appears utterly confounded by what to do with it.

I shift my gaze from the frustrated youngster to a scene
that is beginning to appear frenzied. Floating gulls that have
just eaten repeatedly dip their bills in the shallows, cleaning
them of small food particles. A fight breaks out between
two gulls on a patch of stony wetness. The aggressor clamps
the other bird's beak in its own and begins to tug. Both
birds are screaming and flapping their wings as they pull
against each other with their whole bodies. The attacker
drags its victim several feet. After three or four minutes,
the two gulls abruptly part. Neither looks much the worse
for the encounter. Who won?

Most of gulldom's hierarchical social structure is established and maintained by means of just such fierce-looking
yet relatively harmless jousts. This is not to say that the
birds don't injure one another. But more often than not,
the skirmishes, like some of the gullish calls I hear around
me throughout the day, are warnings that stave off fatal
conflict.

Herring gulls, who have nested in the Sound only since
1942, are one of two resident gull species. The other is the
enormous and handsome great black-backed gull. But
these two are not the only gulls we see. My favorite non-
nesters by far are the laughing gulls, who are seated quite
demurely now on their own Sunday Grand Jatte. Though
their laugh can approach hysterics, everything else about
the birds seems refined. As they float, they balance far forward on their breasts with their black tails held up at a
dramatic angle. Often they look like nineteenth-century

ladies in bustles, especially as they adjust their wings over their posteriors soon after they come to rest on the water. All that's missing to complete Seurat's famous scene is a dark, hand-held parasol tucked under a primary feather. I look back at the blue umbrella on shore.

———

From the waters off Guilford, Connecticut, Falkner Island looks like a whale. Its blowhole spews a constant stream of stone, brick, and mortar—a 41-foot-high lighthouse that, while now automated, has nevertheless been continuously active for almost two centuries. Unless the island's eroding ridges can be reinforced within the next few years, the landmark tower will fall down an unvegetated, east-facing slope of glacial debris and across a flat margin of stones into Long Island Sound.

Up close Falkner Island looks beige and white. On this three-acre unit of the Stewart B. McKinney National Wildlife Refuge, every exposed piece of clothing, every bared strand of hair, every bedroll, thumb, neck, shoe that shows up in summer is sooner or later coaxed into the color scheme. The island hosts breeding colonies of terns, 3,000 pairs of common terns and another 150 pairs of the endangered roseate terns. Well-aimed beige-and-white guano, precision dive-bombing, and repetitive calls like shrill machine-gun reports are the birds' natural defenses against intruders who threaten their young.

A ladder attached to a wharf offers access to Falkner Island's west side from a boat. Common terns, who fish from the waters I've just crossed, don't wait for people to reach the top rung before they fire their unmistakable messages. I dashed to the haven of a nearby shed. Splotched

hard hats hung on walls there. Some had bandannas attached to their back rims. The fabric was stiff with guano,
and it reeked. I threw on a plastic poncho, put on the hard
hat with the longest tail, and drew the poncho's hood
around my cheeks as tightly as I could. Then I set out after
the smiling young researchers with whom I'd made the
three-mile crossing.

We started up a path that wound through a sloping
meadow. Orange tongue depressors stuck out of the soil
in several places along the path's edges to mark tern nesting
sites. The bright color was necessary: mottled fluffballs that
hunched in the scrapes matched their surroundings so
completely that they disappeared. By the time we reached
the building at the path's end, I had served as a bull's-eye
five times and narrowly avoided crushing two newly
hatched chicks beneath my boots. That hike left no doubt
as to whom Falkner Island belongs. It made me wonder
how far from the easygoing, all-inclusive mood of The Fish
a person can travel in only a few steps.

I observed concentrated nests through holes in walls.
Large squared openings without glass or screens serve as
windows in the converted Coast Guard engine house that
constitutes the research station. Terns had built almost
all the way around the structure. Two nests lay just outside
the doorway that leads to and from the sun showers and
the unplumbed toilet facilities (there is no running water
or electricity on the island). Any significant movement inside the main building—even snapping photos from well
within the doorway—resulted in a rising din. Only when
all six of us who shared the one-room space remained
relatively still and quiet did the outside screaming lessen.
Even then, and throughout the night, it never completely
stopped.

The island's two species of tern (*Sterna* spp.) are so similar that it takes a well-trained eye to distinguish them. Both are approximately the size of a flicker or similar woodpecker. Breeding adults wear black caps on beautiful, sleek white heads, have tails forked like barn swallows', and show light-gray backs—if the neutral color can be seen as the birds dive headfirst after fish. This is a big "if." Terns are mercurial. They hover one second and drop out of binoculars the next. This means, for me at least, that the common's orange beak and the roseate's nearly black one (its telltale feature) must be spotted while the birds are at rest or it's no use.

Somehow, in spite of the filth and nervous rancor and similarity of birds, the Falkner Island Tern Project is a marvel of efficiency and dedication. If it wasn't, both species of tern on this jot of land might face a future as tenuous as that of the Falkner Island lighthouse. Wildlife biologist Dr. Jeffrey Spendelow, who directs the project's cooperative research, has devoted himself to these creatures since 1980. The data he has amassed and analyzed, along with the concentration of nesters, make this sanctuary (closed to the public) one of the most important on the entire East Coast. Developed waterfront property on the mainland has left little nesting habitat for terns, and herring gulls often claim the appropriate sites first. All of Connecticut's roseate terns and two-thirds of Connecticut's common terns depend on this one National Wildlife Refuge.

The bulk of what Jeff and his associates do on Falkner Island, in work that sometimes stretches into twelve-hour days, involves counting and banding both tern species. Jeff, a hardy-looking man in his forties, goes into the field clad in a hat, a T-shirt, and jeans that have belt loops threaded with the free ends of two long cloth bags. The bags contain the essentials—bands, pliers, calipers. Other pouches hold specialized scales. When Jeff walks, the weighty bags look like orioles' nests in motion.

Jeff doesn't walk, however, as much as he stands, kneels, crouches, and lies flat on the ground while he reaches into one recently set wire-mesh trap after another to gather a bird. Carefully he measures the tern's weight, overall length, wing length, and bill size. He also notes eggs and chicks, plus features or habits that might seem to merit further study. He or someone around him records all this on index cards, each assigned to an individual nest. After Jeff has assessed the condition of a previously unmarked adult, he places an official U.S. Fish and Wildlife band around one thin leg and a carefully noted series of color bands around the other. This second banding is the researchers' way of fingerprinting the birds in order to identify them through binoculars or a telescope, now and perhaps in later seasons.

Banding results have shown that fledged roseate terns don't return to Falkner Island until they reach breeding age, which is usually after three or four years. The results have also shown a trend that excites Jeff when he talks about it: there has been increased nesting success among roseate terns who have adopted the one hundred or so old rubber tires to which Jeff has introduced them.

Unlike common terns, roseates like having some way to conceal themselves while they're nesting. After Jeff found a pair of roseates settled into a tire that had washed onshore, he began paying attention to how well their youngsters fared in the rubber homes. Now the collection of tires, with lips held apart by stones, looks like a beach full of huge chocolate doughnuts erratically iced in white.

Erosion control for the Falkner Island lighthouse is being

designed to incorporate more nesting spots attractive to the roseates, only without the tires. Huge rocks will be jumbled and fitted into the base of the disappearing cliff in such a way that crevices will be created. Above them, where winter waves splash ten to twenty feet into the air, smaller rocks will go in at the most advantageous angle. The hope is that the roseates will find this man-made environment as attractive as the one Jeff was able to provide.

I did not have a spiritual experience on Falkner Island. Quite the opposite. Yet I'm not sorry I spent twenty-four hours there. On Falkner I gained some understanding of what serious research biologists undergo in order to contribute to a body of knowledge. As George Reiger points out in his book *Wanderer on My Native Shore*:

> Wildlife research is glamorous stuff to read about in an armchair where such realities as heat, biting insects, grime, improvised food, and disappointment—the constant disappointment of missed opportunities and simple misjudgment—do not intrude on the coolly worded summaries. Nor do wildlife reports provide many clues to the years of grueling effort that sometimes go into a single insight.

For a moment, I also shared the world of a creature utterly different from myself who, despite superhuman effort and imagination, is disappearing from this part of the earth. Already, maps that show where roseate terns still exist on the North American continent have more bare space in them than I care to think about. Falkner Island, Bird and Ram Islands in Massachusetts, and Great Gull Island at the tip of Long Island's north fork now make up the vast majority of this bird's North American nesting range.

How did it come to this? Roseate terns, more elegant than the unthreatened common terns, are not as feisty. They typically produce one egg to the common's two. Yet roseate chicks, being sheltered, are not as vulnerable to predation as the common's exposed offspring, and roseates appear to derive defense benefits from associating with their more aggressive cousins.

Cape Cod environmentalist John Hay, a chronicler of terns, accounts for a portion of the decline as follows. Off Ghana, in Africa, he reports, roseates are offered as food in markets after being "caught with snares set along a beach, or by means of a hook and line with fish as bait."

Hay speaks of terns as if what is happening to them is a magnification of mainland phenomena, as is often the case with island creatures.

> The dispossession of terns [he writes in *The Bird of Light*] reflects a new and dangerous volatility in the earth environment. Populations forced out of synchronization with their habitats and sources of food have an unstable base to depend on. This is also true of us, who are both the cause and the victims of widespread, global displacement, and are only beginning to recognize that this round world and its spatially balanced communities of life is the only foundation for whatever stability we can claim for ourselves.

In contemplating this avian species, whose disappearance would signal a loss of beauty as well as one more nick in the world's armor of biodiversity, I realize that I am linked to the terns of Falkner Island through something as simple and as complex as the globe's uninterrupted margins. Hay calls these birds "untiring, restless explorers of an earth which has always sustained them." Even if the progeny of the Falkner roseates can hold on a while longer in their insular world, I have little doubt that the birds' ultimate fate is, as Hay suggests, a preview of my own species'. And that my species' notions of a planetary island are often not even acknowledged.

Will we let these feathered creatures go? Have I told them goodbye?

TIDES

"This is the late morning and early afternoon marine weather broadcast for Watch Hill, Rhode Island, to Montauk Point, to Manasquan Inlet, New Jersey, and twenty nautical miles offshore including Long Island Sound . . . The following are some selected high tides for the local area that will be occurring later today: Sandy Hook, New Jersey, high tide will occur at 5:01 p.m.; Willets Point, New York, at 9:25 p.m.; and Montauk Point, New York, at 5:28 p.m."

Twice a day tides visit the shores of Long Island Sound. Their arrivals and departures change their host land visibly, by the moment. The mood of a meadow can alter dramatically from dawn to dusk, but in Jackson, Mississippi, the land itself doesn't shrink and grow.

Consider this. I wake up about 6 a.m. and go straight to the telescope at the front window. Connecting two of the nearby islands is a sand bridge obvious only at dead low tide. Three great black-backed gulls parade across it between internecine squabbles over a sea star. I zoom the lens to full power. Through the circular eyepiece I watch two of the sea star's arms flail from the beak of the largest bird.

I go to make coffee, grumbling because no one emptied yesterday's grounds and washed the cone filter. I do both, get the new coffee chugging and dripping, spill some water on the counter, mop it up, slide a mug in front of me, and lift the pot from its metal base. I inhale as I pour.

The first sip is hot and strong.

I make a couple of halfhearted notes while I wait for the jolt that comes with the third or fourth mouthful. Then I return to the window. The scene has changed. The gulls and sea star are gone, which is not surprising. But the sand bridge across which they padded has also vanished. No sign of it.

How do I deal with this on the page? I can't find the right pronoun for the land around me. It can't be an "it," which implies constancy and continuity. "I love it" or "I see it" involves an objective case that stays put, or at least stays visible. Is the ground a "them," which acknowledges the minute-by-minute mutability of the islands in my view? This will lead to trouble. The islands, plural, are already a "them," a shorthand archipelago. How will I distinguish between this "them" and the upstart one?

The problem is not really one of number. It lies in my early perception of tides. Being a landlubber, I watched land shrink and swell when I went to the shore. I didn't see water rise and fall.

The Sound has slowly changed me. Now I focus on the liquid. Its margins slop onto mainland and island stones like lapdogs that rush a vacant sofa. They leap. They're not allowed to stay.

The dramatically low tide I saw was a full-moon tide, properly known as a spring tide. Though the typical tidal range for my segment of the Sound is a few inches over seven feet, twice a month, under full and new moons, that range expands to almost nine feet. The two-foot difference may not sound very dramatic. But the water it represents entirely redefines the upper and lower margins of land that make up the intertidal zone. The coastal rock on which I lounged through yesterday's flood tide may be completely submerged by a higher flood today. At flood tide tomorrow or the next day the stone may be visible again, but it will feel different to me—borrowed, almost. Or as if it had just returned from a realm to which I will never travel. This ongoing capacity of the moon to change the very shape of continents, through power over the waters that lap at their shores, has been the single most astounding aspect of my life on the Sound.

The moon's gravitational pull is the primary cause of the rise and fall of tides. When the full or new moon is directly over the Sound, her waters are high. This is as easily observed as the disappearance of the low-tide sand bridge. During the ebb I can read in the width of the dark band marking intertidal stones exactly how far the water has fallen. Even on grasses where there are no stones, the tide records its visits in ribbons of contrasting color. On sand it leaves a twisting line of natural and man-made debris.

After a high tide the Sound rotates out from under the moon's direct pull. If the tide is high beneath a 6 a.m. moon, for instance, it is low by about midday, high again in early evening, and low after midnight. The earth continues to rotate and completes its course by six the following morning. But the moon will not be waiting for the Sound in the previous morning's spot. It will have moved on in the same general direction the Sound moved, though not nearly so fast.

The moon requires about twenty-nine and a half days (a lunar month) to make its elliptical swing around the earth. At this rate it makes a little more than 3 percent of the journey approximately every twenty-four hours. By 6 a.m. on that second day, then, the earth must pursue the moon through that 3 percent rotation before the Sound can experience the next high tide. The earth's daily chase of the moon, her "catch-up time," takes about fifty minutes, or just under an hour. This explains why high tide occurs almost an hour later on any given day than it did on the day before. What's referred to as a complete diurnal tidal cycle (the time required to return the Sound and the moon to the position from which they started) is twenty-four hours and fifty minutes, or just under twenty-five hours.

When strong gravitational pull causes a high tide to occur on the side of the world facing the moon, an equally strong centrifugal force causes another high tide to occur on the world's opposite side. If I could dig all the way through the earth from the Sound, I would encounter this second high tide. Imagine the Sound's tide as one of a pair of twins born of the moon but never allowed to see its distant sibling!

During full and new moons, earth, sun, and moon are all aligned. Then the sun's gravitational force is added directly to the moon's. This makes high tides even higher than normal and low tides even lower.

The effects of the moon's gravitational pull on our planet are strongest when moon and earth are closest to each other, and this also contributes to tidal height. The mega-tug that results then produces what are known as perigee tides, the dimensions of which rival those of full- and new-moon tides. At the other extreme—that is, when the moon is farthest from earth—the natural satellite exerts its weakest pull and so-called apogee tides result. Most tide charts note these opposite configurations, which occur about two weeks apart.

The mid-December floods of 1992, which played havoc with coastal communities all around the Sound, were brought about by a combination of meteorological forces (winds and low atmospheric pressure) plus an astronomical configuration that included both a perigee tide and a full moon. In instances when these two phenomena occur at exactly the same time, perigee and full (or new) moon can cause a high tide that is as much as 40 percent greater than normal. In 1992 the two occurred only four days apart, along with a lingering northeaster, and the Sound's tides were as much as five feet above the norm. An issue of *The New York Times* printed during this period included a statement from a commuter stranded in the city by the freak winter conditions. Disgruntled over the breakdown in public transportation, he said, "If we can go to the Moon . . . why can't we get these things right?"

———

Though the global patterns of tidal influence are fixed by astronomical forces, the tides of a given area are complex due to local winds, currents, basin depth, coastline shape, and other variables. Not all places around the world even experience two daily tides. The Sound has two of approximately equal height, and they come and go, go and come, with regularity. Right now I can predict the stage of "my" tide for eight o'clock on Christmas morning four years hence. I even know that nineteen years from now the alignment of sun, earth, and moon will be exactly the same as today, and that the entire cycle will begin again.

To recognize this cosmological dependability is more than just a convenient way to plot the hours when there will be enough water in the Sound for me to reach certain places by boat. To recognize it is to acknowledge a dimension of existence far wider than any I have measured my life against before. Tides are numbers recorded in charts I consult as frequently as I consult calendars and clocks. But they are also the very essence of change within constancy and constancy within predictable change.

Steve tailors tidal behavior to the Sound through a quirky demonstration.

"This is Greenwich," he says. Facing me, he points to my left at a closed book that he balances on its spine on the dining-room table. "This is The Race." On my right he touches what was the stiff backing of a legal pad.

"Here comes high tide." My husband has drawn a breastlike hump on a sheet of paper that he shows me. A child's sailboat looks precariously balanced on the top of the wave. The chest and diaphragm above and below the wave, he assures me, represent two low tides.

Steve slides the sheet of paper slowly along the tabletop from the cardboard Race—at the Sound's eastern end—to the bookish Greenwich, in the west. When the wave he has drawn reaches its destination, he reverses the direction of the sheet. This sends the wave, which in reality is of much longer proportion than he has suggested, all the way back to the Sound's easternmost point. "That double movement takes twelve hours," he announces, "coincidentally almost exactly the length of time of one complete tidal cycle. If the Sound stretched to Pennsylvania, twenty hours might be required for water leaving The Race to reach the estuary's narrow westernmost end. The tides in the Sound would function far less smoothly then, since some tidal currents would be moving east while others were moving west.

"Tides become higher in the western Sound," my teacher continues, "because by the time the water gets there it essentially has nowhere to go, and it piles up on itself. The pinched shape of the western end also contributes to the higher levels."

Dr. Malcolm Bowman, professor of physical oceanography at the State University of New York at Stony Brook, calls the result of this coincidental timing "tidal resonance." He likens the phenomenon to a child's swing being pushed in harmony with its own natural rhythm, and he states, "The size of the Sound is just right for resonance to occur; its natural period matches that of the ocean tide."

———

The moon's reflection in water is a popular image in Japanese literature. As Gwenn Boardman Petersen states in *The Moon in the Water*, "Every literate Japanese knows the words . . . 'The moon is one, the reflections two' and 'to dip up the reflected moon.' " In Buddhist literature, Petersen continues, the moon in the water connotes a thing of no substance, as in the Zen poem in which two monkeys "are reaching/For the moon in the water." Yet the student of Zen, being open to paradox, is encouraged to interpret these words in a way that grants the reflected moon its own reality.

Petersen writes that even "in today's transistorized and skyscrapered Japan, businessmen, housewives, and students occasionally hold autumn moon-viewing parties and write haiku while they listen to insects . . . The 'progressive' may scorn the habit as old-fashioned and artificial," she says, "but the department stores on Tokyo's Ginza still do a thriving trade in chirping insects."

I cannot imagine a more synergistic activity than this moon watch. It engages several human senses and combines a social event with the composition of private verse. We who live along the Sound experience something comparable to this, if without the haiku, whenever we gather to look out across moonlit waters.

One night in July, Steve and I sailed into our cove just as the moon rose to sew a liquid, melon-colored train onto our boat rudder. Several parties of people who were not there when we had departed an hour earlier relaxed on sloops and cruisers. On one vessel a silhouetted figure was smoking a cigarette. I watched its tip glow red when the person inhaled, then traced its downward arc as the smoker's hand descended.

Occasional laughs spilled from boats that were trailing us in, but by the time we moored, we could hear no human sound in the hush that had fallen. The moon was shining twice—once in the sky above us, from where it lit our opened faces, and once as it swam toward us and slowly silvered the world.

What draws us into these mute pods of observation? Is it the moon's beauty alone? A quarter of a century after men pawed the surface of earth's only natural satellite, took her temperature and brought back her stones, that beauty remains unblemished. Certainly it is great enough to hold us, as it has held every culture on earth—from the Celts with their moon-rich mythology to the followers of Siddhartha awakened as the Buddha the morning after a full moon.

Less obviously perhaps, the moon is also the source of a great and rhythmic refreshment we can feel. The twice-daily tides of the Sound cause an astonishing volume of water to move in and out of the estuary—a volume roughly equal to that of 7,500 fifty-story office buildings. Since horseshoe crabs, barnacles, and many other creatures respond to the moon's gravitational pull, surely we must also feel the tug, though we may not always be able to voice its effect on our lives.

Even living things cut off from tidal cycles may still em-

Like lapdogs that rush a vacant sofa, tides leap but are not allowed to stay

body those cycles in some way. In 1980 writer Dava Sobel was isolated for twenty-five days in a sleep laboratory at Montefiore Hospital in the Bronx. Living in windowless, clockless surroundings, Sobel was given time for her body to establish its own most basic rhythms of wakefulness and rest. After an initial period of adjustment she began waking an hour later each day than she had the day before. Left on her own, Sobel adopted a twenty-five-hour day, the day of the moon. She was not the first to do so under the same circumstances.

This suggests that the lunar lineage of our very cells is more intrinsic to our lives than we might think. It implies that we may even be on the wrong schedule when we build all our days around the sun's glare. Salt tides' embrace of the land's margins and the land's acceptance of that advance tap out a beat on the globe, a Mon-day rhythm played against Sun-day time. The mix is jazz, like the syncopation of our own breaths and heartbeats. It rewards careful listening. And the voice heard above it in the wingbeat of swans, in the kingfisher's rant and the gull's cry, is the ancient voice of flux, forever new.

AFTERWORD

The word "strandloper," of Dutch origin, refers to a band of people who once wandered parts of the South African shore. Their diet consisted mostly of shellfish from the strand, the ribbon of coastline that becomes exposed at low tide. Anthropologist Phillip Tobias gives us a picture of them "hunting in rock pools and along the foaming wave edges and in the water." *The Illustrated History of South Africa* paints a less attractive portrait, referring to them as outcasts and rabble who "scraped a living wherever they could find it."

Negative depictions notwithstanding, strandlopers have something very positive to tell those of us who follow a progressive lifestyle near today's Long Island Sound. For whatever else they may or may not have been, strandlopers were undoubtedly well attuned to the habits and rhythms of marine phenomena—tides and seasons, the richness of ocean shores, the life cycles of certain animal species. Developing similar sensitivities among ourselves may ultimately be essential to the continuation of the life of the Sound, as it has become essential to the continuation of the life on much of the rest of the planet.

I sometimes try to capture a contemporary strandloper ideal in a tangible form, by toying with a large Möbius strip I've made and illustrated with stick figures in tableau. My strandlopers celebrate their shared livelihood along the curving strip's unexpected single surface. There are Lycra-clad women and men plucking edible mussels from rocks that shine through the shallows. The blue of the shells in sunlight dazzles them, and the slender boatlike valves fit themselves neatly into the cupped hands of children splashing along in neon sneakers. Nearby a solitary swimmer is jarred by a collision of sounds—the osprey's *Yewk* and the kingfisher's throaty rattle. The swimmer stops stroking and looks up.

It is necessary for me to own a scene such as this, a scene of modern people in harmony with their waterside environment. Without it I feel overwhelmed and powerless in the face of a continuing emphasis, in some quarters, on the Sound's demise. My updated strandloper vision offsets the gloom and empowers me. It doesn't permit me to indulge in naïve wishful thinking, or to lose myself in the romance of the image itself. Rather, it shows me possibilities, goals, glimmerings of the way entire communities can relate to marine and estuarine surroundings of which they consider themselves a part.

The strandloper vision also suggests the need for parallels with a phenomenon such as the Songlines of the Australian Aborigines. These individuals created their world by singing their way through it on foot. By the time they'd completed their journeys, they'd brought to life a land of mythic stature, one with characters and tales worthy of a strong sense of place.

Long Island Sound, by contrast, has birthed few mythic, traditional, or even humorous associations. Where are the narratives explaining the thickest ice, the largest bluefish, the strongest storm? Why is the term "cat's-paw" heard so often? What motivated Florida manatee Chessie, in the summer of 1995, to swim north all the way to Rhode Island, spending time in the Sound along the way? If we can't explain such phenomena, we may need to invent stories and conjure up answers that do explain them and that embody the Sound's magic in the process. This doesn't mean we can contradict scientific explanations; the two

approaches don't compete. It does mean that our own af-
fective culture and communal imagination can be mined
for ways in which to counterbalance the litany of death
often associated with this 110-mile-long estuary.

Long Island Sound is not dead. It has not "crashed" in
the way that Chesapeake Bay crashed. Today's Long Island
Sound, in fact, is probably as clean for swimming and for
harvesting seafood (cautiously) as it has been at any time in
the twentieth century.

The end of World War II marked the onset of this region's intensive coastal development, much of which was
perceived as a ticket to a comfortable lifestyle. The subsequent baby boom was accompanied by huge increases in
the numbers of cars, parking lots, fertilizers and pesticides,
filled wetlands, and other phenomena associated with a cit-
izenry in love with the promises of technology. New
coastal industries, many of them also technologically based,
treated the Sound as a disposal site for polluted wastes at
the same time that natural landscapes capable of absorbing
pollutants were being rapidly destroyed. In short, from
1945 to 1972 the land around the Sound experienced un-
precedented growth of all types, and the water in the
Sound suffered its most visible abuse.

The 1972 Clean Water Act was responsible for restricting industrial and municipal pollution, including the dis-
charge of raw wastes. As a result, the Sound's water quality
improved throughout the balance of the 1970s. At the same
time, it was becoming apparent that other sources of pollutants were not being adequately addressed, and as a result
problems associated with the estuary (which was later designated an Estuary of National Significance) remained. For
instance, the Clean Water Act did not require that sewage-
treatment plants control levels of nitrogen in effluent.

The management plan that resulted from the Long Island

Sound Study, and that New York, Connecticut, and the federal EPA approved in 1994, addresses this and other problems of the Sound. The plan calls attention to what experts refer to as "nonpoint" sources of pollution. The term refers to pollution sources that are difficult to identify specifically and therefore create problems that cannot easily be solved through government action. Many of these problems are caused by contemporary models of those same cars and parking lots and heavily enriched lawns and fields that began to weave themselves into the fabric of our everyday lives in the postwar years. The big difference between the way we perceived those signs of progress during that earlier span of history and the way we perceive them now is that we're beginning to recognize the pounds of flesh they exact from us.

We know, for example, that pesticides and nitrogen-rich fertilizers eventually find their way into the Sound, either through groundwater or as runoff. We know that motor oil washes off pavement and ends up in the Sound, and that toxic household wastes can do the same if they're not disposed of properly. Both types of substances can contribute to habitat degradation. We're even beginning to understand the negative impact of boats' outboard engines. Such awareness allows us to control the damage, if we will.

This book is not a prescription for how to behave near Long Island Sound. Other publications provide information on Sound-sensitive gardening and Sound-savvy driving, on water conservation and wise land use. The book does, I hope, suggest that the way each of us lives, including the water-related habits we acquire and the peace of mind we develop in multiple ways, is brought to bear on the abundant life associated with this body of water. For just as the Sound is a part of our natural heritage, the very fact that some 8.5 million of us live in her watershed makes us her people.

Long Island Sound has a beauty and a vitality that leave me dumbfounded with love. These writings are my love letters. By coming to understand something of the limits and gifts of this water, I have tried to repay it for nurturing my spirit.

ACKNOWLEDGMENTS

Long before this book was in anyone's thoughts, my husband, Steve Buckles, urged me to coax sentences out of barely formed ideas about Long Island Sound. Later he was editor, computer and boat-engine whiz, and top advisor. More than any other person, Steve, with his fine sense of balance, has made it possible for this project to come to fruition. The journey we've shared along the water has been an even greater source of joy for me than the Sound.

My mother, Mary Harmon, has always been a beacon and a benchmark for me. Her remarkable grace and generosity, her marriage and home, her professional life, and most of all her perceptions and values have been such important sustaining influences that in many ways this book belongs to her.

The same forces that brought me to the Sound led me to people who increased my understanding. Dulcy Brainard, Roland Clement, Jackie and Guy Fiske, Elsie Wheeler, Art Glowka, and Tom Horton took an interest in *Margins* when it was still in the thinking stage. They helped me to work further. Friendships that grew enrich my life.

My agent, Jacques de Spoelberch, believed in the book from the start and has been an indispensable support. His editorial imagination and seasoned judgment are just two aspects of his wide-ranging talent. I value our friendship greatly.

To be judged by the high publishing standards of Farrar, Straus and Giroux has been both humbling and exhilarating. My editors, Jonathan Galassi and Ethan Nosowsky, have guided me through this project with extraordinary grace. I thank them sincerely. My thanks also to Roger Straus III, Debbie Glasserman, and Jeff Seroy for the important roles they've played.

The public librarians of southern Connecticut have been immeasurably helpful. In particular, reference librarians Blanche Parker, Maura Ritz, Janie Rhein, Mary Fox, and Kate Buckardt have spent innumerable hours on my behalf in pursuit of arcane information. Kathy Stalker and her staff have gone the extra mile. I owe all of them, as well as Louise Berry, an enormous debt of thanks.

Many other individuals helped me in ways as various as providing introductions and (while I was buried in field guides) keeping me stocked with the best tomatoes and rhubarb in New England. They include Bruce Ando, Avery Brooke, Jane and Russ Kinne, David Challinor, Lige Parker, Walter Taylor, Helen Steinkraus, Martha Hammonds, Anne and Jack Stone, Vinnie and Maria LaVecchia, Kay Barksdale, Pamela Lape, Reuben Wuensch, Gardiner Green, Tom Blake, Susan Faulkner, Mary and Gil Robbins, John Ruskey, Phyllis Hawkins, John Casey, Jacquelyn Lazo, Sarah and David Dorrance, Steve Weinberg, Joe Leo, Scott Jamison, and Donald Fraser.

Many scientists, naturalists, and other people whose professions link them with Long Island Sound took considerable time to share what they knew and in many cases to review parts of my manuscript. Some of them appear in this book, but others do not. The latter include Carolyn Hughes, Mark Tedesco, Jim Kent, Ralph Lewis, Jessica Gurevitch, Lauren Brown, Catha Grace Rambusch, Roger Swain, Sheila Connor, Jack Alexander, Katherine Powis, Paul Merola, Brian Swift, William Sladen, Jay B. Hestbeck, Julie Victoria, Macel Simmons, Hardy White, Chat Phillips, Dave Hopp, Rob Jones, Oddvar Nygaard, John Sculley, Terry Backer, Malcolm Shute, John Volk, Melissa Beristain, Chester Arnold, Paul Fell, Karl Schuster, William Niering, Tom Steinke, Ron Rozsa, Scott Warren, Woody Reed, Irv Mendelssohn, Mark Bertness, David Sutherland, Don Repe, Helen Roselli, Charles Yarish, Pat Walker, L. Jane Walley, Ralph Grams, Paul Casey, Jack Schneider, Bob Brooks, Rick Schreiner, John Atkin, Willard S. Moore, Jean Thompson Black, Ted Augustine, Sam Sadove, and Steve Gephard. I thank them all wholeheartedly.